going
off
script

ALSO BY GIULIANA RANCIC

I Do, Now What? (with Bill Rancic)
Think Like a Guy

going off script

—

HOW I
SURVIVED A
CRAZY CHILDHOOD,
CANCER,
AND
CLOONEY'S 32
ON-SCREEN
REJECTIONS

—

giuliana rancic

THREE RIVERS PRESS
NEW YORK

Copyright © 2015 by You and I Productions, LLC

Published in the United States by Three Rivers Press,
an imprint of the Crown Publishing Group,
a division of Penguin Random House LLC, New York.
www.crownpublishing.com

Three Rivers Press and the Tugboat design are registered
trademarks of Penguin Random House LLC.

Originally published in hardcover in the United States by
Crown Archetype, an imprint of the Crown Publishing Group,
a division of Penguin Random House LLC, New York, in 2015.

Library of Congress Cataloging-in-Publication Data
Rancic, Giuliana.
   Going off script : how I survived a crazy childhood, cancer, and
Clooney's 32 on-screen rejections / Giuliana Rancic. — First edition
   1. Rancic, Giuliana. 2. Television personalities—
United States—Biography. I. Title.
   PN1992.4.R3575A3 2015
   791.4502'8092—dc23
   [B]
   2014048904

ISBN 978-0-553-44668-5
eBook ISBN 978-0-553-44667-8

PRINTED IN THE UNITED STATES OF AMERICA

Book design by Elizabeth Rendfleisch
Cover design by Christopher Brand
Cover photograph by Peter Yang
Hand lettering by John Stevens

10 9 8 7 6 5 4 3 2 1

First Paperback Edition

To those who give me life:
Anna and Eduardo, Bill and Duke

I was born a celebrity. It was the summer of 1974, a Saturday morning in Naples, Italy, where my father, Eduardo DePandi, was a master tailor and my mother, Anna, was a housewife. My brother, Pasquale, was seven years old and already anointed king of the world, much to the outrage of my five-year-old sister, Monica. I was two weeks overdue, but my mother kept that to herself, determined as she was just to go about her business until I decided to make my entrance, whenever that happened to be. What's an extra three or four months in the womb, right? Mama DePandi was never one to complain, even when she was swollen like an Oompa Loompa and stuck in our cramped third-floor walkup apartment with no air-conditioning in the torpid August heat.

On Italy's southern coast, summer weekends are always hot and unhurried, generation after generation following the same rhythm, and the same rituals. Come Saturday morning, the men and children traditionally head to the beach while the women stay behind to fix a huge picnic feast, which they then lug down to the shore, appearing en masse like an advancing army at lunchtime.

When my mother's water broke on the beach the morning of my birth, I'm told that she just kept serving her famous frittata. Then, without a word, she suddenly got up and discreetly walked into the sea, hoping to swim off the labor pains. No one had ever seen Anna DePandi go into the water during lunch before. My father hurried in after her.

"Anna, what's going on?" Babbo called out.

"Nothing, nothing," she insisted, as if she were suddenly an Olympic medalist preparing to do a few warm-up miles before casually swimming across the sea to Tunisia.

"Are you in labor?" my father demanded.

"No," she insisted, turning back to the beach and not bothering to mention the contractions. "Let's eat." Italians invented comfort food, and our thinking is that there's nothing a few hundred carbs can't cure.

Mama kept up the pretense that nothing was wrong as long as she could, but I was hell-bent on joining the party, and the picnic came to a screeching halt as her contractions worsened. I was very nearly born in traffic on the way to the clinic, where a midwife waited to deliver me, contrary to my sister's account of highly skilled dolphins doing so at sea (a story I fervently believed until I was something like twelve). Maybe the dolphins would have been less shocked than the humans by my size: thirteen pounds! If I hadn't been her third baby, my poor mother may not have survived, considering that she didn't have the luxury of an epidural and got nothing more than the equivalent of a single Advil to kill the pain. Not only was I huge, but I came out with a full head of dark hair, too. I basically arrived as a toddler.

I was named after my mother and her older brother, my Uncle Giulio. As a child, I took the lack of a middle name as an open invitation to find my own. I gravitated toward stripper names. Roxy was a recurring favorite. At birth, though, everyone just called me Pacchiana, which loosely translated to "large peasant woman with a red moon face." Neighbors lined up out the door waiting their turn to come see the giant baby when my parents brought me home, and my mother proudly passed me around for closer inspection. It's hard to picture this scene now in a Purell-ified world where we don't even dare touch a shopping cart at a grocery store without sanitizing it first, but Mama's approach to building up her newborn's immune system was more along the lines of "Oh, sure, hold her, sneeze on her, set her on the floor if your arms get tired . . ." But no one ever did. I was the neighborhood star, and it seemed like no one would ever get enough of me and my chubby cheeks.

Sadly, that initial wave of public interest and adoration lasted for only eighteen months. By then, the only part of me still freakishly large were my feet, which were crammed into big, black orthopedic shoes. Pictures of me back then show this poor, sweet little girl sitting there with her dainty pierced earrings and froufrou dress, with her face nearly obscured by the black clodhoppers sticking out in front of her like skis. It's not like I was expecting red-soled baby Louboutins, but seriously? Not long ago, I came across one of my old baby photos. I kicked into *Fashion Police* mode and interrogated my mother about this footwear horror, demanding some answers: Were they trying to hide evidence that they were secretly binding my feet in hopes I wouldn't grow into the size ten I became before I even hit puberty? Did Mama have some torrid fling with a clown when the circus came through town, and was I their secret love child? Mama waved off my indignation, trying to pretend there was nothing unusual about dressing an infant in old man oxfords. I still don't buy it. But clearly I was traumatized by it: trying to overcompensate for my large baby hooves no doubt drove me to become the shoe whore I am today.

My fickle local fan base reappeared once my full head of dark baby hair turned into golden corn silk; I was once again a huge hit. A blond kid in southern Italy is very rare. Like, traffic-stopping rare. Vespas are pretty much the only thing with a motor that can navigate the narrow streets of old Naples, and boys and young men would roar around piled three to a scooter. Sometimes they would stop to gape at me and my golden hair while I was on the stoop playing with my doll, and my maternal grandfather, Antonio, would come charging out. "You get away from her! Don't even look at her!" I was the apple of Nonno's eye. He adored me, and the feeling was mutual. My very first memory is of standing next to him, while he's talking to people about how pretty I am, how special, that I am his angel. My grandfather was also my first fashion icon. He was really tall and elegant, and wore a top hat. He just put himself together so beautifully, and carried himself with such pride, even though he was a simple man who worked at a train station food cart. Nonno was my first heartbreak, too. He died suddenly at the age of seventy-five; I was nine years old when I kissed him good-bye forever.

My grandfather was a great man, and I think my mother saw a lot of him in my dad. My father has many of the same qualities, including the sweet temperament that can flare in an instant, turning him into a raging Italian bull. (Different variations of the Vespa boys would discover that years later—stay tuned for a very special episode of *Giuliana Hits Puberty*.) Dad was the oldest of five children born into a struggling family in postwar Italy. His parents would have to hide the bread and ration it out so their hungry kids wouldn't climb up on the counter and gobble it up.

Young Eduardo loved school but was forced to find a job at ten so he could help support the family. He was put to work in a tailor shop, where he picked up scraps and cleaned. When he didn't return to class, one of his teachers showed up to confront his father, Pasquale. Eduardo was a really bright boy and a very good student, the teacher explained. He had potential, and his parents were making a big mistake not to give him the education he deserved. "Are you going to help pay the bills?" Pasquale asked the teacher before telling him to mind his own business, and Eduardo started working in the fourth grade. My father is still one of the smartest men I've ever known, and his ability to focus so keenly on any challenge before him made him a master tailor at a young age. He had his own shop while still in his twenties, and his exquisite custom work would eventually make him sought after within the powerful circles of Washington, D.C.'s elite. He and my mother, a pretty brunette (at the time) with brown eyes and great curves, met when Anna was just fifteen and Eduardo was twenty. Once they fell in love, it was forever. They're in their seventies now, married fifty years, and they still dance together and laugh at their private jokes and don't like to go anywhere without each other. I want my marriage to always be like theirs.

It's funny, but when people ask me to describe Naples, one of the first images that always pops into my head is of old marble steps riddled with chips and cracks, a fairly common sight in a city tested by the wrath of both man and nature. Maybe the steps got seared into my memory because children just naturally explore the ground beneath them more than adults. The streets were where we played, and the stoops were our vantage point for any neighborhood drama. As a little girl, I couldn't possibly have grasped what those ruined steps were telling the world, but as a grown woman, I would one day cling to their truth, understanding that Naples was beautiful not despite her scars, but because of them.

There was a coziness to my Italian childhood that I wish Bill and I could replicate for our son, Duke. Everything revolved around the two things Italians treasure most: food and family. What I would give now for those lazy weekend lunches on the beach like the one on the day I was born. As a child, I would watch hungrily as the women unpacked a feast from their baskets and totes. Out would come fresh baguettes and hunks of cheese, fresh tomatoes, bottles of wine and liters of Coke, and, of course, heaping platters of antipasti—slices of fatty salami, small mountains of shaved Parma ham and salty prosciutto, bowls of cured olives and peperoncini, maybe some artichoke hearts and pickled vegetables. The mamas and aunties and grandmothers always brought extra helpings of their signature dishes to share with the extended family. Even now, my mouth waters when I think of the delicious frittata Mama used to make by mixing cold leftover pasta from the night before with eggs and parmesan, then frying it all up in extra-virgin olive oil before wrapping slices of the gooey pasta pie in aluminum foil like a sandwich. I can still taste the warm, tangy cheese and hear the sound of waves crashing in the background as my family laughed and argued and laughed some more, while the women fussed over us all.

I had cousins by the dozen. My uncles Giulio and Michele were the grand adventurers of the family—moving first to London, and later America—but the rest of us saw no point to leaving: Naples was world enough for us, and we held it close. It was as much who we were as where we lived. It seemed like the whole neighborhood was family, either literally or figuratively. My grandparents lived next door. Aunts, uncles, cousins were always coming and going. Apartments were usually so overcrowded—multiple generations living in homes with just one or two bedrooms—that there was no place for the kids to play, really, except outside, and everyone kept a collective eye on us, especially the nosy, toothless old women who tended to live in the tiny one-room flats on the ground floor of the apartment buildings.

At the end of our block was the baker who delivered the fresh cornettos we would have for breakfast each morning, dunking the custard-filled croissants into cups of hot latte. The fact that I started drinking coffee with milk at four probably explains a lot about why people always think I have so much energy and can balance a million things at once. But hey, wine was on the lunch and dinner table and I was free to drink that, too, so it all evened out. Anyway, after breakfast, we'd go grocery shopping. Like all the other housewives, Mama would lower a basket attached to a rope off the balcony, and one of the little boys who worked for the grocer would scurry over and run back to the store with the list and money tucked inside. He would return with the groceries and change, and we'd hoist the basket back upstairs. The same system worked for the greengrocer. We'd yell *"Fruttiere!"* down to the street, and the fruit vendor would hurry over and take our order. If only I could put together my favorite chicken chopped salad with as little effort today.

The best time of day was late at night, after dinner, when everyone would gather at the nearby Piazza del Plebiscito to socialize over drinks or coffee. The men would smoke cigars, the women, cigarettes. The kids would all run wild, jumping in the fountains and playing hide-and-seek amid the eighteenth-century colonnades while our parents talked. Bedtime was whenever you fell asleep, whether you laid your head against your grandmother's chest, a café table, or your own pillow. European kids are expected to adapt to the adults' schedules, not the other way around. We'd be at the piazza till one in the morning. Life was all about family, fun, eating well, and staying up late.

School wasn't a priority, at least in my family. My mother, like my father, had never gone to high school, dropping out in the sixth grade. Anna grew up with four brothers and an older sister. She was especially close to her brothers Giulio and Michele, who were in their early twenties when they went to London to work as casino blackjack dealers, despite the dire warnings from everyone back home that straying so far from the motherland would surely lead to ruin. Far from failing, though, my uncles were just getting started on the road to success. From London, they were recruited to work in the Bahamas at the Britannia Hotel, which had a glamorous, 007-style casino then, with a hint of mystery and suave danger. That was before the place turned into the Atlantis, which is basically a theme park with roulette wheels and waterslides. Giulio married a Brit named Angela, and Michele married a Frenchwoman named Marielle. I always considered them such cool couples; Michele and Marielle were sort of beachy, boho people, while Giulio and Angela were more conservative and ritzy. Giulio got an opportunity to become a partner in an Italian restaurant in Washington, D.C. Tiberio's became the hottest table in town and spawned multiple spin-offs. At the same time, Michele opened his own popular restaurant, Picolo Mondo, on K Street near the White House. The two feckless brothers with wanderlust were huge success stories. Giulio lived with his young family in a stately mansion with original Warhols on the wall and two Rolls-Royces in the driveway. Michele was raising his family in a more modest house on a lakefront across the Potomac, in a posh Virginia suburb. Both of them loved their sister Anna dearly, and urged her and Eduardo to come to America to chase their own dream.

"Let's just go for vacation in the summer for two weeks and see what it's like," my father suggested one day. My brother, sister, and I were overjoyed by the prospect.

"Are you going to be in Hollywood or New York City?" my cousin Riccardo asked me. We assumed those were the only two cities in America, and that they were right next door to each other.

"I don't know," I replied. "Probably Hollywood." In Hollywood, we knew, TV and movie stars strolled the streets. In my six-year-old imagination, this meant I might run into Olivia Newton-John at the café and let her dunk her cornetto in my latte. Or maybe Scooby-Doo would walk me to school. My exposure to celebrity in Naples (other than my own questionable fame, of course) was limited to soccer stars, beauty queens, and the pope. In that order, actually.

Uncle Giulio persuaded my parents to buy tickets, and we boarded a plane for America. None of us had ever flown before, and my only memory of the flight is of my mother's utter terror when we were forced to make an emergency landing due to an issue with one of the exit doors. Enter my lifelong fear of flying. When we finally landed in neither Hollywood nor New York, I didn't even notice, I was so excited to see my uncles and cousins again. I had never seen a house as big as Giulio's, other than the Royal Palace that anchored the Piazza del Plebiscito back home, but as far as I knew, no one actually *lived* there. Giulio's kids each had their own bedroom and bathroom, and the family room alone was bigger than our whole apartment. I couldn't believe how beautiful it was.

The uncles were certainly rich enough to have put us up in a nice hotel, but in an Italian family, that would be considered unthinkably rude—something Bill had to struggle with early in our marriage when the relatives descended—so we set up camp in Giulio's basement. Monica, Pasquale, and I usually ended up sacked out in our cousins' rooms. It was like one big, extended sleepover. The older kids loved to reenact *Grease,* but I would invariably disrupt the show by randomly jumping up to shout and sing, "Go, greased lightning!"

"Stop it! Sit down! You're the audience!" everyone would yell at me.

"I don't want to be the audience!" I pouted. "I wanna be Olivia Newton-John!"

"No! Monica's Olivia Newton-John! Shut up and be the audience!"

The adults, as usual, talked late into the night while the kids ran amok, and at some point during that vacation, it was decided that Eduardo would open his own men's clothing store and tailor shop in D.C. My parents called a family meeting and told us the big news: we were moving to America! They would go back to Italy to pack our things while we stayed behind with our cousins.

I was too young to feel scared by the big upheaval, or upset that I wouldn't have a chance to say good-bye to my friends back in Naples. I'm sure Monica and Pasquale dealt with more conflicting emotions, since they were already in junior high, but I was thrilled. I was the giant baby bigfoot golden-haired special angel child—what could possibly go wrong, ever?

After six months at Giulio's house, we ended up settling into an apartment building on a busy thoroughfare called River Road, which ran through Bethesda, Maryland, and across the D.C. line. We were on the Maryland side, and instead of a 19th-century piazza, there was a 7-Eleven across the street. My father soon opened a shop called Eduardo's in a fancy mall in Georgetown and quickly became the tailor to politicians, athletes, and other well-heeled Washingtonians. His star was rising just as mine came crashing down.

Enrolled in public school, I didn't know a word of English, so I spent my days doodling at my desk. Nobody could pronounce my name, so the teachers decided I would be Julie from then on. (Was it so impossible to just add the extra three letters, people? It's not like *ana* is hard to say; it's phonetic, for godsakes.) But wait, there were lots of Julies, so I would have to be Julie D. The other kids thought I was stupid, because I didn't speak or understand anything they were saying. I was Julie D., the weird mute girl with (still) big feet. Even my golden hair was unremarkable now: I was drowning in a sea of little blond girls, and most of *them* had blue eyes to up the ante. Stripped of my identity, my voice, and my singular claim to beauty, one thing about America was perfectly clear:

My fifteen minutes were up, and I was only six years old.

chapter two

In America, I became a latchkey kid. Babbo and Mama would work long hours at the shop, and, keeping with Italian custom, we never had dinner before 9:30 at night. Over our bowls of fresh pasta, Babbo always asked us whether we had learned any new English words and phrases that day. Monica and Pasquale were taking language lessons at Berlitz, but I was on my own, daydreaming at the public school either in the back of the classroom or with four other ESOL kids sitting around a table. My parents assumed I was young enough that English would just come naturally to me, and amazingly, it did. For the first time in my life, I felt superior to my older brother and sister, and I loved rubbing it in during Babbo's evening quizzes, piping up with an ever-growing repertoire of words and phrases while Pash and Mon still spun their wheels on "Hi, how are you?"

The importance of learning this strange new language had become painfully clear to me that first Christmas in the States, when Uncle Giulio took me and my siblings along with his three kids to Toys R Us for a dream-come-true shopping spree. "You have five minutes to go get whatever you want," he told us. My brother, sister, and cousins all sped off to stockpile as much high-ticket loot as they could—bikes, electric cars, Ataris, video games. Vincent, my brainiac cousin, homed in on jigsaw puzzles and all the best board games. I made a beeline for the dolls.

My heart was set on one thing and one thing only: a baby doll with bodily functions. It had to be able to pee and go poo. I was certain I had seen such a doll on a TV commercial, but I didn't know what it was called. I started turning over boxes to see if any dolls had the necessary holes. I couldn't read the English descriptions, but the pictures promised me that some could blink, or cry, or even crawl. You could change their diapers, but there was nothing in them. That did not meet my quality-control standards. I didn't want to pretend. I wanted reality, dammit. I gladly would have taken an actual baby, but my parents weren't cooperating, and Toys R Us didn't have a human trafficking aisle. So I proceeded to pick up doll after doll, determined to find the holy pooping grail. Legions of Barbies smirked prettily from their chic townhouses and sporty convertibles, but Barbie didn't even wear underwear, let alone diapers. I could have gotten her a Cinderella ball gown and made her run off with the Incredible Hulk on an Erik Estrada CHiPs moped. But that is NOT. WHAT. I. WANTED. Instead, I stood rooted there in the middle of the toy store with my empty cart until my mother came and found me. "*Piccerella!*" she cried. "Little one." I usually took comfort in her pet name for me, but time was running out on Uncle Giulio's beat-the-clock extravaganza, and sympathy wasn't going to cut it. "Everyone has full carts!" Mama fretted, trying to goad me into action. "Look, here's a baby doll you can give a bath and feed, how about that?" I shook my head, on the verge of tears. I didn't want the food to go in as much as I wanted it to come out. Was it so much to ask for a doll with a working digestive tract? "But I saw it on TV," I wailed. If it was on TV, it had to be real, right?

My mother flagged down a salesperson for help, only to remember too late that neither one of us knew enough English to even begin to explain the problem. "Hi, how are you?" we politely asked, before breaking into excited Italian, pointing at our v-jays and pleading "pee-pee, pee-pee!" The salesperson smiled, nodded reassuringly, and gestured for us to follow. *They have it! I'm going to get my doll!* I thought, grinning in gratitude at this savior who was leading us so purposefully straight to . . . the ladies' room. Back I dashed to the doll aisle, with Mama now nearly as frantic as I was (not to mention utterly humiliated, but that was more her than me). We passed Monica and Pasquale drunk on greed, pushing their teetering carts toward the register. Finally, Mama and I found a doll that could actually pee after you gave her a bottle. Thrilled with the prospect of changing a diaper that was at least wet, I hurried back to the checkout lane to join the rest of the family. "Is that it?" Uncle Giulio asked in surprise. I nodded and happily cradled my prize. "Where's your cart?" the other kids wanted to know. They couldn't believe I had wasted all my time looking for a single toy. How dumb *was* I? But I was satisfied. I knew exactly what I wanted, and once I had it, that was all I needed. Nothing else mattered. That one-track mindset would end up leading me to many of my sweetest triumphs and most bitter disappointments throughout life. And the pissing doll definitely went into the win column.

While we were nowhere near my uncles' league, our fortunes rose quickly in D.C. Babbo couldn't have chosen a better time to open up shop as a master European tailor in the nation's capital. The frumpy Carter administration had just been voted out, and the inauguration of President Ronald Reagan was ushering in an era of formal entertaining and couture style that put Babbo's craftsmanship in high demand with the A-listers. His clientele soon included big-name athletes, politicians, pundits, and rainmakers. We moved across the Potomac River to a townhouse in the Virginia suburb of Springfield, where our modest end unit seemed as grand as the White House itself to me. I had my own room for the first time. Aside from tending to my incontinent doll, though, there wasn't much to keep me occupied during the long afternoons and evenings I spent by myself after school while my parents worked and my siblings went about their teenaged lives. I was lonely and bored, until I made my first—and most loyal—friend in America. Her name was Barbara.

Barbara kept me company every day, and she always spoke to me clearly and directly. Her voice was pleasant, and she never tried to make me understand unfamiliar words by speaking louder or more slowly. Barbara was everything I yearned to be someday: pretty, in-the-know, and completely unflappable. She was cool in the face of any calamity. And calamity, I learned, was all around me. All the time. The emergency landing when we were flying to America was just a taste of the dangers that loomed here. People were constantly getting shot down in the street, or run over in crosswalks by drunk drivers or city buses, or carjacked at gunpoint, or tied up and beaten by home invaders who took their valuables. They were horribly burned in house fires ignited by Christmas trees, and trapped in wrecked cars, and buried beneath collapsed buildings. They became lost for days in snowbound mountains, scorching deserts, or storm-tossed seas. Children were routinely kidnapped while walking to school or shopping with their parents. People got eaten by sharks, alligators, and sometimes zoo animals. They were fatally struck by lightning while playing golf, or shot by crazy postal workers. In America, the most unimaginable nightmares came true every single day. I had this all on very good authority from Barbara.

I had never actually met Barbara, but I admired her deeply, trusted her implicitly, and mimicked her earnestly for hours on end in front of my bedroom mirror. Barbara Harrison anchored the evening news on the local NBC affiliate, and watching her broadcast was the highlight of my day. I had to be the only second-grader in America more familiar with the Falklands War than the Fonz. The live footage and packaged features on the news always kept me riveted to the TV screen, and, of course, the images illustrated what everyone was talking about as they said it. Even better, the reporters spoke in short, simple sentences. English began to make perfect sense, and I became the first in my family to master it. I was just too terrified to leave the house and use it.

"Mama, I need you to come home right now!" I would implore, dialing the shop so often and with such rising panic that my parents would eventually have to give up and send Mama to rescue me from the serial killers, home invaders, and Freddy Krueger psychopaths I was sure were trying to break in that very second. Monica was supposed to be watching me, but her m.o. was to offer me five bucks to keep my mouth shut while she went to hang out with her friends. "Listen, you little brat, you're going to stay in the corner and watch TV," she would warn me. "I swear," I would promise, snatching the bill from her hand. She pretty much always got a full refund, and hell to pay from our parents. I'd last maybe an hour at most before freaking out and calling my parents to rat my sister out. The fear factor was actually worse when my siblings were there. They preferred R-rated horror movies to the evening news, and once you've seen *Friday the 13th* for the fourteenth time, the only thrill left is in convincing your little sister that it's a documentary based on a true story.

Oddly enough, even though Naples has often ranked at or near the top of the list of Europe's most violent cities, the mafioso bloodshed and street crime never seemed to faze me there. We would go back every summer to visit, and I remember one time when I was eight or nine years old, and a bunch of us were playing at my friend Rosaria's apartment on the top floor of our building in the old neighborhood. Suddenly, we heard a commotion outside, and Mama, Babbo, and all the grown-ups started yelling up at us from the apartment balcony below. "*Bambini, bambini!* Get inside! Close the door!" Of course, we all immediately ran outside to peer over Rosaria's terrace and see what was going on. I saw a man with a hat on extend his arm and shoot someone, then get in a car and drive away. I saw the other man's body fall. It scared the shit out of me, but I didn't want to look like a baby, so I followed the other kids back inside to finish watching our cartoon. (Denial is second only to soccer as a national sport in Italy.) I don't recall any sirens or police crime tape or homicide investigators swarming the neighborhood. That's not how it worked. In Naples, the game was six degrees of Mafia, and even if you were an eyewitness to murder, you minded your own business. This was a town where eleven-year-old boys drove getaway vans.

On our first trip back to Naples, I appointed myself chief cultural critic, and kept up a running commentary on how inferior Naples was; after barely a year, I was a bona fide ugly American in miniature. "*Che schifo,*" I complained about the garbage everywhere. "How gross." The familiar racket of Vespas, vendors, and kids playing soccer in the street was also suddenly intolerable. "Listen to all this traffic!" I whined. "People should be arrested for making so much noise!" My Italian relatives, friends, and old neighbors all got the same unsolicited advice: "You should move to America with us," I loftily urged them. "America is clean. Naples is disgusting."

The second summer back, I went from insufferable to insufferable and creepy. I must have been in the throes of some weird giant-baby flashback, because as soon as we were back in Naples, I started badgering my mother to buy me a pacifier, which I suspect she finally did only because the advantage of plugging my mouth shut outweighed the humiliation of traipsing around town with a tall-for-her-age nine-year-old sucking on a binky. It wasn't as if she could just dart into a CVS or Walgreens to buy one with no questions asked. In Italy, drugstores are tiny neighborhood *farmacias,* whose owners know and greet each customer by name.

"Ciao, Anna! What are you looking for?" the pharmacist asked as soon as we walked in.

"Oh, nothing, really, just a pacifier," Mama breezily replied. As an actress, I ranked her right up there with Naples's most famous daughter, Sophia Loren. No one would have guessed how epically pissed she was at me right then.

"Whose baby?" the pharmacist wanted to know. He knew every binky-sucker in a ten-block radius. "How old is the baby? Is it just starting to use a pacifier?"

I had a bad feeling about the direction this was taking. It was as if I could hear Mama's last nerve snap.

"Listen," she confided to the nosy pharmacist. "Our baby is nine years old! It's for this crazy person next to me! Do you have pacifiers for nine-year-olds?"

"Mama!" I protested, too late. The pharmacist was looking at me in disbelief. Like I was some kind of freak, instead of a perfectly normal third-grader with a perfectly reasonable request.

"Why you acting crazy, Giuliana?" the pharmacist asked me. I tried to make up some feeble story on the spot about wanting it for a doll. To be honest, I couldn't fully explain why I wanted it. I just thought it would be fun to chew on all day. Obviously there was some mental issue going on there, and three decades later, I still do not want to know what it was, thank you very much. The binky is the whole reason that I don't want to be hypnotized to get over my fear of flying, even though I hear there's this great hypnotherapist in Santa Monica who could cure me in a few sessions. I'm too scared of whatever else might get dredged up, attached to the end of that stupid pacifier. I can just see the hypnotist telling me to relax, and to picture the plane's engine revving up, and then suddenly I blurt out: "I was touched!" When I relayed this whole hilarious (I thought) scenario to my fake therapists on the E! crew, everyone fell silent on set and said there was nothing funny about it. What they don't get is how overactive my imagination is, and how I trained it from a very young age to visualize things that hadn't happened—like me being crowned Miss USA, and anchoring the evening news—so my childhood dreams would come true. What if that same mechanism has some trick lever I don't know about, and under hypnosis I falsely accuse someone—say, Cookie Monster—of molesting me? I'd rather take an Ambien and sleep through a long flight than risk revealing some deep-rooted shit during a hypnosis session. The pacifier was just my gateway tranquilizer. I popped it into my mouth as soon as we left the *farmacia,* and no amount of ridicule from my family could make me stop.

Back home in the States, I at least had the good sense to lose the pacifier, but I was still decidedly weird. I had earned that label back in the second grade, when my teacher asked the class to draw a picture of what we wanted to be when we grew up. All the boys drew astronauts or firemen or basketball players, while all the girls drew mommies or cheerleaders or veterinarians. I drew my floating head behind a big desk with a microphone on it. "I want to be an American anchorwoman," I announced in my thick Italian accent. Everybody giggled. "Julie, that's so sweet," the teacher chided me, "but to be an anchorwoman, you can't have an accent. You have to speak perfect English. How about a Redskins cheerleader?" I was devastated. If I closed my eyes, I could see myself delivering the news. I wasn't about to ditch my imaginary TV career for a couple of pom-poms. I just needed more practice, was all. I redoubled my efforts.

When I wasn't mimicking Barbara Harrison at home, I sat in front of my bedroom mirror pretending to be Oprah. I would act like I was interviewing Matt Dillon. I loved him from *The Outsiders*. And Ralph Macchio from *The Karate Kid*. I would ask them if they had a girlfriend, what they liked in a girl. Blondes or brunettes? Would they ever marry a regular girl or would they only marry a celebrity? Basically, the "hard-hitting" questions I still ask on the red carpet. Then, when Fake Oprah was done interviewing all her invisible, famous guests, I would flop across my bed with my head hanging over the edge and listen carefully to Eddie Murphy's *Delirious* album on my record player. Eddie was an excellent English coach. Eddie taught me how to curse like an American. Upside down. My whole family cursed frequently and extravagantly in Italian, and speaking any language without the ability to swear would have been like singing opera with just a one-octave range. Once again, Berlitz was miserably failing Monica and Pasquale, who were being drilled on crucial vocabulary lessons ("Is that your dog?" "How much are the oranges?") while Eddie Murphy was showing me how to effortlessly drop the f-bomb in any situation. So that honky bitch of a second-grade teacher could just kiss my sweet Italian ass, because I was going to be the best fucking anchorwoman in the U.S.A., goddammit. And Miss USA, too. I was going to be Miss U Expletive S of Undeleted A, too.

Just to clarify: Beauty queen wasn't so much my Plan B as it was my companion career to Plan A, unless, of course, there was a network out there with the foresight to have their anchors deliver the evening news wearing tiaras and ball gowns. Pageant mania ran in my family. We'd get out our pencils and paper, make a big bowl of popcorn, and settle in for a happy night around the TV to cheer on our favorite contestants and mercilessly heckle the rest. Babbo was the most intense, especially during the Miss Universe pageant, which we had watched back in Italy, too. Babbo would work himself into a lather when Miss Italy appeared. "She is a dog!" he would rail. "This, a country full of so many beautiful women, and this is who they chose?" The judges must have felt the same way, because Italy never even made the finals when we were watching.

I got pretty good at predicting the winner and runners-up, and I fantasized endlessly about someday standing on that stage myself wearing the Miss USA sash and crown. I had some naive notion of making the entire country proud of me (while I blew kisses in the spotlight). I wouldn't be the dumb immigrant kid anymore. I would win everyone over. I didn't fantasize about mere approval—what I wanted was public adulation. I had seen what that was like when I was a little girl in Naples and went out with Mama to watch a parade one day. I was nearly swept away by the cheering crowd, but I was too little to see who or what was causing such a commotion. Processions were always winding through the streets in honor of some saint or another, but the size and fervor of this particular crowd signaled something more exciting than another flower-bedecked statue of St. Francis or the Virgin Mary being carried on a platform through town. People were literally weeping with joy, and I jumped up and down, trying to see over their heads.

"Who is it, Mama? Is it the pope?" I asked. As Catholics, we were more dutiful than devout, but I couldn't think of anyone else who might spark such mob hysteria on the streets of Naples.

"No, it's Maradona, the greatest football player in the world!" Mama told me. I wasn't into soccer, but this Maradona's adoring fan base really impressed me.

"Oh, Mama, isn't it wonderful that the greatest player in the *whole world* is from here?" I cried, catching the crowd's wave of what I now understood to be patriotic pride. Mama looked down at me in puzzlement and shook her head.

"He's not Italian," she shouted over the cheers. "He's from Argentina!"

I wouldn't have been able to put words to it then, but something clicked and my subconscious took note:

Local approval good.
Universal approval better.

Throughout my childhood, I never once wavered from my twin ambitions of anchorwoman and Miss USA, even as my friends changed their minds a zillion times about what they wanted to be when they grew up. It was like the Christmas doll: This was what I wanted. It was all I wanted. Period, end of story.

I had no clue how I would actually get what I wanted so desperately. I'd have to figure that out later, but I had utter confidence in my own abilities. That was something of a miracle in and of itself, since no one else seemed to have all that much faith in me. As the baby of the family, my dreams were considered "cute" well into adulthood. Everyone treated my aspirations like a joke—*Giuliana on TV?*—and I was doomed to be seen as precocious instead of passionate. Since they didn't realize how serious I was, my family couldn't have known how hurt my feelings were. Besides, the DePandi family already had a star, and her name was Monica. My older sister was smart, beautiful, and hilarious.

Monica and I were mortal enemies, but she was also the object of my grudging admiration and envy. Monica had inherited our father's discerning eye and exquisite taste. Style was always something I would have to work hard to achieve, but for Monica, it came naturally. So naturally, I borrowed her stylish things—without what might, in a court of law, technically be considered permission or anything remotely resembling it. It would be stupid not to take advantage of the years' worth of experience Monica had in the fashion department. She was basically the prototype for Suri Cruise. From a very young age, my sister would insist on designer clothes, and my parents would give in to her demands. We were all spoiled, but Monica could pitch a fit like no one else if she was denied. And there was no arguing that she had superior taste. If Dolce & Gabbana had made diapers when she was a baby, she would have worn the samples.

Much as Monica's shameless materialism made me cringe whenever she wanted a new Versace top or yet another pair of buttery leather boots, my disgust never stopped me from sneaking into her closet when she wasn't home. Junior high started later than Monica's high school did, so I would wait for her to leave, then go back upstairs to change into something cool of hers. I was always careful to put things back exactly where I found them later that afternoon, and I even took care not to wear perfume or scented deodorant that would give me away. I'd show up in homeroom, and jaws would drop. Once, I borrowed a pair of cowboy ankle boots, which I proudly wore with slouchy white socks and shorts—not exactly a flattering look for my skinny legs and surfboard feet. My classmates fell over laughing and called me "Rodeo Raheem," a name that made as much sense then as it does now. "I'll be laughing in a year when everyone is wearing this!" I shot back. You better believe, every other kid had a pair of those ankle boots a year later. Monica had a knack for forecasting fashion trends. She could also accessorize with the brilliance of a *Vogue* stylist. I shopped at the Gap and

Limited, but Monica worshipped Neiman Marcus and, given the amount of our parents' money she spent there, the feeling was surely mutual. Even if she wanted to buy a basic white shirt, it had to be the highest quality. She loved the finer things, but to get the finer things, it took money. Cash was her drug of choice. When I was twelve, she even stole the seventy dollars I had saved from leftover lunch money and odd jobs around the neighborhood. When I went to my secret hiding place behind the stuffed animals on my bedroom shelf and the money was gone, I let out a banshee wail that brought everyone running.

"She stole my money!" I shrieked at Mama. "Call the police! I'm calling the police right now so they can arrest her!"

Monica was unfazed. "Oh, stop being so dramatic. I needed it, big deal."

Mama frantically dug into her purse and produced a sheaf of bills. "Here, Giuliana, it's okay, look, here's seventy dollars. Stop crying now."

"No," I keened as Monica smugly walked away unpunished yet again. "I want *my* money!" Mama couldn't possibly understand my indignation and fury; she let herself get fleeced by Monica on a daily basis and did nothing. Every morning as we got ready for school, Mama would ask us the same question:

"Okay, how much do you need for lunch today?"

"Forty," Monica would answer, shooting me her death-ray look. Mama would just hand her a couple of twenties without ever voicing dismay at the price of sloppy joes on a high school cafeteria tray. I felt like the silent bystander to the same mugging every morning, and would try to even things out by insisting that I only needed a dollar even as Mama tried to cajole me into taking five. I would often sneak loose change or a few dollars I had saved back into Mama's purse later. It's hard to explain why. I realized we weren't poor, of course; after a year of renting in Virginia, my parents had bought a beautiful colonial house with a pool in Bethesda, a posh Maryland suburb. And contrary to my beloved grandfather's early proclamations, I was no flaxen-haired angel from heaven: I just wanted, in my childish way, to somehow pay Mama back for all she and Babbo sacrificed to give us whatever we wanted. I believed in karma even before I knew the word for it.

Now that I'm a mother too, I get it that Mama's need to appease Monica no matter how brazen or bratty she acted probably had a lot to do with having seen her child suffer, and wanting, in any and every way possible, to make it all better somehow. I despised Monica for her attitude back then, but I know today that it would absolutely shatter me if I ever had to see my son endure the pain my sister did as a child.

Monica was in grade school when she was diagnosed with scoliosis, a curvature of the spine that tends to run in families, most typically affecting girls. The causes are usually unknown, and the treatment, in Monica's case, consisted of spending junior high in a full-torso metal brace, day and night, in hopes her seventy-two-degree curve wouldn't worsen as she grew. Her seventh- and eighth-grade school pictures show the rod with its metal bar and neck ring sticking up out of her turtleneck sweater. Kids couldn't help but stare. The physical pain was awful, too. The bowing of the spine causes chronic back pain, but if the C- or S-shaped curve of scoliosis gets bad enough, the rib cage can press against the heart or lungs, causing potentially life-threatening complications. Over the course of a miserable year, the brace did what you would expect such an ugly contraption to do to a young girl's self-esteem, and nothing at all for Monica's spine. When she was thirteen, we all went to Children's Hospital in Boston so Dr. John Hall, a renowned orthopedic surgeon out of Harvard, could operate on her. When she woke up, I remember my tough sister moaning and crying in agony. Her body was encased in a cast. From a corner of her hospital room, I watched, wide-eyed and terrified, as Mama and Babbo tried helplessly to comfort her.

"Can you open the window for me?" she begged. "I need you to just open the window."

"You want some fresh air?" the doctor asked.

"No, I want to jump out," Monica answered. "I want to die." I knew, even at eight, that she meant it. Her pain was unbearable to see, much less feel. After a slow and excruciating recovery, an even tougher Monica emerged from the cast. Life, she seemed to be declaring on a daily basis, owed her one. And, by God, she was going to collect.

When it came to pulling a fast one, though, even Monica was no match for our brother, Pasquale.

Pasquale turned fifteen two years after we left Italy, and on his birthday, he informed my parents that in America, all kids got cars when they could drive. And just so they knew in advance, he helpfully added, Pasquale would be wanting a Porsche Turbo convertible. Red, of course. Sure enough, even though the fanciest car in our Virginia neighborhood would have been maybe a Trans Am, and even though our parents drove a modest car, four months shy of his sixteenth birthday, Mama and Babbo tapped into their savings to give Pasquale a Porsche 944 lipstick-red convertible, fully loaded. Pasquale then insisted on having professional photos taken of him posing alongside the Porsche in a black leather jacket and black driving gloves. Off he roared to the tenth grade. It didn't take long for the school to call Babbo.

"What do you think you're doing?" the principal demanded. "He can't drive that car to school!"

"Whatta you mean?" Babbo said.

"It's not legal," the principal argued.

"No, Pasquale, he can drive!" Babbo insisted. "He has piece of paper that says he can drive."

"No," the principal tried to explain. "What he's showing you is a learner's permit. It does not allow him to drive by himself."

Pasquale wasn't even grounded for his b.s. job, and he was allowed to keep the car. According to my parents, this was all the principal's fault, not his. My parents remained more perplexed than perturbed. What was this paper that said Pasquale could drive but couldn't drive? And what kind of a permit denied a boy permission to drive his own Porsche Turbo? The possibility that Pasquale had done anything wrong was not entertained. "That guy's an idiot," Babbo assured Pasquale. "Drive anywhere you want, just not to school." Pasquale was the prince, the one and only son.

Overindulgent as they were, Mama and Babbo were also extremely overprotective and often illogical when it came to our social lives. It took a long time to convince them to let us go on sleepovers, or even to football games at the school. House parties were forbidden, but nightclubs were allowed, probably because it was considered such a harmless diversion for teens in Italy, where you only had to be thirteen to get in. Every summer, we spent time on Ischia, a beautiful volcanic island in the Bay of Naples. The older kids would all go dancing at the club while the parents socialized late into the night at their own nightclubs or outdoor cafés. "Take Giuliana with you," my parents always ordered my sister. Monica would dress me in cute clothes and apply full makeup to try to sneak me into the teen club her crowd favored, but it rarely worked, and I usually ended up dancing outside with my friends to the music we could hear booming through the walls.

My parents always refused to leave Ischia before the season there was over, which meant I was always starting school two weeks late in the fall. I would badger them to go back to the United States, but they didn't see the point: I could make up my schoolwork, but we would never get this time with family back if we relinquished summer now. But I wasn't the kind of student who could catch up easily once I was behind, and my grades always suffered.

The kind of freedom I enjoyed in Italy didn't carry over to the States, but I didn't object: I understood that they were two very different worlds. I remember sitting on a hill with some friends at recess one time in the eighth grade and feeling my blood rise when the American kids started in on how strict my foreign parents were, and how unlucky I was. "My parents are smart, because they know what we'll do if they let us go to parties and have sleepovers, you idiots," I said. "They're the best parents in the world, because they'd do anything for me." I never touched drugs, or got drunk, or slept around—not because I was afraid of how my parents might punish me, but because I was so scared of disappointing them. None of the three of us kids wanted to ever lose their respect. I still feel that way. But as I entered adolescence, I found a different way to rebel: I became a prankster. In that category, I had way more imagination than common sense, and, for a change, I was utterly fearless. From the age of about twelve on, I occupied a place due north of mischievous and barely south of felonious on the bad-behavior spectrum. I was always hatching crazy, elaborate, sick schemes. Grandma and the Play-Doh Penis Incident was one of the earliest installments of my prankster life.

Whenever my parents brought my maternal grandmother over from Italy for a visit, Nonna Maria would share my pink Laura Ashley bedroom with me, sleeping in the twin bed across from my own. Posters of my favorite celebrities were tacked to the walls. Along with Madonna and whatever boy band was hot at the moment, I had a life-size cutout of another one of my heartthrobs—basketball star Manute Bol. I wasn't obsessed with basketball, but I was crazy about Manute. At seven feet, seven inches, he was one of the tallest men to ever play in the NBA, and with the polished ebony skin and sinewy build of his native Dinka tribe back in Sudan, one of the most striking. My replica of Manute hung over Nonna's twin bed. I loved Nonna dearly; she was the one who had taught me to pray as a small child, and every night, we would kneel on my bedroom floor together to thank God for all our blessings, which we would tick off one by one. Tender as it was, that connection we had did not immunize poor Nonna against my wicked sense of humor.

One night when I was twelve, I was hosting a sleepover with friends, and we were all giggling and listening to New Kids on the Block in my room while Nonna snored contentedly in her bed. We decided that we needed to make Manute more noticeable than he already was. I broke out the cans of Play-Doh, and my friends and I went to work. Soon, I was climbing over my sleeping grandmother with our masterpiece in hand, ready to be affixed to Manute. It wasn't a perfect match: Manute's complexion was nowhere near the "flesh" color of Play-Doh (seriously, are there actual human beings that sickly shade of melted Dreamsicle?), and the generous appendage we'd sculpted for him kept falling off onto Nonna's pillow. Eventually, it stuck to him more or less where nature intended it to, and we fell asleep and forgot about it, until my mother walked into my room the next morning.

It was always hard for my friends to gauge just how much trouble we were ever in at my house, or if there was trouble at all, since my whole family routinely conversed in high-decibel Italian with the kinds of theatric gestures Americans usually save for sudden heart attacks, shocking news, or declarations of war, not requests to pass more linguine. The casual swearing also threw most outsiders for a loop, especially when I bothered to translate it for them. My mom could smile like Mrs. Brady, tell me something in Italian, and I'd smile, nod, and say something back, and a friend would nudge me and want to know what she'd said.

"Oh, nothing, she just called me a dumb little bitch," I'd shrug.

(Shocked silence.)

"Omigod. What did you say?"

Another shrug.

"I told her to go fuck herself."

I picked up a ton of junior high street—okay, cul-de-sac—cred as the girl who was allowed to curse. In two languages, no less. Being considered cool was something new and exhilarating to me, and since all adolescence had given me so far was acne, braces, and a bad perm, I was eager to work with whatever little scraps fate tossed me. "Did you know Julie can say fuck and shit and piss at home and not get in trouble?" a friend boasted one day at the lunch table. I confirmed that I had blanket potty-mouth immunity, and offered to prove it by taking any doubters back to my house for a live demonstration. Mama was in the kitchen and greeted us warmly.

"Mama, I'm allowed to say 'fuck,' right?" I asked. Mama said yes, of course, why not, and went about her business.

"Mama, I can say 'shit,' too, can't I?" Another distracted nod. I then turned to my friends like a magician about to perform the grand, saw-the-beautiful-girl-in-half finale. "Now I'm going to say 'cunt' in front of my mom," I announced. My friends gaped as I proceeded to do just that. Mama, having never heard that word before, couldn't have cared less. My audience was hugely impressed. I smirked triumphantly, and was still reveling in my newfound coolness when I heard a roar and felt myself being picked up by the ankles and thrown to the floor.

"Don't you ever cuss at her, you fucking little shit, if you ever call Mama that again I will fucking kill you!" My brother, six foot four and seven years older, then proceeded to swing me head first against the wall while I screamed at the top of my lungs. My friends looked on; this show just kept getting better and better. "Pasquale, why-a you killing your sister?" Mama shouted over the commotion, stopping short of actually forbidding Pasquale to murder me.

Pasquale's God status made him the perfect fodder for what would turn out to be by far the worst prank I ever pulled. I was twelve or thirteen, and I was up in my room talking with my friend Matt Donnelly when I got the brilliant idea that we should prank my mother. "Okay," I instructed Matt, "let's conference-call my mom, and you pretend to be a police officer." I went over his lines with him, and we dialed Mama. I could hear her pick up downstairs.

"Do you have a son named Pasquale DePandi?" Matt asked in his best serious adult voice, identifying himself as an officer with the Montgomery County Police Department.

"Yes?" Mama answered. "What-a this is about?"

Matt drew a deep breath. He was a natural. I listened, excited for the punchline.

"I'm so sorry to tell you, he died in a car accident."

Up in my room, I heard a boom, followed by a prolonged wailing. "Noooooooooo," Mama howled. I raced downstairs to find her weeping on the kitchen floor.

"Mama! Mama! April Fool's! It's April Fool's Day!" I cried.

"Noooooooo, nooooooo," she kept screaming through her tears.

"It's a joke!" I assured her, hoping she would find my fake glee contagious. "Pasquale is alive!"

"Waaaaaaa?" Mama jumped up and began beating me with every kitchen utensil within reach—wooden spoons, metal spatulas, a random cheese plane. She hurled pans at me as I fled her wrath. Fast-forward to me as an adult, getting ready to go on *The*

Arsenio Hall Show with my husband, Bill, and sharing this memory with the producer, who thought it was hysterically funny and urged me to tell it on air. Arsenio hadn't heard it and didn't know what was coming when he followed the prompt his producer had provided. When I finished telling the story, he looked stricken and said something like "Oh." The studio audience was uncomfortably silent, and when I looked past the lights, I saw a sea of moms glaring back at me. *Oops.* The only two people laughing were Bill and the wicked producer backstage.

I don't even have a great moral to the story. The important life lesson I took away from this episode was to think before I pranked, and avoid targeting old-school immigrants who have no idea what April Fool's Day is and have zero awareness of child protection laws in this country. I was outgrowing these childish practical jokes, anyway. Soon, I would be entering high school, and it was time to mature. That meant broadening my horizons, and graduating from prankster to aspiring juvenile delinquent. Sex, drugs, and drinking remained on my taboo list, which narrowed my options somewhat, but the bad behavior I did engage in, I turned out to be very good at: It's not that I didn't get caught stealing cars; I just always managed to get away. I was sort of a one-girl *Dukes of Hazzard* in greater Washington, D.C.

My first escapade behind the wheel was honestly more of a favor than a felony. Monica had gone off to college in Boston, but her best friend, Niki, was still like part of our family and treated me like a kid sister. As I grew older, Niki would become both a mentor and friend to me. So when she found herself in a pinch and needed a ride to the airport, I was flattered that she turned to me for help as a stand-in for her absentee BFF Monica. I generously offered Niki my parents' Mercedes. We got to the airport, and it only then seemed to dawn on Niki that someone—thirteen-year-old me, to be exact—would have to drive the car back home. "Don't worry, you'll be fine," Niki assured me. The airport was a good twenty miles from Bethesda, on the Virginia side of the Potomac River, but you could take surface streets and avoid the dreaded Beltway. This was all pre-GPS and iPhones, of course, but I was sure I knew the way. It didn't take me long to get lost in one of D.C.'s sketchier areas. This was when the District was considered one of the most dangerous cities in America, racking up nearly five hundred murders a year, and here I was, an eighth-grader joyriding her daddy's Mercedes through a neighborhood where people got shot and killed for their sneakers and Eddie Bauer jackets. I clipped a curb while making a turn, and a police car appeared out of nowhere behind me, lights flashing and siren whooping. I rolled down my window.

"License and registration," the officer said.

"Oh, shoot, I forgot my license," I said. "Can I just give you my name and birthdate?" I rattled off Monica's information, and he went back to his car to check it out. I had a quick flash of myself posing for a mug shot in striped jailbird pajamas, and my whole school finding out—they'd probably use it in the yearbook—but it wouldn't really matter because my parents would kill me, anyway, and I wouldn't have to face my classmates again. Just as the cop walked back up to my window, another car suddenly shot past us, tires squealing. "Holy shit!" the cop swore. "It's your lucky day," he told me before running back to his patrol car to give chase. I somehow found my way home, and Mama and Babbo never missed me or the Mercedes.

I had something of a Roadrunner versus Wile E. Coyote relationship with the police. I got pulled over again when I went joyriding in my friend Liz's family station wagon (with Liz riding shotgun, of course). I slammed the gas and fled as the policeman was getting out of his squad car. He gave chase, but I lost him in the leafy neighborhoods of Bethesda by wheeling into a driveway and pulling into a random garage whose door was open. I turned the lights out, and Liz and I crouched down in the seat for twenty minutes to be sure the coast was clear. Knowing I had shaken the police gave me the best adrenaline rush ever. I was such a little gangster, I even made it a habit to take the license plates off whatever car I was borrowing without permission (or a license).

On yet another occasion, Liz, my friend Alison, and I heard about a party we wanted to go to late one night during a sleepover freshman year. Securing that particular ride had put my formidable acting experience to the test, since it was Alison's grandmother's car we were borrowing, the keys were on her grandmother's nightstand, and her grandmother was asleep in the bed next to them. Alison had been a less than enthusiastic accomplice (*"Are you crazy? We can't steal Nana's car!"*), but I was persuasive (*"Sure, we can! Watch this!"*). Liz and I tiptoed into the room. Nana was not the heavy sleeper my own Nonna had been—she definitely would have noticed a Play-Doh penis plopping onto her pillow—and she stirred as we inched our way inside her bedroom.

"Alison, honey, is that you?" she murmured.

"Yes, Nana, go back to sleep," I whispered sweetly. "I just need a tissue. I have a runny nose."

"Okay, honey. The Kleenex are on the nightstand." Zoom, off we went. And back we came a few hours later, with no one the wiser.

I had an uncanny ability to pretend nothing out of the ordinary had ever happened, and I could fool even the people who knew me best.

It was a survival skill that was about to be put to the test.

chapter three

"N ext. Uh, huh, uh huh. Okay. Next." The school nurse was calling us forward one by one in gym class to check our posture. I waited nervously. I had always avoided doing self-checks in the mirror or asking my parents to see if my spine was straight, terrified that what had happened to my sister might happen to me. I silently prayed for the school nurse to nod in approval and write down on her clipboard that Giuliana DePandi was normal. When it was my turn, I stepped up, waited for her to look me over, then moved aside for the next kid in line.

"Julie, hold on a sec. Bend over," the nurse said, pulling me back and running her hand over my spine. "You need to go to the doctor. You have a curve."

I was thirteen. The same age Monica had been when she had had to have her surgery. I kept picturing myself wearing her old brace, or on an operating table. My mind replayed that day in Monica's hospital room when she had been in such agony she had wanted to kill herself. I feared the pain more than anything. I walked out of school that afternoon fighting tears as I imagined how my mother would take this devastating news. Mama refused to believe it at first—that old Italian denial—and made me bend over in the kitchen so she could see for herself. An orthopedist confirmed the school nurse's finding: I had scoliosis. I was no longer just skinny and awkward: I was crooked. Monica cried. The good news was that I only had a nineteen-degree curve, and Mama and Babbo were against putting me in a brace, having seen one child suffer through that ordeal already for nothing. It was decided that we would just take a wait-and-see approach with me; if the scoliosis didn't worsen, I might never need anything more than some ibuprofen now and then for backaches. That was the best-case scenario. But my body quickly betrayed me, and as I hit puberty, my right hip rose higher than the other, jutting out at an angle. One side of my chest protruded, which may have been less noticeable if I were curvy to begin with, but that wasn't the case, so I would stuff my bra with Kleenex to try to even things out into something that did not look like a 32A through a funhouse mirror. I was all twisted, and every day the first thing on my mind was how to fool everyone into thinking I was straight.

I didn't tell any of my friends about my diagnosis, and built my new wardrobe going into high school around oversized sweatshirts. Babbo had to start tailoring one leg of my jeans so they would fit right, but needle and thread weren't going to fix the way tops hung on me. I wanted to be like everyone else, to blend invisibly into the unremarkable river of kids hurrying to class or hanging out at the mall. I wanted to not make myself sick with worry before my annual X-ray and MRI, when the specialists monitoring my scoliosis would decide whether it was bad enough to warrant the same excruciating spinal fusion my sister had undergone.

Nonna had taught me as a little girl that prayer should never be a selfish act, but I figured I could sneak in a personal favor as long as it wasn't a biggie and I made sure to express gratitude for all the blessings I already had. So I asked God to just let me be normal. Average was all I was asking. I wasn't going to get all greedy and pray to wake up as Brooke Shields's secret twin. Just please, God, Jesus, Mary, the Holy Ghost, and whatever saint is eavesdropping, could I not be lopsided?

As I grew, though, the occasional twinges turned into a chronic backache, and it got harder to deny the impact the scoliosis was beginning to have on my everyday kid life. I was a soccer goalie and junior varsity cheerleader, but I didn't dare tell my coaches or teammates that diving for the ball was killing my hip, or that jumping up and down at a football game could leave me gasping for breath. I didn't want anyone, including my own parents, to suspect how bad it was actually getting, so I just accepted every fresh or worsening symptom as my new normal. My life was turning into one big masquerade, and I was self-taught in the art of illusion. I learned to camouflage my misshapen body by casually leaning against walls when I could, so the jutting hip became part of a contrived slouch. *"Stand up straight!"* I was forever being urged by people who had no idea I couldn't. "Oh, whatever, I'm just tired," I would shrug. Nonchalance was the key to my whole act, my best survival skill. The more something mattered to me, the more I would pretend it didn't.

I actually envied classmates who were overweight or had to wear thick glasses—millions of people in the world could relate to them. They had the option of making time their ally instead of the enemy; you saw it every fall, when a lucky few would return to high school a social caste or two higher than the semester before after losing weight or getting contacts or finding a good dermatologist over the summer. But scoliosis was a different level of ugly. Scoliosis was the kid with the brace trying to drink out of a water fountain in the movie *Sixteen Candles*. Scoliosis was people staring. It was the voice inside their heads and mine, saying *Eeew, you're a freak*. Scoliosis meant I was deformed, and that was something I never wanted anyone outside my family or orthopedist's office to know. I accepted what I took to be the cruel truth—that I was ugly—but that didn't mean I had to publicly admit it. Pity was the last thing on earth I wanted.

I masked my deep insecurity by becoming the funny chick, that nutty Italian girl who was every guy's pal but never more. I secretly crushed on virtually every one of those "just a friend" boys but rebuffed any of them who showed interest. I'd go to the school dances or out clubbing using my sister's ID, but I always got off the dance floor if a slow number came on. I knew if I let a boy touch me, my freakishness would be exposed. No bra stuffing or expert tailoring of a homecoming dress would change the crooked contours of my body beneath it. I imagined the surprise and disgust a guy would feel when he felt my jutting shoulder blades, or put his hands on my hips to draw me closer, then discovered that one hand was inches higher than the other. It was much easier to suck down the loneliness and let everyone run with the assumption that I was playing hard to get. "Oh, Julie is so picky," my friends would say. The upshot was that I had a really good reputation that I didn't necessarily want. All my friends were hooking up while I watched from the sidelines of the popular crowd, forever the best supporting actress in everyone else's movie. I wasn't crying myself to sleep, though, or partying my way to oblivion like half my classmates did every weekend. I was sure that my time would come later.

Weirdly enough, for all my insecurity and self-consciousness, still burning inside me was that same stubborn conviction I'd had since the age of seven, that I was meant to be on camera.

I wanted everyone to look at me; I just didn't want anyone to
see me.

Walt Whitman High School was notoriously competitive, full
of kids whose parents had been meticulously assembling them
from a Build Your Own Overachiever kit since birth, and nobody would have suspected for a millisecond that I was just as
ambitious—if not more so—than the classmates vying for vale-
dictorian. At Whitman, achieving a perfect GPA wasn't impres-
sive enough; kids felt pressured to pile on enough honors classes,
early college credits, and whatever else it took to achieve *above*
a 4.0 average. It was the academic equivalent of being a size 0
in Hollywood: the quest for a beyond-perfect ideal that existed
only because they created it out of their own desperation.

I was such a lazy student, I could barely maintain a D average. I couldn't even muster a C in Italian. And the class was
mostly conversational! How could I be incoherent in my native
tongue? This just went to prove how stupid school was. Even
getting kicked off the cheerleading squad for flunking a typing
class (yes, typing) didn't serve as a wake-up call. Nope, my dis-
mal academic record didn't bother me one bit. I regarded high
school as my social life, and the classes I was required to take
were just annoying bases I had to touch on my way to news-
caster stardom. All those hours I saved not studying or doing any
homework gave me lots of time to daydream, and my goals did
not require me to perform autopsies on pickled frogs or measure the angles of rhomboids for no apparent reason. When my
tenth-grade geometry teacher wrapped up an intense class once
by asking if anyone had any questions, I raised my hand. "When
will we ever use geometry in the real world?" I wanted to know.
The teacher launched into a long tirade about the various ways
geometry would come in handy, but let's be honest, I had asked
the question that was on everyone else's mind, too, and I was
too busy glorying in the instant peer admiration I had won to

actually listen to the answer. I was sure that geometry had nothing to do with Barbara Harrison's continued success. The same anchorwoman I had admired in second grade was still on air ten years later. So there you have it.

There weren't any easy or obvious ways to get a head start on my news anchor career while still in my teens, but there were plenty of ways to prep for my companion goal of being crowned Miss USA. What I loved about the Miss Universe pageant system was that it didn't pretend to be about scholarship or talent—it was about stone-fox glamour. One of the best parts of watching the pageants was the carte blanche permission they gave you to just enjoy doing what you were going to secretly do anyway, and judge someone you didn't know based entirely on how attractive you thought they were, without having to factor in whether they were a gifted pianist or planned to use their prize check to pay for dental school. From what I could glean, modeling seemed like a logical starting place for a future Miss USA. I was tall and skinny, so maybe there was some hope.

When I saw an ad for the Barbizon School of Modeling in the paper, I begged my parents to enroll me. I would even get a certificate upon completion of the course. I could frame it as proof I was a real model. One brief interview and twelve hundred dollars of my parents' hard-earned cash later, I was in! The weekly classes were the highlight of my week. I would learn how to get in and out of the backseat of a car elegantly (in case the paparazzi were shooting me arriving at a premiere). I also learned how to sashay down the runway based on what style of clothing I was modeling. Evening wear? Slow and seductive. High-fashion sportswear? Fast and fierce. My personal favorite was safari wear (because you never knew when you might get booked for the one Banana Republic fashion show of the year—hard to believe, but in the eighties, Banana Republic actually sold safari-inspired fashion). The key to modeling in a safari-themed fashion show, we were instructed, is to appear "focused on a mission." I would imagine I was on a mission to find monkeys and bananas in the jungle. Monkeys were my favorite animal as a kid, and bananas were my fave fruit, so . . . bam! Mission accomplished! I wasn't merely a model, I was Academy Award material.

After a couple of months, Barbizon announced that we were ready for our photo shoots, which we could then use to assemble a portfolio to send to Eileen Ford and other top modeling agencies in New York that were *waiting to hire us*. Cindy Crawford was probably losing sleep over the very prospect. When I walked into the photo studio with my ten modeling school classmates, my eyes nearly popped out of my head. There were racks of clothes and fancy props. Everything from sequined gowns and boas to cocktail dresses and statement necklaces. It was even better than my sister's closet (Monica would never be caught dead in feathers). One by one, the stylist and photographer sized each of us up and decided what our "look" would be—not just for the photos, but for all modeling eternity. Their choice was what we should carry forth into the industry if we wanted to become the superstars Barbizon had prepared us to be.

First up was the pretty blonde who was a little short to do high fashion. She was handed a cute peasant top and jeans and told her look was "catalog fresh." Catalog fresh? I felt bad for her. I had heard that girls in catalogs made decent money, but nothing like the fortune tall girls like me could rake in on the runways of New York, Paris, and Milan. The next girl was labeled swimsuit. That definitely would not be my fate, given my curved spine. Next up: runway. *Okay, there's room for two of us, no big deal.* Then came another catalog. Finally it was my turn. The two Barbizon reps looked me up and down. Then they looked at each other, and then at me, up and down again. Then they did something that they had not done with any of the other girls. The photographer and stylist walked away and started whispering.

Some girls would no doubt see this as a bad thing, but I was not one of those girls. My imagination hit the "Play" button on its favorite biopic in progress, and I saw them walking back to me with huge smiles on their faces as they looked me dead in the eyes and told me I had what it takes to go to New York and become a supermodel. My brilliant potential defied any label. This had to be how Naomi Campbell felt the first time she walked into a modeling agency, and now this was happening to me. It was the most exciting moment of my fourteen-year-old life until a voice rudely interrupted my reverie. "Julie," the bitchy voice said, "you are what we call an athletic model. You're tall and lean like an athlete, and we see you modeling a variety of athletic wear in catalogs." It was bad enough I was being told I was a catalog model, but to be told I would basically be modeling for the Sports Authority's newspaper inset was even more of a blow than modeling mediocre fashion pieces in the annual Spiegel catalog.

Before I could start crying, they thrust a sporty outfit into my skinny—*lean*—arms along with a tennis racquet, a white Izod visor to squash down over my short permed-mushroom bob, and size ten white tennis shoes that looked like a size fifteen with my teeny-tiny bony ankles poking out. Not a cute look. But Barbizon was not done with me yet: They stood me in front of a white screen and started throwing tennis balls at me, urging me to swing energetically. I kept missing and the tennis balls kept hitting me, and I tried to fend off the Barbizon attack by twisting the racquet every which way but up. It was awful.

I waited a month for the contact sheets to arrive, praying that maybe a couple of shots had miraculously turned out fabulous. When the envelope finally came, I opened it upstairs in my bedroom and immediately started bawling into my favorite stuffed animal, a dog named Curly who was named after my first real dog, Curly, who was run over by a school bus when I was eight and replaced by another little poodle, who was also named

Curly. Neither the stuffed Curly, the memory of the late Curly, nor the concerned face licking of the current live Curly could begin to console me over my sabotaged modeling career.

Every single picture in the Barbizon shots showed me with my eyes shut tight or a look of sheer terror on my face. I didn't even look like I was playing tennis. I looked like I was using the racquet as self-defense while being attacked, like Tippi Hedren in Hitchcock's movie *The Birds*. And I was so shell-shocked over being labeled "athletic," I hadn't even realized how awful the outfit I was modeling actually was. The least they could have done was dress me in a flirty little tennis skirt, but nooooo. I was defending myself from killer birds while wearing what appeared to be prison pajamas—an oversized shirt with broad stripes and matching Bermuda shorts. Both were at least four sizes too big on me. I called Barbizon to ask for a reshoot. They agreed, for an extra five hundred dollars. Pass. I was done.

Even I could see that putting my career in Barbizon's hands was not going to get me anywhere other than another expensive level of Barbizondom, so I cut out the middleman and became my own junior talent agent. Every Sunday, I would settle in with a stack of Chips Ahoy to dunk in my latte while I carefully scoured the classifieds section of the *Washington Post*, looking for audition notices. These cattle calls invariably took place in some conference room of a nondescript office building in a skeezy part of town, but Mama would always give in to my excitement and patiently wait for hours until I was rejected yet again. The biggest one was the casting call for the lead in *Return to the Blue Lagoon*, which I thought I was perfect for even though my acne, scoliosis, and bad eighties perm made me look more like Bon Jovi's hideous sister than Brooke Shields 2.0. When we showed up at the audition, all the pretty almost-Brookes and their barracuda mothers looked at Mama and me as if we'd misread the ad and thought it was a remake involving the black lagoon, not the blue one, and I was trying out for the "creature from" role. No callback on that one. Or the next one or the next. I had a hard shell, though, and just kept going to whatever audition I could. When I spotted a casting call for a feature film called *Broadcast News*, my one-track mind was officially blown: this had to be fate! I persuaded Mama to drive me downtown to wait in a long line yet again. When my turn came, and the casting director asked how old I was, I tacked on a couple of years to match the minimum age requirement and said I was sixteen.

"Okay, you got it."

"No way!" I blurted. Thank God, I had the good sense to shut up before they reconsidered, and I eagerly agreed to return the following Saturday at six in the morning to start filming. The adrenaline rush was probably going to keep me awake until then anyway. When the big day arrived, I got to the set and found out that I was going to be an extra in the scene where a young Albert Brooks delivers his graduation speech ("Thank you, and go fuck yourselves"). I would be a member of the graduating class he was addressing, which, at the rate I was going, was as close to a commencement ceremony as I'd ever get. It took over four hours to shoot the brief scene. Everyone else sitting there in a mortarboard and gown grew increasingly bored and miserable, but I had this huge smile plastered across my face. I was so happy to be on camera, I couldn't *stop* smiling.

I ended up getting the close-up, and when the hit movie came out, I made like I was starring in it (Holly Hunter was just photo-bombing). My face flashed across the screen in approximately half a blink, and most of my friends never even saw me. I can't remember what I got paid, and my sister probably stole it, anyway. None of that mattered: I had been on screen.

Every time I interview Holly Hunter, I have to resist the urge to blurt out, "Do I look familiar, Holly? Remember when we were in *Broadcast News* together?" But she isn't exactly the easiest interview in the first place—very serious, hates personal questions, redirects with one-word answers—and I don't think she would be amused by my silly childhood pipe dreams. *Broadcast News* turned out to be a huge hit, but not my big break. I never got another part, and, contrary to Barbizon's big promises, I never got any callbacks for modeling jobs, either. As a suburban badass, however, my star just kept on rising. I was fifteen when I picked up my first stalker-fan.

Officer Pervy, as I came to call him, had pulled me over on yet another one of my grand theft auto escapades. This time, at least it was my own parents' car I jacked. They had gone out to dinner in their Jeep Cherokee and left the Mercedes behind, and my best friend Andrea and I decided to go cruise River Road, the major thoroughfare that connects suburban Maryland to D.C. We headed for the Universal Church of Bored Teens Up to No Good, aka the 7-Eleven. Just as we hoped, a group of bad boys stood smoking outside, obviously waiting for a German luxury car full of good girls to show up. I homed in on a boy named Lance. He had black hair, shocking blue eyes, and pale skin. He wore an old T-shirt and baggy jeans with about three inches of his boxers on full display. When it was time to go, I was so busy trying to be cool as I pulled out of the parking lot that I accidentally jumped the curb turning back onto River Road. The all-too-familiar flash of police lights instantly appeared behind me.

My streak of juvenile delinquent luck had just run its course. I tried the forgotten-license trick using my sister's name, but I screwed up her birth date. After running my bogus information, the cop ordered me out of the Mercedes.

"What's your name and who are you?" he demanded.

"Let me explain," I began. He cut me off.

"We're not explaining anything." He noticed the 7-Eleven boys watching us.

"Who are those guys?" the cop now wanted to know.

"They go to Monroe," I answered. Monroe High School was as close as you could come to being on the wrong side of the tracks in Bethesda, which wasn't saying much.

"What are two pretty white girls doing with thugs from Monroe?" the cop said. It wasn't so much a question as a not-so-subtle racist remark. Two of the Monroe boys were black. I deflected the interrogation by shrugging and saying we didn't really know them. Which brought Officer Pervyracist back to the central issue: Who was I?

I attempted to plead the Fifth and refused to provide contact information for my parents.

"You can either tell me, or I lock you up for driving without a license," the cop said.

To his surprise, I pounced on Door #2.

"I need to be behind bars when my dad shows up," I explained. I wasn't kidding. This was not a Mama-with-kitchen-utensil kind of offense.

The cop cracked a smile, and I sensed my opening.

"I'm telling you, Officer, I'm a great driver! I'm Italian. Like Mario Andretti. Driving is in my blood! My birthday is on August 17, and I'll pass the driving test without missing a point, I swear." I had learned from enough trips to the front office at Walt Whitman that fluttering my eyelashes, dusting off the Italian accent, and tossing in a few *ciao bella*s went a long way when I needed damage control. I had stellar flirting skills, and zero shame. It was a useful combination.

"Okay, I'm going to let you go, but here's the deal," Pervy said. "On August 17, you are going to take your driver's test, and if you don't pass, I am going to come find you, and when I find you, you are going to be in trouble. Then I'm going to arrest you." I thanked him profusely and was sent illegally on my way. Pervy followed closely behind to make sure I drove straight home.

My sixteenth birthday rolled around, and the second I got home from school, I began lobbying to go to the DMV. The hurdle wasn't so much getting Mama to agree to drop everything and take me ASAP—it was waiting for her to corral every other blood relative within a thirty-mile radius to go with us. In an Italian family, you never know what is going to be decreed a major life event requiring the presence of not just parents and siblings, but grandparents, aunts, uncles, cousins, and friends who count as "just like family."

My entourage of a dozen or so spectators assembled noisily in the DMV parking lot as I climbed into the car with the examiner. I smiled brightly. The examiner regarded me with flat shark eyes. Charm was going to get me nowhere with this one. For the next fifteen minutes or so, I chauffeured her around the prescribed course, executing every three-point turn, blind-spot check, and lane change perfectly. When I slipped smooth as butter into a tight parallel parking space, the examiner let out an involuntary "Beautiful!" and I knew I had nailed my test. As I drove into the homestretch, I could see my family shouting, clapping, and jumping up and down. I was so excited, I started giving them thumbs-up, and accidentally blew right through the last stop sign. I put the car in park, gushed my thanks to the examiner, and waited for her to hand me my prize. She sneered at me triumphantly.

"Do you not know what you just did?" she demanded. "You just ran that stop sign."

What? I looked back over my shoulder and spotted the trick stop sign.

"Holy shit, noooooo!" I said by way of apology.

"Yep. And that is not good, so maybe you better tell your

family to stop acting all crazy." They were still jumping up and down. This was starting to play like a *Saturday Night Live* skit. I couldn't believe one little mistake was going to cost me my license. No way was I going down without a fight.

"This is the worst day of my life! And on top of it, you are being such a bitch!"

"Oh, really?" She looked down at her clipboard and furiously jotted something down. "That's an automatic sixteen points taken off for Attitude. You're done," she concluded, thrusting the failing score sheet at me.

"Are you fucking kidding me?" I shrieked.

"You better stop cussing," she warned.

"No! This is fucking ridiculous! I want my fucking license!"

She got out of the car and marched up to my parents, who smiled proudly, assuming she had come to congratulate them on raising such a wonderful driver.

"Your daughter has a real attitude problem," she informed them. "I failed her for running a stop sign and for her nasty behavior. She just called me a bitch." Everyone else stopped jumping and applauding. Babbo briefly studied the examiner and considered her complaint before responding.

"Well, that's-*a* because you *are* a beetch!" he shouted.

Oh no, here we go, I thought. The only thing that could possibly make the situation any worse would be if Officer Pervy made good on his threat and swooped in to cuff me. Mayhem was prevented only because DMV Beetch realized that a couple of carloads of crazy Italians would easily take out every examiner on duty in a parking lot brawl. We all went home to finish celebrating my birthday. If I laid low for a while, I might be able to retake the test and pass before Officer Pervy hunted me down.

I flunked the second time, too, but without the drama.

I was relieved that Officer Pervy had forgotten all about me and my little unlicensed driver escapade, which, after all, was nothing compared to all my other unlicensed driver escapades. Just before I was eligible to take the driving test for a third time, I came out of school one afternoon to see a familiar face waiting for me.

"I hear you failed your driving test," Officer Pervy said. It was pretty obvious why he hadn't shot up the ranks and made detective yet. Half the school knew I had failed. Freshmen knew I had failed. I nodded my head and tried to look dejected. Officer Pervy had a pretend sad smirk on his face. "You hungry?" he asked. "C'mon." He took me to my favorite fast-food joint, Roy Rogers, where he watched me eat chicken legs dipped in mayo and smack my fingers while I chattered on about my fascinating life as a high school student.

The third time was a charm at the DMV, but Officer Pervy didn't forget about me. He would pop up every so often to take me out for fast food, and I would tell him about the kids at school—who was smoking, who was hooking up with a football player, who got busted for making out in a bathroom stall. As far as looks went, Pervy was never going to make the cut for a first responders calendar: he was fortyish and paunchy, with brown hair and a mustache. Nonetheless, I still thought it was proof of my coolness that a cop actually seemed fascinated by my stories and wanted to pal around with me. One day, he showed up in the Whitman parking lot while I was hanging out with a bunch of my friends. He kept trying to signal me to come over. "What's that cop doing here?" my friends wondered. "What's he want?" I shrugged along with them, and ignored Pervy's insistent gestures. Finally he called out, "Giuliana, can I ask you a quick question?" I sauntered up to his car.

"What?" I asked. I could feel my friends watching while pretending not to, everyone urgently speculating about what kind of trouble I had managed to get myself into.

"What did you want to ask me?" I asked Pervy again. He

fidgeted with a bag in his hand and looked nervous. Our relationship was 100 percent platonic, but we both understood without saying so that the power had shifted between us many McNuggets ago. He was no longer an authority figure. Now he was just an adult who seemed awkward and confused.

"Uh, well, I, uh, have a new girlfriend, and I was hoping you could tell me whether I should give her flowers or lingerie for Valentine's Day. What do you think?" He pulled a red teddy from the bag.

"Omigod, definitely lingerie. That's so sexy!" I felt grown up to be asked for such advice. "Okay, so, I have to go now! Good luck!" I turned and rejoined my friends.

"What was that all about?" one of them wanted to know.

"Oh, nothing, he just wanted my opinion about some lingerie for his girlfriend," I said. There was a collective outcry of "*Eeew!! Gross!! That's so creepy!!*" My friends convinced me that there was nothing innocent or remotely normal about a uniformed cop taking a sixteen-year-old girl out for after-school snacks in her short shorts and seeking her advice about underwear. The next time Pervy appeared out of the blue, I breezily waved at him and kept walking, and that was the end of that. I didn't need or want his attention, anyway; I had a boyfriend.

I was dating Lance, the 7-Eleven bad boy. Lance was one in a series of losers I gravitated toward. I was all shoot-for-the-moon when it came to pranks or outrageous behavior, but when it came to romance, I purposely aimed low. Little ventured, less lost. I boasted a perfect record of never being dumped only because I was accomplished in the art of preventive dumping. I never wanted anyone to see me hurt. My working assumption was that anyone who chose me would never want to keep me, except maybe the bottom-feeders who couldn't get anyone else. If I sensed that a guy I liked was losing interest, I would bolt before he publicly confirmed how unworthy I was by leaving me first.

When I pulled the plug on a relationship, everyone was going to know. I was not the type to beat a quiet retreat. Even the DMV knew that. Not everyone was that perceptive. There was Sam, for example. Sam was a cute Middle Eastern boy who hung out with the Euro crowd of kids whose parents were diplomats, World Bankers, and the like. Sam and I were briefly a couple in my senior year, until I left early one night when we went clubbing, only to hear later that he had made out with one of my friends, a hot Latina named Sophia. The next day, I went to school ready to kill them both. I waited for Sam after first period and slapped the crap out of him in the hallway in front of an appreciative audience. After second period, I found him again and did the same thing. Sam offered a very sincere apology and begged my forgiveness, which our hallway audience also appreciated. I started to melt, then changed my mind.

"No! You know what? I'm going to slap you every period!" He had five more to go.

I got a hall pass during third period, and spotted Sophia through the glass of a classroom door. I started gesticulating wildly until a few kids noticed me, and my mimed message was somehow relayed across the rows of desks to Sophia. Sophia looked up to see my angry face in the window. "*I am going to kill you,*" I mouthed, slashing a hand across my throat for emphasis. I then gestured for her to come out into the hall for her murder. Sophia shook her head. I gestured more vehemently. She pretended to pay attention to the English teacher droning on about Shakespeare. I decided that if Sophia wasn't going to come out to get killed, I was going in. I opened the door, marched up to her desk, and dragged her out of her seat. She resisted by trying to hold on to anything in her path, like desks and heads. The teacher stood frozen in shock. Things like this did not happen at a school like Walt Whitman.

Once in the hallway, we both fell to the floor, and a pathetic girl fight ensued with hair-pulling and screaming. We scuffled until the teacher broke it up and sent me to the vice principal. I got suspended and was told to go home. I left campus, but kept coming back after each period to slap Sam, who had run out at lunch to buy me roses in hopes I would stop beating him up. I threw down the flowers and slapped him anyway. I was the crazed woman scorned, the one you see on *Dateline*. I finally forgave Sam after the seventh-period slap, and we went to prom together before I broke up with him for good. With Lance, though, what happened was much darker, and finding my way out was more complicated.

At first, things were fun. Lance's best friend, Brandon, was the hottest guy in the world. Brandon was always sweet to me, and dating Lance felt like I was sort of shadow-dating Brandon. Just being in Brandon's circle was motivation enough for me to pair up with Lance. Compared to the rich, preppy boys who went to Walt Whitman, though, Lance and his pals were definitely more urban than suburban. They frequented the sketchy hip-hop clubs that sprung up in warehouses on the ragged fringes of D.C., and favored an underground band called the Junkyard Boys. I thought listening to Vanilla Ice made me street. When I heard Lance blasting the Junkyard Boys from his boom box, I thought he was the epitome of cool. I became a Junkyard Boys fan, too, banking on a cool-by-association ploy that fooled no one but yours truly. Lance may not have been a threat to society, but he was just enough danger for me.

The abuse started out as a joke, just Lance being an asshole, and me being the tough-cool chick who could handle it. "You're so ugly. You know how fucking ugly you are, right?" Lance would say, and I would laugh along with him. But the more often he said those words, the sharper they became, any pretense at humor filed off their edges until nothing but the sharp thin blade remained. No one had ever spoken to me that way before.

I acted like I knew how to take it, but I didn't. I would laugh it off and tell Lance to fuck off, too, but then I would go home and cry. I would stare in the mirror at my swollen, red eyes, my mouthful of braces, my bad skin, and skinny, crooked body and see that Lance was absolutely right: I was ugly. The Giuliana the world saw was nothing like the beauty queen and anchorwoman who lived in my imagination. Even though, at sixteen, I was fully Americanized, the insecurity of being a foreigner, of always lagging behind in school and not quite fitting in, never left me—it lingers to this day. I still felt different, never as pretty or talented or intelligent as the other girls. Lance wasn't telling me anything I hadn't secretly known all along.

I never told my family that I had a boyfriend. Babbo would have flipped out. I remember sitting around at dinner one night with the TV on, all of us watching *Beverly Hills 90210*, and Brenda kissed her boyfriend. My father was horrified. "He's kissing her in high school? That's terrible! That's wrong! Giuliana, just so you know, you won't be doing things like this until you are much older!" I nodded earnestly. "Yeah, I know, Dad. She's a *puttana*. And so are the other girls on this stupid show, Donna and Kelly." I'd been dating and kissing boys on the sly for some time by then, but I knew the wisest course was to just agree with my parents and then do whatever I wanted when they weren't looking.

One time, my mom came home earlier than expected to find Lance and all his hoodlum friends splashing around our pool, drinking and playing loud music and being rowdy. When Mama walked out on the patio, a boy who looked like he had served time for murder happened to be jumping up and down like a crazy person on the diving board. My mom yelled at me and kicked everyone out. She would have really freaked if she knew one of those losers was my boyfriend.

Much as Lance enjoyed an audience when he was humiliating

me, the emotional abuse was worst when we were alone. Lance would rip me apart, telling me how hideous I was. He would shove me into the bathroom and yell at me to face the mirror.

"Look at you, look at your face. You see how fucking ugly you are?" he snorted, laughing at his own bad luck. "Your body's disgusting! No one else would ever want you!" I didn't fight back. I knew it was true. I wish I knew what makes a young girl or grown woman allow some loser who will never be half the person she is to take his own insecurities out on her. I stayed with Lance for nearly a year, letting him voice all the worst things I already thought about myself. I was a dog. Worse, I was dog vomit. I was stupid, and I was fucking ugly. I never told my friends about the abuse. Something that painful, you just block out and don't share. Not even—especially not even—with your overprotective Italian father. Babbo was arriving home for lunch once just as a friend was dropping me off after school. One of my platonic male friends in the backseat had shouted out to him, "Mr. DePandi! I love your daughter!"

Babbo stopped on the porch.

"Whatta you say?"

"I said I LOVE YOUR DAUGHTER! She's the best!"

"Just-*a* minute!" Babbo turned to go inside. I had a hunch what was coming.

"DRIVE! GET OUT OF HERE! NOW!!" I yelled at the boys.

Babbo reappeared with a baseball bat and began running at their car. They took off, and Babbo kept chasing them.

I should have told Babbo about Lance.

Instead, I found the motivation to leave only after Lance cheated on me with a private school girl and I found out. Her name was Jill, and I sent word through the girl grapevine that she needed to meet me at the 7-Eleven. I fully intended to kick her slut ass. We both showed up with our girlfriends, like it was

West Side Story or something. Jill turned out to be this sweet little five-foot-tall thing who I probably could take down with a single Slurpee to the face. She immediately started apologizing. "I didn't know," she said. "He duped us both." We decided to conquer instead of divide. "We should do something fun," I suggested.

I pretended everything was fine, and went to Lance's house. Of course, he wanted to make out in his bedroom. When I dangled a pair of handcuffs I had bought, just for this occasion, at an adult toy shop in Georgetown, his eyes lit up. He must have thought I was really coming out of my shell. I cuffed him to the bed and quickly stripped him, promising him I had a big surprise. Saying he was excited is an understatement. I yelled for Jill, who was waiting outside.

"Surprise, Lance, it's your other girlfriend," I said when she walked in. It was pretty obvious we didn't have a threesome in mind. I leaned over him, and it was as if all the hurt and shame that had been building inside me for the past year suddenly crystallized into disgust—not with myself, for once, but for this worm splayed out now in front of me.

"You total piece of shit," I said. "Don't ever fuck with me again."

Then I spit on him. Again and again. And not just "Oh, my mouth is dry" kind of spit. I'm talking deep-rooted, nasty loogies right to the face. "Jill, spit in his face," I said.

"No, I can't," she protested.

"This piece of shit lied to us, used us, and treated us like garbage. The least you can do is spit in his face." Jill, at my urging, finally mustered up the courage to spit a big fat one right between the eyes. It was brilliant.

"You cannot leave me here!" he shouted. "My parents are going to find me!"

Actually, it was his older sister.

Years later, married with a houseful of kids, he sent me a message on Facebook.

"Congratulations, Julie. I knew you could do it!" he wrote.

I did what I should have done with Lance the minute I met him: I dragged him straight to the trash.

High school ended, for me, not with the proverbial bang or whimper, but with a frantic Hail Mary pass to end all Hail Mary passes. It was the last week of school when the principal summoned me to his office.

"You have forty-five absences this year," Dr. Marco said.

"But it's senior year. You're not supposed to go to class senior year!" I objected. Seriously, what handbook was he using here?

"You're failing every subject."

"But I proved myself!" Even I didn't know what that was supposed to mean, but it sounded righteous. I could probably sweet-talk my way up to D minuses or do some makeup work over the summer.

"No, you're not graduating," Dr. Marco reiterated. "You can't fail senior English and graduate."

I was mortified. What was going on here? I'd been skating for four years, and only now they're telling me there's no ice? I might have been less surprised if I hadn't made a habit out of intercepting any mail from school and burying it in the trash without bothering to open it.

"But I already have a party planned and I have my dress and everything," I sputtered. "Please, Dr. Marco, I'll do *anything*!" The principal sighed heavily. Whether it was pity for me or pity for the teachers who would get stuck with me for another year if I didn't graduate, I'll never know, but Dr. Marco sent for the English teacher to see if a treaty could be negotiated.

It was the same teacher whose class I had interrupted to jump Sophia. Who knew it was *my* class, too? Hey, I had forty-five absences. She looked like one of those grandmotherly nannies who turns fifty shades of psycho when the parents leave and drowns the children in the bathtub. Beady eyes behind old-fashioned spectacles, mousy hair in a tight bun. She addressed Dr. Marco as if I weren't standing right there.

"Miss DePandi has a total disregard for Shakespeare," Psychobun declared. "She never read *Hamlet* along with the other seniors. If she wants a passing grade, she needs to recite the soliloquy in front of the class. Without a single mistake."

Home free.

Two things I happen to excel at are juggling and memorization. I taught myself how to juggle off a cheesy tutorial tape I bought at Circuit City, and I still like to show off my moves on the red carpet or to any interviewer who'll let me. I will challenge some star to a juggle-off while wearing a ten-thousand-dollar couture gown. They almost always agree, because really, who's going to turn down a five-foot-ten circus seal in Valentino? Memorization, on the other hand, isn't something I trained myself to do: It's just a freak talent I've always had. I can look at a page of script once and my mind will take a picture of it. I cracked open my like-new English lit book, read the soliloquy through a couple of times, closed the book, went to class, and recited it perfectly.

Diploma accomplished.

Next stop, Miss USA.

chapter four

I was right: You didn't have to have talent, perfect SAT scores, or the spun-sugar heart of a Disney princess. From what I could tell, as long as you weren't a call girl, coke addict, or drag queen, you had a shot at becoming Miss USA. You could be the fugliest girl in Maryland, but as long as you had a pulse and the $1,500 entry fee, you were more than welcome to enter the state pageant. *At last*, I thought, as I sat down with my official paperwork. I went to work happily filling in the blanks. Name, gender, address, birth date, high school attended. *Done, done, done, done, done.* Citizenship.

Sound of cartoon brakes screeching inside my head.

Whaaa?

Shocking true fact: You have to be an actual American citizen to become Miss USA. Let's be honest here. It's not like you're actually *representing* the country in some official capacity, right? How many international peace talks have been brokered by nineteen-year-olds wearing rhinestone tiaras and silk sashes? This was stupid! I wanted to be Miss USA, dammit, not secretary of state.

If there was a sneaky way around this hurdle, believe me, I would have found it. After all, guile had worked its evil magic when I wanted to be a homecoming princess during my senior year at Whitman. I had simply run off a couple hundred Xerox copies of the nominating ballot and filled in my name on each one, trying to alter the handwriting, until my fingers cramped. I was great at signing my mother's signature to fake excuse notes or report cards she never saw, but I didn't have the patience for mass-production forgery. I stuffed the ballot box after letting myself into the front office after school with a key I'd gotten hold of in some clandestine manner several semesters earlier when I needed to do an emergency interception of interim report cards. Whitman was a huge school, and plenty of kids—my crowd included—would never be caught dead actually voting for something as lame as homecoming court. I correctly assumed that plenty of ballots would go to waste if I didn't put them to good use. So I forged and waited. When they announced the homecoming court over the intercom, there was a noticeable pause before the final nominee's name was read: ". . . and finally, Julie DePandi." You could hear necks breaking in my classroom as each kid turned to look at me in disbelief. It was me and four straight-A, goody-two-shoes popular girls who couldn't believe I was crashing their ball. I was not what Whitman considered queen material. "A little rough around the edges" would be putting it diplomatically. My friends were all laughing themselves sick, waiting for me to let them in on what was surely one of my infamous pranks. *What a bunch of bullshit! What'd you do, dude?* Forgetting momentarily that I had, in fact, rigged the vote, I was deeply offended. Was my nomination *that* unimaginable? "What do you mean? No!" I protested. "I don't see what's so funny. People *love* me!!"

Needless to say, I came in a distant fifth.

Older and much wiser now, I wasn't about to watch my Miss USA/Universe dream crash and burn on takeoff. I suppose I could have gone back to Naples and tried to make my way to the Miss Universe stage as Miss Italy, but then who would my father heckle on TV? Besides, I had already played the Italian card once on the pageant circuit. That particular fiasco had been put into motion when my sister entered the Holy Rosary Miss Pomodora contest at our church. In her pink taffeta gown, Monica was by far the prettiest one—and the obvious choice to represent tomatoes in our parish—but the catechism teacher's little sister won instead. I vowed to avenge my family's honor and become Miss Tomato as soon as I was old enough. When that time came, however, I changed my mind: Nope, I was going bigger. I was shooting for Miss Italia USA! That was a real pageant, held in that American mecca of pageantry, Atlantic City. I pestered my mother into buying me a gorgeous black-and-white striped silk dress at Saks. I wish I still had that dress today; I would wear it on the red carpet in a heartbeat. The only way I got Mama to agree to spend so much money on it in the first place was to assure her that I would win and pay her back with my cash prize. Little did Mama realize, the dress cost far more than the money I would receive and I knew this. My secret plan would be to wear the gown with the tags still on, avoid perspiring, then return it after the pageant for a full refund. (Yeah, I know: if there had been a Miss Tacky award, I would've won it.)

The gown looked fabulous, and maybe if it could have competed without me, it would have at least made runner-up. Not only did I lose, but to make matters even worse, Saks was on to me and refused to take the dress back. I confessed to Mama, who was fuming, but was more upset over a rumor she had heard about the winner being related to the organizer. Between Miss Holy Rosary Tomato and Miss Italia USA, we developed a full-blown conspiracy theory about pageants at the lower level being corrupt. This had Mafia written all over it, we concluded. I had milked, or possibly even started, rumors in high school that I was a Mafia princess, but this latest outrage forced me to sever all imaginary ties with them now. The Cosa was no longer Nostra. This despicable organized beauty pageant crime syndicate would be exposed for all the world to see once I became Miss USA (and possibly Miss Universe). I would get the first hand-written apology ever signed by the Mafia. I would then report it on the evening news myself.

But none of that glory would be mine if I didn't become an American.

By this time, I had spent most of my life in the United States. My accent had vanished, I could sort of hit the weird high notes of "The Star-Spangled Banner," and I had dressed up like Madonna for four consecutive Halloweens as a kid. I belonged to America, whether America was admitting it or not. This was home, and I truly loved it, and my life here. That said, I still felt torn about formally becoming an American citizen. Italians are fiercely proud of their heritage. I never wanted to surrender my nationality, make it somehow less a part of me. Italian was so much more than my citizenship: it was my identity. *I'm Italian* explained why I have a hot temper, why I adore fine wine, fast cars, beautiful clothes, fabulous food. Why I think *The Godfather* is the most beautiful movie of all time. (Because it's so Italian, about family and loyalty and passion all boiling on high at the same time. And yeah, there is a lot of violence and he did kill his own brother and all, but he deserved it.) I reconciled myself to dual citizenship, relieved that at least I would not be required to formally renounce my native land unless Italy declared war against the United States again, which seemed unlikely seeing how embarrassing that had proved the last time.

I sent for the citizenship booklet provided by the Immigration and Naturalization Service, and studied harder than I ever had in my life. Granted, that wasn't saying a whole lot, but I needed this. When the day of the big test came, I nervously sat across from the examiner and waited for him to start firing questions about the Constitutional Convention at me. My heart was pounding. What if I mixed up my Roosevelts or mountain ranges?

"Okay, so what is your name?" the examiner asked. I spelled it for him.

"How long have you lived here?"

"Since I was a little kid."

"Okay, you're good to go."

I was dumbstruck. That was *it*? What, did the INS subcontract the screening process out to the Barbizon School of Modeling? C'mon, throw some tennis balls, I can take it.

"Wait, wait!" I practically shouted at the examiner. "Don't you want to ask me some *real* questions?" What about the two longest rivers in the country, the thirteen original colonies, Ben Franklin's résumé, the rights guaranteed under the First Amendment? If I didn't use my archived knowledge of the Louisiana Purchase and the Federalist Papers right then and there, when would I ever? Where was the trick stop sign?

"Would you feel better if I asked you questions?" the puzzled examiner asked.

"Yes! I mean, no! Thank you!" I forced myself to zip it and leave before I got myself deported under some "undesirable lunatic" clause.

I was the first in my family to get U.S. citizenship, but I don't remember it being a big deal. It wasn't, in our culture, considered a rite of passage, like getting your period or learning to drive. The entourage of relatives didn't accompany me to the citizenship test or to my swearing-in ceremony in Baltimore. I drove there alone and clutched my little souvenir flag along with my fellow new Americans. I was expecting to be in a pissy mood, but once I was in that big room with all those people who were so proud, tears streaming down their faces, it made me a little weepy. It suddenly hit me that I was living in a country of incredible potential and opportunity, a country that had helped my entire family realize their dreams. First my uncles, then my parents, followed by my older siblings, who were both happily launched on their own careers by then. I looked at all these over-joyed strangers and wondered what their dreams were. We all wanted something from this, right?

My Hallmark moment was too little, too late: Karma has a way of dealing with jaded little teenage bitches who regard American citizenship as nothing but a box to check so they can enter beauty pageants. I found myself an official contestant in the Miss Maryland USA pageant, all right, but I also found my-self marching and saluting while wearing a sailor hat embla-zoned with the letters *USA* in puffy paint, a cheesy white T-shirt tucked into denim shorts, and white Keds in an opening number so awful I would agree to Pine-Sol injections directly into my brain if I thought it would scrub away the memory. It was noth-ing like the glamorous, high-production opening numbers I'd grown up watching on the Miss USA and Miss Universe pag-eants. My favorite had been a riverboat number from Miss USA. The contestants came out holding these gorgeous masks to their faces, which they revealed when their names were announced. They were surrounded by professional dancers and singers. And now I was skipping around stage in a cheap sailor hat in some DIY state pageant.

Most of the contestants were more experienced and less inter-ested in a possible Miss Congeniality consolation title than I was.

My roommate was nice enough—I think she went on to become an adult-entertainment star, or maybe just a Hooters girl—but most were cutthroat. One girl even slashed the gowns of two other contestants. I was a little insulted she didn't consider me worthy of sabotage. In the official pageant program, I thanked my family, my parents' business, and my dog Curly for their support. I hadn't even tried to rally any outside sponsorship. I went home crownless but undefeated.

Lose or not, I did learn important life lessons from the seasoned pageant girls in Miss Maryland, like how to use this special butt spray so you wouldn't get a wedgie during the swimsuit competition. That was the least of my worries about appearing onstage in a swimsuit, though: I experienced a fluke growth spurt at the start of college, and my curved spine was more pronounced than ever. I had to get special permission to wear a one-piece in the pageant so my uneven hips and protruding shoulder blades might be less noticeable. I entered the competition again the following year and made it all the way to the semifinals that time. I choked on the supposedly idiot-proof interview question: What would you do if you were Miss Maryland?

A genius answer immediately popped into my mind about how the title would give me the access I needed to help deserving people in the community, but for some reason, when it was time to speak, the word *access* was deleted from my brain. "Well, I, uh . . . If I was given the title," I stammered into the microphone, "that would give me the . . . *key* I need to the city and the state, and that, um, that would be great because I can go in different places and help!"

I heard shouts of *Bravissima!* from the audience—only my Italian family was cheering. The judges, meanwhile, all exchanged confused looks before quickly looking down in unison to consult the official pageant guidelines. You could practically see the giant thought bubbles appearing above their heads:

Key? What key? It says here they get a Caboodles makeup kit and a free year of tanning, but there's nothing about any key!

I gave up my Miss USA dream after that. Being around the hard-core pageant queens had made me realize that it didn't matter how much work you put into it; if you weren't the prettiest, you weren't going to win. These girls were gorgeous, and I knew I wasn't ever going to win on looks alone. When I got to E! years later, I would actually end up judging Miss USA in 2007. Donald Trump, the pageant's owner, addressed the judges before the show. "We're going to find the most beautiful girl in the country tonight!" he declared. He sat right behind me in the front row and watched the entire pageant. The winner was a super cute girl I gave straight tens who went on to work online at E! as a reporter before becoming a red-carpet hostess for ABC.

I had spent my high school years daydreaming about becoming an anchorwoman, but I never sought any guidance on how to go about achieving that goal. The University of Maryland had a well-regarded journalism program, but my near-negative GPA and low SAT scores ruled out my chances of getting accepted there. Or to any other college with or without a communications department, for that matter. I was restless. I had ten years' worth of ambition pent up inside me, and no place to unleash that energy. I wanted something to happen. I wanted my real life to begin. It was Monica, of all people, who swooped to the rescue. Since she had moved out on her own, we had switched gears from mortal enemies to devoted friends.

After finishing her studies at Boston University, Monica had gone to New York City to pursue a career in, no surprise, the fashion industry. She was instantly snapped up by the House of Versace and had quickly risen through the ranks to become a U.S. rep working out of corporate headquarters on Fifth Avenue. She was living the Carrie Bradshaw life while sharing a one-bedroom apartment with a college friend named Larissa. Larissa had become an FBI agent, assigned to a task force investigating the Colombia drug cartel. A fair number of the drugs themselves were busy making their way up the nose of Monica's boss, Donatella Versace. The Italian designer, by her own (much later) admission, was a coke fiend who was midway through an eighteen-year binge when I wiggled my way into her company as a temporary receptionist. When I first encountered Donatella, however, I knew nothing about the drugs and was too naive to figure it out—I assumed she was just batshit crazy. Why else would anyone have security guards block off the entire women's room and plaster a sign on the door reading RESERVED FOR DONATELLA?

At lunchtime, Donatella would have her male assistants don white gloves to serve her greasy Chinese takeout on exquisite Versace dinnerware. One time, I witnessed one of Donatella's infamous nuclear meltdowns when she accidentally locked herself out of her smoked-glass office. It began with a scream that brought the whole office running. "My cell phone is in there!" she shrieked. "I need my fucking phone!" Everyone instantly started scrambling to find another key to the sacred domain, but the still-shrieking Donatella merely stood there and pointed at one of her huge security guards. "Go!" she ordered him. "Get me in there!" There was a sudden shattering of glass as the guard kicked his way in. The whole office froze, and we all gaped in stunned silence. She had been locked out of the office for all of thirty seconds, tops. "What are you all looking at?" she snarled. "Get someone to fix this fucking door." I see Donatella at the Met Gala all the time now, but I'm too nervous to say anything. She's a crazy gangster diva. There is absolutely no one else like her. I think she's fabulous, but I know the firepower of an Italian temper, and with Donatella, you do not want to wander across the shooting range. She wouldn't remember me, anyway: my stint as a fashion industry receptionist lasted about as long as a cheap knockoff, and I quit after just a few months before they could fire me. It turned out that I had very little aptitude—and even less motivation—for taking phone messages. If it's that important, they'll call back, right?

Things were equally tense at home. I was living with my sister and her roommate in their tiny apartment. Every night, Monica and Larissa would go out barhopping. Occasionally I would tag along with my fake ID. Larissa would wear some hot little dress, which she accessorized with a concealed weapon. I thought Larissa was awesome. The feeling was not reciprocated. When you're a sexy, single twentysomething, having your roommate's teenage sister camped out on the couch can get old pretty fast. Plus, I'm a slob by nature, so I wasn't exactly trying to ingratiate myself by being helpful around the apartment. I finally wore out my welcome when the phone rang late one night. I pounced to answer it, because I was waiting for a call from a hot guy. I could barely hear the voice on the other end.

"Larissa," the voice whispered urgently. "Larissa?"

"No. Can you call back in the morning?"

"Larissa, it's me, I have information for you . . ." At that moment, the call waiting beeped, and I clicked over; it was Hot Guy.

"Sorry, she's sleeping," I told Larissa's caller. "Call first thing in the morning, okay? *Gracias!*" I hung up on her and went back to flirting with Hot Guy.

Larissa was up by then and came charging out of her room to interrogate me. "Did I just get a call?" she demanded.

"Yeah, it was some young girl with an accent but it's cool, she's gonna call back in the morning!" I replied with a dismissive wave.

"IDIOT! THAT WAS MY INFORMANT!" I felt bad. I had assumed it was some relative who could wait. Who gets urgent work calls at midnight, anyway? (Answer: FBI agents do.)

New York and I just couldn't find our groove, and I left before the summer was up. I hated how hot and loud it was, and how rank it smelled. I fled back home to my Laura Ashley bedroom and enrolled in community college. I was starting to grow up a little, and knew I had to get serious if I wanted a future for myself. I made the honor roll for the first time in my life and got accepted to St. Mary's, a small public college on Maryland's Eastern Shore. There was no journalism or communications major at St. Mary's, but I was thrilled to land a gig at the campus radio station. I hosted the after-midnight show, when every student within listening range was either asleep or getting wasted. Since I had spent my childhood broadcasting to nonexistent audiences in front of my bedroom mirror, I was a natural for the job. Between songs, I would talk and talk and talk, with no one listening. Then I would convince myself that they were out there, and just too star-struck to engage with such a big-time deejay. As the lonely minutes ticked by, I would start begging people to call in. "If you've ever been in love, call me, let's talk," I'd coo into my mike, waiting for the phone to light up. Nothing. "If you have ever taken a breath of air, call me." Silence. "If you have lips call me. Call me even if you have only one lip!" Nothing. "If you're at St. Mary's College and hear this, for the love of God, please call me!" Nada.

I was ecstatic when I was finally promoted to the evening shift. I still wasn't getting any callers, but the possibility seemed more real in prime time, and the better hours meant my friends could come up and hang out with me in the deejay booth, which resulted more than once in dead air because I was too busy acting cool to remember to play another song when one ended.

Dead air might have been a better choice than what turned out to be my dinner-hour swan song. I love hip-hop and R & B, and on the night in question, I thought everyone else would enjoy my favorite 2 Live Crew hit as much as I did. The catchy chorus was soon thundering across the crowded dining hall:

Me so horny, me so horny, me so horny,
Me love you long time

The song gets a whole lot raunchier after that.

Finally the phones lit up.

So did my boss, who came running into the booth. "Turn that off!" he yelled. I didn't think he needed to get so worked up over it; this was Maryland, not Florida. Some D.A. in Florida, I vaguely recalled, had successfully prosecuted 2 Live Crew on obscenity charges, and record clerks selling the controversial album were actually arrested. The conviction would eventually be overturned on appeal by the U.S. Supreme Court, but that day was still nearly a decade away, and even if I was willing to fight the good First Amendment fight on behalf of horny rappers, my station manager, Me So Uptight, was not. It was time to change schools again, anyway. My transcript was decent enough for me to get accepted at last by my first-choice school, the University of Maryland, where at long last I became a journalism major.

That summer before my junior year, I was hanging out in the little espresso bar in the back of my father's store one afternoon when I heard a customer come in to pick up some tailored suits. I peered over the little half wall and spotted a handsome guy around my age. He smiled at me, and we exchanged pleasantries before he left. The store manager hurried up, breathless with excitement as he told me who the visitor was. "He asked who you were! He wanted me to give you his number if you ever wanted to call." I was flattered, but not willing to show it. "Just have him call me," I told the manager. He did, and just like that, I had a date with one of the hottest bachelors in town.

The son of a prominent car dealer who was a regular customer of my dad's, Richard was two years older than I was. He had attended an exclusive private prep school and had his pick of the prettiest debutantes in D.C., not to mention neighboring Maryland, Virginia, and Delaware. He was widely known as a party boy who liked to tear around in Lamborghinis and Ferraris, but I was the one who was going to prove to be hell on wheels in this particular romance. Richard picked me up in a grampa boat of a Chrysler off one of his dad's lots. *Smart,* I thought, realizing immediately that I was being tested. He may have been downplaying what he had, but I wasn't going that route, myself: if the shorts I wore for our first date had been any skimpier, they would have been a thong.

Richard and I had instant chemistry. That very first night, he asked me what I was doing over the summer before going back to college that fall.

"I just started working at Houston's," I told him. I'd been hired as a waitress, but I took food orders the way I took phone messages and had been demoted to hostess after just one shift. I didn't mind. Better clothes and more opportunity to chat with customers, I figured. Let someone else deliver all those house salads and glasses of Chardonnay.

"Well, I hope you had fun, because you're going to be quitting that job to spend more time with me," Richard informed me. His confidence was a more natural fit than the cocky swagger of boys I'd fallen for in the past. With Richard, my "type" did a seismic shift from bad boy to businessman. There was definitely something to be said for grown men dressed in nice suits instead of hoodlums in baggy jeans with three inches of underwear showing. True to Richard's prediction, I quit my job that week to spend more time with him. I loved the envious looks from other women when we were out clubbing or eating at the hottest new restaurant in D.C. With his impeccable clothes, olive skin, blue eyes, and seductive lips, Richard looked like he had stepped out of a Ralph Lauren ad. And he was as generous as he was good-looking: he loved to take me on shopping sprees to Neiman Marcus. It all seemed too good to be true.

When September rolled around, I answered a roommate-wanted ad with Student Housing and moved into a student apartment with three other girls for the semester. On my second night there, I took a break from unpacking to get ready to go out. The new roommates wanted to know more about my boyfriend.

"What's he do?" one of them asked.

"He works for a car dealership," I said.

"Oh, that's sweet, good for you!" they said, exchanging quick stifled-laugh looks that said *loser*.

The condescension was cut short by the deafening roar of a motor gunning outside our open balcony door. "What the fuck?" my roommates said in near unison. We all ran to the balcony to see who was causing the commotion. I had a good hunch. Sure enough, there was Richard sitting in a red convertible Ferrari. He smiled up at me and waved.

"Be right down!" I shouted over the rumbling engine.

"He works for a car dealership?" one of the roommates asked skeptically.

"Yeah," I said with what I hoped was supreme nonchalance. "He *owns* the car dealership. And," I added as a little *take that, bitches*, P.S., "something like thirty others."

Academically, I didn't have such an auspicious start at UM. Leafing through the course catalog, I had been on the lookout for sliders, and a class called TV Westerns 101 had caught my attention. Watching TV shows for college credit sounded like an easy A if ever there was one. In hindsight, I probably should have watched at least one western before committing to an entire semester full of them: they basically pitched me into an instant coma. There were bawdy women of ill repute, but no one ever had sex. There were saloon brawls, but no one ever bled. There were cattle ranches but no steakhouses. The plot lines of TV westerns generally involved the hero and his men giving chase on horseback to the villain and his men, until the latter were caught and/or shot (again without bleeding) or hanged from the gallows (minus any gruesome sound effects or entertaining word games).

I hated westerns. And the one I hated above all others was *Bonanza*, which, in terms of popularity and longevity, was like the *CSI* of its time. So of course *Bonanza* turned out to be the topic for our final paper in TV Westerns 101. Half of my grade would hinge upon my scholarly dissection of life on the Ponderosa. The Ponderosa, in case you are blissfully unaware, was a large ranch in need of a good landscaper and a decent security system: viewers saw lots of dirt and tumbleweeds, but never anything actually being ranched, per se. Nevertheless, rustlers seemed to make off with the off-screen herd of cattle every other episode or so. Maybe it was an insurance scam—don't ask me, I never stayed awake through an entire episode. Ponderosa patriarch Ben Cartwright spent most of his time organizing posses with his wildly mismatched sons from different mothers. There was big, dumb Hoss and sorta hot Little Joe (where and who was Big Joe? And while we're at it, why wasn't anyone investigating the deaths of three Mrs. Cartwrights in a row?). Ben also had a third, prodigal son named Adam who showed up every tenth posse or so. Despite all this galloping, brawling, and gunslinging, the Cartwrights never broke a sweat (or, obviously, bled): Ben, Hoss, and Little Joe wore the same exact clothes on every episode. And the show ran for fourteen seasons. Where was *Fashion Police* when the nation needed it? I couldn't find a damn thing to say about Bonanza when I went to write my final.

On the day our professor was handing back our graded papers, he skipped mine. "Giuliana DePandi, can I see you in my office, please," he said at the end of class. I showed up all smiles, extending my hand and introducing myself—a necessity given the degree of my participation all semester. "Hi! How are you?" I said brightly. He cut right to the chase.

"You're in trouble for plagiarism."

"Huh?" I responded. "Plagiarism?"

He then informed me that I would have to appear before some sort of university tribunal the following Monday morning. They were sending me to the college gallows!

"What makes you think I plagiarized anything?" I cried. I was in a state of disbelief: I would never stoop to plagiarism! And I was mad as hell that the geek I had bought the paper from had done so. With reckless abandon, it turned out. The professor pulled out first one book and then another, opening them to giant swaths of text he had marked. There was maybe half a page worth of original material in my ten-page treatise. For three hundred bucks, I had expected originality. That was a good chunk of the grocery-and-extras allowance my parents gave me for the semester, which I had managed to sock away thanks to Richard's generosity when it came to picking up checks. I wondered if there was a way to report dial-a-cheater for consumer fraud. Lucky for me, it turned out that the professor wanted to avoid the bureaucratic time-suck of an ethics trial, and he offered me a plea bargain, instead: I could accept a D for the full semester's grade. I gladly snatched it up and rode off into the metaphoric sunset.

I was never one to be scared straight, and the only lesson I learned about cheating was that if you wanted to do it right, you had to do it yourself. Or, in my case, with a trusted accomplice. I recruited Richard to help me with an elaborate scheme to ace a botany final I was dreading. The reason I was dreading it was because—minor detail—I had never actually gone to botany class. What did succulents have to do with journalism?

The idea was to wire me up so I could relay the final exam questions to Richard via a hidden mike, and he would consult my notes and radio back the correct answer. If I had spent half the time I spent researching recording devices just studying the damn textbook, I would have been fine. Luckily, Washington, D.C., provides excellent shopping opportunities for both amateur and professional spies, so I was able to pick up what I determined to be a reasonably good two-way radio set. Come the big day, I squashed a baseball cap down over my long hair to conceal the earpiece in my ear. The cord was taped down my back, leading to a battery pack clipped to the back of my bra. Then another wire ran down my arm to my wrist and the tiny mike I would read the exam questions into for Richard. Growing up in greater D.C., I had seen the Secret Service in action plenty of times, and I was confident I had this. Richard was hiding in the stairwell closest to the lecture hall, standing ready with his spy gear and the botany notes I'd bought. (Remember, this was pre-Internet!) I sauntered into the classroom and settled in for the big test. I wasn't just going to pass this course; I was going to get an A-plus! I pretended to cough while covering my mouth and dictating the first question to Richard:

"What is cytokinesis?"

My ear was filled with loud crackling, then Richard all but shouting.

"Wait, repeat that!"

I put my wrist up to my mouth and softly read the question out loud again. Everyone within a three-row radius seemed to respond with an annoyed *"Ssh!"* which only piqued the interest of the TAs who were posted as test monitors throughout the lecture hall. The nearest one shot a suspicious glance my way.

"They could hear you in my ear!" I hissed at Richard. Secret Service my eye. We were the friggin' Penguins of Madagascar.

"What did you say?" Richard crackled back. Now the TA was staring hard. I flipped over my exam, scanning the questions. There were eighty of them.

"I still can't hear you!" Richard squawked.

Now the TA was striding toward me. I was busted. There was no way this was going to work. I gathered my things, left the blank exam behind, and walked out. I found Richard in the staircase barking into his microphone: "Giuliana? Are you there? What was the question again?"

"It's over," I said, unplugging us both. "This was a horrible plan. Let's go get a burger."

I got a C.

Okay, maybe it was a D.

Bumbling spy episode aside, Richard had the kind of style that made it easy for me to forget that I was just another struggling student, anyway. His sophistication always rankled the frat-party college boys in my apartment building, and they made a sport out of coming outside to heckle me whenever Richard showed up in whatever fabulous fresh-off-Daddy's-lot car he felt like flashing that day. I'd hear shouts of "gold digger!" as we drove off laughing, killer sound system blasting. I didn't care what anyone called me; I was Richard D.'s girlfriend—*the* Richard D.—and I wanted everyone to know it. When Richard arranged a sweetheart deal on a leased Lexus for me, commuting to campus made a lot more sense than paying rent and sleeping on a twin bed in a room shared with a girl I barely knew, so I moved back home.

My parents adored Richard, his adored me, and it was all very lovey-dovey except for the part where Richard and I tried to kill each other on a regular basis. Our honeymoon period lasted about as long as one of Ben Cartwright's marriages. Both of us tended to jump to conclusions, and both of us were insanely jealous. If I wanted to go out with my girlfriends, Richard would race over to my house and be sitting at the kitchen table with my parents, waiting up for me at two in the morning.

"Where have you been?" he would demand. Mama and Babbo would wait expectantly for my answer. Veteran snoops who had spent years brazenly listening on the other line (without even *trying* to be quiet) whenever I was on the phone, they were thrilled now to be included in practically every episode of my relationship drama, courtesy of Richard, who doled out guest passes just to sway the popular vote in his favor. Sometimes I just wanted to kill him. Sometimes I attempted to.

Richard lived in a fancy apartment above the garage of his parents' mansion. One night, after another one of our epic fights, Richard, utterly exhausted, yelled at me to go home just before slamming his bedroom door in my face. No one slams a door in my face. Oh, I would go home all right. Right after I wedged this chair up under the doorknob so Richard couldn't escape and then turned the heat up as high as it would go with the fan on full blast. He was probably already asleep, and could just roast away like a baked potato for all I cared right then. I sped off.

Once home, I knew who was calling when the phone rang at one a.m., waking my parents.

"Ma, I got it! Hang up!" I hollered upstairs. Mama was already on the line when I cut in.

"No, no, Anna, don't hang up!" Richard was imploring.

"I don't understand," Mama was saying sleepily. "Here's Eduardo."

"Richard, what's-*a* the matter?" my father asked.

"Eduardo," Richard began, "your fucking daughter . . ."

"Dad, hang up!"

". . . tried to kill me!"

"Giuliana, she do-a what?"

"SHE TRIED TO BOIL ME TO DEATH!"

"What-*a* you boiling, Richard?" Babbo was perplexed. Was Richard making pasta?

"Me! She was boiling me, Eduardo!"

"Giuliana, she put-*a* you in water, Richard? How she do that?"

"Dad! Don't listen! He's drunk! Hang up the phone!"

"Why-a you get in the boiling water, Richard? I no understand."

"Your daughter is fucking crazy!"

"Ha-ha! April fools, Dad! We are playing a joke. We can all hang up now!"

"Oh. You so funny, Giuliana. I go back to sleep now. Good night, Richard!"

A week after the heat incident, I don't know who grabbed whose neck first, or why, but Richard and I had a choking standoff.

"I'm going to kill you!" I gurgled, veins bulging, eyes popping.

"I'm going to kill you!" Richard rasped back.

"You let go first!"

"No, you let go first!"

We agreed to both let go on the count of three, and continued to consider ourselves the perfect couple.

We were still together in my senior year at the University of Maryland when I was studying for final exams one November night. I'd been reading in bed for hours, then finally got up to brush my teeth around one o'clock. When I went to stand, though, my body refused to straighten. I fell back onto the bed on my side and tried to deep-breathe my way through the searing pain in my spine. The next day, I made an emergency appointment with Dr. John Kostuik, my orthopedist at Johns Hopkins. He ordered X-rays and an MRI and delivered the news I had been dreading since junior high.

"You're going to have to have the big surgery."

"What's the alternative?" I asked hopefully. I thought of all the physical therapy exercises I'd been told to do over the years but had blown off. Maybe I could do a crash course now. I was terrified. After so many years of dread, denial, and tentative hope, it was as if the monster had finally won. I was cornered.

"The alternative is to live in pain and have it get even worse and eventually have to do the surgery anyway," Dr. Kostuik said.

I was still desperate to negotiate.

"I'm graduating in the spring and then really want to go to graduate school. Can it wait three years?" I asked.

The doctor shook his head. "You'll curve another one to three degrees a month," he said.

"I can't even wait and go to my graduation in a few months?"

"No." My spine was collapsing in on itself. I couldn't wait three years, or three months. Even one month was gambling.

Surgery was scheduled for January 6, 1996. The operation would last around eight hours. My entire back would be splayed open. A couple of times a week for several weeks leading up to D-day, I had to give blood to the bank for the surgery. There was no way to pretend anymore that this wasn't happening. I had no delusions about the pain that was awaiting me, and I was terrified.

Snow was forecast the morning of the surgery, so my parents drove me to Baltimore the night before, and we stayed in a hotel a few miles from the hospital. We woke up to a record-breaking blizzard that ended up causing $3 billion in damage and 154 fatalities across the Northeast. The roads were almost impassable even with our four-wheel drive, and we were late for pre-op. The hospital felt eerily deserted, with only essential staff called in. Dr. Kostuik stopped in before I was rolled to the operating room.

"What degree will I be?" I asked. My curve was at forty-five degrees. How uncrooked could he make me? Fifteen degrees or less would be fantastic.

"I think I will be able to take you to ten degrees," Dr. Kostuik reassured me.

As the anesthesia pulled me under, I found the nerve to urge him to do better.

"Can you make me zero degrees?" I groggily asked.

"Zero?"

"I know you can do it. Please make me zero and take my awful curve away for good."

"I will try," he promised.

I remember waking up during the surgery, seeing faces and lights hovering over me, and hearing an urgent voice say "She's awake!" before I plunged back down again, feeling scared. When I came to again, my bed was being pushed to the recovery room. I saw Dr. Kostuik smiling at me.

"I made you straight," he said. "I made you a zero."

That first night, I was certain I was dying. There was only one nurse working on the orthopedic floor because of the blizzard, and it felt like forever before she gave me my painkillers. Within an hour of swallowing the two horse pills, I was gagging. I spent the next three hours dry-heaving. It felt as if every single stitch was ripping open and every already traumatized muscle along my spine was being wrenched. The blood vessels in my eyes burst. I was a weeping, hysterical mess. The pain overwhelmed me. It was far worse than I had ever dreaded or imagined—a blinding pain, white-hot and relentless, like being mauled from within by some wild animal. No morphine in the world could carry me away. Thumb frantically pumping, I would dispense the maximum dosage as soon as it was time, then beg the nurses to *do something*, give me something, anything, because the morphine wasn't cutting it. Monica took the train down from New York and slept in a chair in the corner of my room. I could hear her crying for me. She was the only one who understood what hell I was going through, and how desperate my helplessness made me feel. I would sit up all night, my eyes fixed on the wall clock, waiting for the doctors to make their morning rounds, not wanting to risk being asleep when they came for their five-minute exam. I was convinced they would find some way to conquer the pain.

"Giuliana, go to bed," my mother would chide. "Nothing will be different tomorrow."

"No, Mama, we're going to have an answer," I would insist. The pain was something tangible and solid to me, a puzzle to solve. They just needed to work on it harder, and then I would be fine again.

"Good morning! Hi, hi, hi!" I would greet the doctors. "Listen, I wanted to ask you if there's something you can give me instead of the morphine," I pleaded. "It's not working."

"We'll look into it" was the answer they always gave. I would then fire off questions at them that I had etched in my brain the entire night before. "When will I start feeling better? How bad are my scars? When can I leave the hospital? Will I need more surgery? And most importantly, is there anything more you can do for the pain? I'm dying here!"

I'd harass the nurses for the rest of the day, buzzing them to check and see if my doctor had sent over a new medicine for me.

"Nope," came the response, always.

I spent two miserable weeks in the hospital. The streets were still snowy and frozen from the blizzard when my parents packed me up in the back of their Jeep Cherokee for the hour-long ride home to Bethesda. We pulled up to the house and the Jeep stopped. My parents had been keeping vigil at my bedside, so no one had been home to shovel since the blizzard, and now the driveway was a treacherous bobsled run of solid ice. There was no way I could hobble my way to the front door, and it would likewise be too dangerous for my father to carry me.

Of course, my parents had planned a surprise homecoming party for me—because that's exactly what everyone who is delirious with pain and hasn't showered in two weeks hopes for after major surgery—so the house was full of relatives, friends, and neighbors. The uncles all poured outside to contemplate the ice situation, which, being Italian, meant yelling over each other and waving their hands around a lot.

"Take me back to the hospital," I demanded from the backseat. "You cannot get me into the house." I was starting to fear that Plan B would turn out to be abandoning me on the driveway glacier like one of those orphaned baby seals with pleading eyes in *National Geographic* specials.

After more yelling and gesticulating, the geniuses came up with a solution: they would get a chaise lounge from the pool and carry me up the driveway like Cleopatra. As if. I knew it would never work like that. My objections were overruled, and I soon found myself being dragged, bumped, and slid along the uneven ice while screaming bloody murder. Everyone came out of the house to watch and shout advice while my lounge-chair pallbearers continued to argue and curse in Italian as they slipped, fell, and dropped me along the way. I was still yelping in agony and fury by the time they got me up the stairs and deposited into my bed. Then they all went back downstairs to celebrate my homecoming. Our cleaning lady, Bianca, had come over to help with the festivities, and she and her three-year-old daughter were the only ones still upstairs.

I was happy to be left alone. All I wanted to do was try to

sleep and enjoy a little peace and quiet. But first, I needed a drink of water.

"Mama," I called out. "Mama, I need some water, please!"

No one heard me over the party. I tried calling more loudly, but I was still weak, not to mention dehydrated. I'd stop, gather strength, then mewl again. *Dammit, I should've gotten a bell*, I thought. Finally, a small head poked inside the doorway. Bianca's little daughter.

"Hi, sweetie," I said in my most syrupy voice, trying to coax her inside. "Can you go get Mama?"

The toddler stared at me blankly.

"Mamacita? Donde esta tu mamacita?" I tried.

She giggled and stepped inside the room.

Good, good, we're getting there, my hopeful brain assured my thirsty body.

She plopped down on the floor, watching me, and giggled some more. A grown-up in bed in the middle of the day! Who couldn't get up from bed! Funny grown-up!

"Mi mama," I said with growing urgency. *"Emergencia!"* Lassie would've been halfway to the farmhouse by now, what was with this heartless kid?

"Tengo mucha suerta," I explained, grasping my throat for emphasis, which did nothing to clarify the situation, since I had just used the Spanish word for luck instead of thirst.

She laughed some more, then got up, walked over to my bookcase, and started pulling my old stuffed animals off the shelves. She brought them to my bed and began piling them on top of my immobile body.

"No, no, no, *por favor!*" I croaked in my parched-throat voice.

She put the next batch over my face.

This was starting to go south in an old black-and-white horror film kind of way, like *Whatever Happened to Baby Jane?* where Bette Davis buries paralyzed Joan Crawford up to her neck in sand at the beach and dances around her singing a children's song.

By now, Terror Toddler was giggling up a storm as she scooped up whatever she could find in my room to pile on top of me—dirty socks, old issues of *Vogue*. I was her personal Legos base, and she was building a tower on top of me. She had figured out that I couldn't move and there wasn't a thing I could do to stop her.

"Cut it out, you little shit," I snarled past a mouthful of Curly, my favorite stuffed poodle. After she added a few record albums, picture frames, and more dirty clothes from my hamper to her living sculpture, I sensed that my tormentor had left the room. Now all I had to do was get someone's attention so they could come rescue me. "Maaaaaammmmma," I whimpered. I tried blowing Curly off my face. Relief flooded through me when I heard the rustle of someone hurrying through the door.

Not Mama.

The enemy had returned.

This time, she had bottles and cans piled in her tiny, evil arms. She had gone down the hall to raid her mother's cleaning supplies. Now bottles of Windex and cans of Scrubbing Bubbles were added to the growing tower o' death on top of me.

"You're a *puta diablo*, get out of here you little bitch!" I said. "*Diablo*. You understand that?"

Then, just as she started to make her way to me with the dreaded bottle of Windex, blessedly, I heard my mother's voice.

"What's going on here?" Mama asked.

"Ma, you *abandoned* me! This little bitch was about to blind me!" I wailed, but she either couldn't hear me beneath the mountain of debris, or, more likely, she was pretending not to so she wouldn't have to face her own guilt over leaving an al-Qaeda sleeper cell to babysit me.

"Are you playing?" she chirped brightly. "That's good! You're feeling better!"

The rest of my two-month recovery went somewhat better. I made a half-assed attempt to do the prescribed physical therapy exercises but bitterly stopped trying when I discovered that the surgery hadn't magically made me two inches taller and super-model material. Mama was fetching homework from my professors and would hold my books for me or spoon-feed me lunch while I worked. Babbo never saw through my lies about my feet feeling numb, and gave me foot massages on demand. I wasn't about to suffer nobly. I held court from my bed all day. Monica's old high-school bestie, Niki (the one I had played airport chauffeur to when I was thirteen), lived only five minutes away and came by every day to help me with my schoolwork and watch Chris Farley and David Spade in *Tommy Boy* for the four hundredth time. It never failed to crack us up, and I can still recite the entire movie from memory. Not that anyone ever takes me up on the offer. Laughter and good company were definitely the best medicine for me.

Not such good company was my boyfriend, Richard, who showed up for the first time two days after I got home.

"Hey, how you feeling?" he asked with what I took to be faux concern.

"Huh. Nice of you to finally come see me," I groused.

"Are you fucking kidding me? I was at the hospital!" he objected.

"No, you were not." I had no recollection of Richard ever coming to the hospital, and it was just like him to blow it off because of the blizzard and figure it would be fine to wait for me to get home. He hadn't even called me at Johns Hopkins.

After the water-deprivation homecoming incident, I had gotten a bell for my nightstand. Now Richard started going crazy ringing it, until Mama appeared.

"Anna! Tell her I was at the hospital!" he begged her.

"He never came to see me, Mama!" I argued.

Mama wanted nothing more than for me to marry Richard, and she was willing to defend him to the death. Richard was almost like a son to her. And, like Pasquale, a son could do no wrong. She turned to admonish me.

"How can you say this?" she scolded.

Richard and I went round and round, until finally he said, "I'm leaving! You're a bitch!" and pulled the pillow out from under my head in frustration. I howled in pain. Mama gave me a "drama queen" look, and Richard stalked out. I silently vowed to boil him again as soon as I got my strength back. Once I did, however, I decided to spend the energy on more urgent business: I needed to take my final exams so I could graduate.

My surgery was a wake-up call and a life changer. If I hadn't had the operation, I wouldn't have my career. For starters, it corrected the way my bowing spine had pushed out my upper chest on one side and made my shoulder jut out. There is no way I could have camouflaged that deformity in the strapless designer gowns that are such a staple of my working wardrobe: you can't wear an empire-waist dress at every awards show. More important, though, my long recovery gave me a lot of time to truly *think* about my future instead of childishly fantasizing and believing it would magically come true. I had done all right at University of Maryland, ending up with a solid B average, but I hadn't done anything beyond that to make myself ready for the working world. I had been too caught up in my social life to get an internship or entry-level job at a local TV station like so many of my classmates had done, and I hadn't done any kind of networking. I knew I needed more experience to even get a foot in the door. I started doing some research from my sickbed.

I got a handicapped parking pass, wobbled my way to classes, and somehow made it through exam week. But managing the stadium for the graduation ceremony was a huge ordeal. The pain was overwhelming, but it wasn't going to stop me from showing up and getting my diploma in person. Once it was in my hands, I sat back down with a big grin on my face. I had a huge secret that I had been keeping to myself:

I wasn't really done.

lthough we weren't officially engaged, there was a general assumption on everyone's part that Richard and I would get married after college, and I would join him in the family business once I realized that my cute little goal of becoming an anchorwoman was nothing but a pipe dream. As far as my parents were concerned, I had my college degree now, so I should be happy. I'm not so sure that my Bachelor of Arts had that much more significance to them than my Barbizon certificate. They were proud, to be sure, but in the way they were proud of whatever their children did, whether it was Monica making a name for herself in the New York fashion world, or me graduating from college, or Pasquale singing opera and building his own business. I didn't feel a sense of completion, though. I was still a work in progress, and some polishing needed to be done before I was ready to launch myself into the world as a real journalist.

I knew a master's degree would make me more marketable in a competitive industry, but when I lightly tested the waters over going to graduate school, the response from Babbo and Mama was something to the effect of "You have a degree, why-*a* you need another one? Marry Richard!" I decided not to ask them for the money, or to even tell them that I'd already applied to American University and had been accepted. They had spent their whole lives giving and giving and giving to all three of us kids. Besides, I was twenty-one years old, and it was time for me to start becoming financially independent. So I quietly took out a student loan for the full tuition and charted my own course. I would devote the next two years to learning everything I possibly could about broadcast journalism. No more frivolous classes in sailing or bowling or, God save me, botany: this was my chance to truly immerse myself in the subject that had grabbed me at the age of seven and never let go.

I was still envisioning myself as a news anchor someday, reporting authoritatively from D.C. with one of those cool backdrops of the Capitol dome lit up behind me. What went on inside that dome bored me to tears, though, to be honest. Politics, policy, government—it seemed like there was too much galloping around and kicking up of dust without anyone actually getting anywhere. The Ponderosa all over again. True to form, it would take a megadose of public humiliation to clarify things for me.

One of the things that made AU's journalism program so attractive to me was the emphasis on practical experience, especially at the graduate level. One day, I was assigned to take a camera crew and report on a press conference being held by Senator Ted Kennedy. I was supposed to try to get the esteemed senator to answer a question during the Q and A period following his remarks. As soon as I heard those magical words, "The senator will now take a few questions," I flew into hyper, arm-waving, choose-me-choose-me mode. I hadn't done any real preparation. I wanted to ask a question to be noticed in the room, not because I was dying to know the answer. I was so caught up in my frantic attempt to get Kennedy's attention that I didn't even realize that I had it when he said, "Yes, you in the back." All the other cameras and reporters turned to catch my question, while I stood there sputtering like an idiot trying to think of one that hadn't already been asked and answered. "Uh, uh," I stalled. Kennedy waited patiently and smiled politically. "Yes?" he prodded.

"Senator Kennedy, what do you do for fun?" I blurted.

The professional journalists in the room collectively sniggered and gave me a professional "Are you fucking kidding me?" look. Senator Kennedy's smile twitched at the corners.

"What do I do for fun?" he repeated, now clearly bemused by the dumb kid he had just been trying to give a break.

"For instance," I forged ahead, suddenly channeling Mike Wallace, "where were you last Friday night at eleven p.m.?" I could feel the collective disdain in the press corps shift to collective confusion—the real journalists and probably the senator himself had to wonder for a split second whether I was an undercover reporter for some sleazy tabloid that actually had something on Kennedy. But I had no hidden agenda. *C'mon, help me out here, what the hell do you do for fun? Order in pizza and watch movies? Play cards? Do you like Jenga?*

The senator's response, which I didn't even hear over the prayers I was saying inside my head to please God, just please get me out of here, was something banal and charming, something along the lines of having a nice dinner, eating too much dessert, and getting to bed well before eleven. I went back to school and put my segment together. Afterwards, the dean called me into his office for a little chat.

"I think your style may be better suited for Hollywood than D.C.," he said.

At first, I was mortified—not to mention deeply insulted. Compared to my previous misadventures in academia, I was a serious, nearly straight-A student at AU. Still, the more I thought about it, the more I came to believe that the dean might be on to something. I had always loved pop culture, and I had grown up with MTV. I thought of Downtown Julie Brown as sort of a badass little sister to Barbara Harrison. And while entertainment journalism didn't really exist on television in the early 1990s the way it does today, with entire networks like E! built around it, public fascination with celebrity was at an all-time high, thanks to Princess Diana and her rocky royal marriage. Identifying my niche was exciting, but how to stake my claim in the emerging field was baffling. Traditional news reporting had an established path that aspiring TV reporters could follow to success—intern at the biggest station you could, land your first job at a local affiliate, then move to increasingly bigger markets until you could crack a network job. But there were no maps yet pointing the way from Bethesda, Maryland, to *Live From the Red Carpet*.

My personal life was equally unresolved.

Richard and I kept bumping along in our Mr. and Mrs. Smith relationship. The good times were still good, and the bad times were still epic. He still considered himself in alliance with my parents to bring Giuliana into line, and I considered myself in alliance with Satan to punish the stupid shithead for even trying. I wanted to not care, but Italians are hardwired to be passionate, so indifference was never an option. I could love Richard or hate him, but there weren't any stations on my dial in between those two channels yet when it came to romance. Which is why I went berserk when Richard didn't answer my calls late one night when I was holed up in an editing booth at AU working on a final project.

All those times he had accused me (falsely) of cheating, and obviously it was all just a smokescreen so he could secretly hook up with—what? Some scheming salesgirl from Parts and Service? I didn't even have time to flip through my Rolodex of imaginary rivals before a friend called and mentioned that she had just seen Richard with some woman at the Tel Aviv Café in downtown Bethesda. Proof! I immediately jumped into my leased Lexus and raced to the restaurant. Sure enough, Richard's Ferrari was parked outside, and through the open windows facing the street, I could see Richard sitting at a table staring into the eyes of a gorgeous brunette. He was busted big-time, and I was going to kick his two-timing ass. And hers. I stormed up to the table. He looked up at me in surprise, but tried to play it smooth.

"Hey, what're you doing here?" he said. "I thought you had to study."

"What're *you* doing here?" I countered. (Great comebacks usually come to me instantaneously, but not in this case. Bill often complains that I bring a machine gun to snowball fights.)

"Honey, Brenda and I were just—" Richard said before I jumped in and started screaming at him and the brunette who was smiling nervously.

"You bastard! Is this your whore?" I screamed, "Your little *puttana*?"

"Honey," Richard interrupted. "Calm down. You're overreacting. You two met once before. Brenda is a family friend. She's our realtor! Why don't you join us?" Oh shit, she did look familiar after all. But it was too late to cave in and apologize. Besides, family friend or not, this little ho looked like she wanted a piece of my man.

"You want me to join you and your *puttana* whore?" I screeched. Brenda started to say something, but I cut her off.

"*You* shut up!" I may have flunked *Bonanza*, but I had *The Godfather* down pat. The whole restaurant was watching now, or pretending not to while they fake-ate their baba ghanoush. At this point, I suddenly remembered meeting Brenda and having a few laughs with her and her boyfriend (Oh crap!), but I was deep into Woman Betrayed mode by then, and I had an audience, so it wasn't like I could just sit down and order a kabob.

"Honey, you're embarrassing yourself," Richard tried again.

"Who's going to be embarrassed now, punk?" I shot back. I went to slap him across the face, but my fist was half-closed and I missed, anyway, so I ended up slap-punching him in the ear, instead. Hard. He was clutching it in pain when I stalked outside to write FUCKING PIG in hot pink lipstick on the windshield of his Ferrari. I then started kicking his doors, all the time cursing out loud like a deranged bag lady in high heels. If there had been a horse nearby, I would have put its head in Richard's front seat.

Fury spent, I finally got in my car and went home just in time to answer the ringing phone. My dad picked it up at the same time.

"Hallo?" I heard him say.

"Eduardo, Ed, Ed, listen to me, your daughter . . ."

"What-a Giuliana do, Richard?" Babbo interrupted.

"She physically abused me! She punctured my ear drum!"

"Your drum?"

"Dad! He's drunk, hang up!" I hollered upstairs.

"She punched me in the ear and broke my eardrum!"

"Giuliana play-a your drum and she break it?" Babbo seemed to think I had formed a thrash-metal band while working on my master's.

"My ear!" Richard repeated.

It ended as it usually did, with my parents clucking sympathetically while trying to figure out what the hell Richard was talking about before finally giving up and wishing him *buonanotte*. If he could call, he was still conscious, and if he was conscious, I hadn't offed him, so no harm, no foul on the DePandi parental scorecard. We would all live to fight another day. That day came the week of my AU graduation.

Since my epiphany courtesy of Ted Kennedy, I had concluded that Los Angeles was my only hope if I wanted to break into entertainment journalism. I had toyed with the idea of moving there but was certain my parents would never allow it, and doing it without their blessing and financial support seemed unfathomable. But the thought kept tugging at me. I had a $150 student voucher with TWA, and since the struggling airline had already gone through two bankruptcies by then, I figured I'd better use it or lose it. I booked a one-way ticket on a flight that would get me into L.A. at one in the morning on Friday the thirteenth of June, 1997.

Once the flight was booked, I started to freak out. I couldn't believe I was actually going to do this: I had no job, no prospects, no place to stay, and barely enough savings to cover a week's worth of cheap sushi. Not to mention I was a fearful flier and flying on Friday the thirteenth was the dumbest idea on earth, but that was the cheapest ticket I could find so I had to suck it up and do it. Moving to L.A. for good was such a far-fetched idea, I was sure my parents would say no, and I would just end up staying in Bethesda and marrying Richard. I was so terrified, I half wished they would stop me. Then I remembered what that would look like: Richard had already suggested I start learning the family business by selling tires and rust-protection packages at one of his lots as soon as I was out of school. My graduation ceremony was on Sunday. Three days later, I dropped my bombshell.

"I've got my master's, I paid for it all on my own, and now I'm going to follow my dreams and go to L.A. and I'm leaving on Friday night," I announced. In Italian, it sounded even more dramatic.

My parents looked at each other, then looked at me. When Babbo finally spoke, we both had to fight back tears.

"You proved yourself, Giuliana. Honestly, I can't believe you had it in you. You've achieved so much. There's nothing you can't do."

The conversation with Richard was not so heartwarming. There were no protestations of once-in-a-lifetime love. No vows to follow me to the ends of the earth. He was more dismissive than despairing. Why in the hell was I pulling such a ridiculous stunt?

"Your parents will never let you go," he said petulantly. He was twenty-five, but sounded twelve.

"Guess again, I already told them and they're thrilled," I said.

"Okay, let me call you back," he replied. I didn't have to wait long before he rang again.

"I've discussed it with some people," he began.

"What people?" I asked. (He ignored me, but I later found out his "people" were his employees at the dealership.)

"They told me if you go to L.A., you're a prostitute."

"*What*? What do you mean?" I may not have had a job lined up, but the leap from master's degree straight to streetwalker seemed unlikely and not a little insulting.

"You're going to become a whore," he concluded. The only way I could possibly succeed, he and his "people" had determined, would be if I slept my way through Hollywood. That's how it worked. Ask any auto dealer.

"Okay, well then, I'm going to go become a prostitute, so see you later!" I slammed down the phone. Richard D. could rust in hell. We were over.

I spent the next day packing everything I could into two cheap suitcases and called random hotels in L.A. until I found one I could afford for a few nights. Mama and Babbo had given me a couple hundred dollars, and I had a student Visa card with a five-hundred-dollar limit. I was almost twenty-three years old, and I wanted to do this on my own.

On the flight west, my cheap seat turned out to be in the back of the plane, next to the toilets. I made friends with a fellow passenger, an Angeleno who asked where I would be staying.

"Downtown at the Hotel Figueroa," I said.

"That's skid row," he told me. "Downtown is a horrible area. You need to find someplace else. Seriously, you're checking into some crack hotel!"

As soon as we landed, I found a pay phone in the airport and called my sister collect. Monica frequently traveled for her job, and she would surely know the name of a decent hotel where I could stay in Los Angeles. It was four a.m. in New York. The phone jolted her out of a dead sleep.

"Jules, what's wrong?" she said as soon as she heard my voice. I explained the situation, and asked her if she'd heard of the Hotel Figueroa.

"You can't go downtown!" she confirmed. "Tell the cab driver to take you to the Mondrian on Sunset in West Hollywood."

By the time I got to the Mondrian, it was two a.m., and the bar was closing. The lobby was filled with chic, gorgeous people. The Sky Bar, I soon learned, was the white-hot hottest spot in L.A. I stood dumbstruck as Jason Priestley from *Beverly Hills 90210* drifted past. A pretty African American woman approached me.

"How can I help you?" she asked in that polite icy way that lets you know right away that you are a lowly mortal who does not belong in so magnificent a place.

"Um, I need a room, please?" I ventured.

"I'm sorry, we're oversold," she promptly answered.

"Well, could you just please look to see if there's anything at all? I don't care where it is, if it's next to the elevator or whatever, I just need a room because I was booked at this hotel downtown but I didn't know downtown was dangerous and now I don't have any place else, could you just check again?"

"Nope, no rooms," she repeated. "I'm sorry."

"I'll just stay one night and I'll leave first thing in the morning. I just landed from Bethesda, Maryland, and I don't have the energy to walk three thousand miles home tonight," I half joked. I was desperate, jet-lagged, and beyond exhausted. She heaved an annoyed sigh, consulted the computer again, and came back.

"Okay, one room, one night," she relented, adding, "it's two hundred fifty-nine dollars a night."

"Thank you so much, thank you," I said. I handed her my student Visa card. She came back a few minutes later. A line of good-looking but impatient pissed off people had formed behind me and my suitcases.

"I'm so sorry, but your card's been declined."

It turned out that the Mondrian charged $259 a night, but put a hold on another $500 for security. My student Visa couldn't manage it.

"Look, I just need a place to sleep, I promise not to trash the room and I'll be out first thing in the morning," I pleaded. "I won't even use the shower!"

"There are a bunch of cheaper hotels if you just go down Sunset," the clerk suggested.

"Okay, thank you so much," I said. As I started to gather my things, tears began streaming down my face. *I should never have come*, I thought. *Maybe Richard was right; I am going to become a whore.* I was too embarrassed to turn around and walk back out through the throng of beautiful people. The pretty clerk sighed again.

"Okay, I'll give you the room and give you my rate and not take the $500. It'll come to $179." I thanked her and booked two nights; it seemed stupid not to make maximum use of the great discount she was offering.

The next morning, I went out and commandeered the pool phone to make free calls, dialing everyone I could think of to see if anyone knew anyone who needed a roommate in Los Angeles. A friend of a friend of a friend had a Canadian friend named Justine who hailed from a wealthy family and was trying to become an actress or model or something and might help. I dialed Justine. Justine was incredibly bitchy.

"Who?" she said.

I explained our eighteen degrees of separation and my dire situation.

"I don't know anyone who wants a roommate," Justine said impatiently.

"Well, if you happen to hear of anything, could you call me, please? I'm at the Mondrian," I said.

"Wait, you're staying at the Mondrian?"

"Yeah," I said, hopefully. This bit of information seemed to warm Justine up noticeably.

"So you can get into the Sky Bar," she mused aloud. "Okay, I'll come by to get you at ten and we'll go to dinner and then the Sky Bar."

I spent the day by the pool in my bikini, napping off my jet lag. I finally roused myself long enough to go to the poolside bar for some water. I heard a man's low whistle behind me as I waited.

"Wow, that's unbelievable. How'd you get that?"

Some stranger was examining my scar. I wheeled around. Not technically a stranger after all. I recognized him immediately.

Johnny Depp.

"It's beautiful," he said. "It's fucking cool. There must be some story behind that."

Johnny Depp wanted to hear how I got my scar. This was the kind of "how we met story" that Letterman would eat up when Johnny Depp and I became a power couple. This was a moment that was destined to change my whole life. It was why fate had made sure I got that one night at the Mondrian. And I knew that fate would not want me to screw it all up by telling Johnny Depp that I had scoliosis. Johnny Depp wanted a fucking cool story to go with the fucking cool scar.

"Oh, yeah. I was bungee jumping off a bridge and the bungee snapped," I said nonchalantly.

"What, are you fucking kidding me?" Johnny Depp was hooked. "Where?"

"The Potomac River," I said.

"You must've gotten huge money off that lawsuit," Johnny Depp surmised.

"No, it was illegal," I said. "It was at night."

"Whoa!" Now Johnny Depp was *really* impressed. Hell, I was impressed with my improvisational skills. I was a fugitive bungee jumper with incredibly bad luck and a fucking cool scar, and I wasn't done yet.

"Yeah, with a bunch of Australians." (When in doubt, blame the Australians. Hey, it made as much sense as the rest of the story, and Australia just adds three cups of crazy to any lie.)

I got my water. I willed myself to walk away from Johnny Depp. Who does that? Who just exits a most amazing conversation with a movie star? *The cool chick with the fucking cool scar,* I told myself. *The one Johnny Depp will be so intrigued with, he will beg to see again. The one who will become Mrs. Johnny Depp and live a fabulous life and bear his fabulous children.* I kept walking knowing he would yell after me. *Slower, slower. Give him a second.*

Johnny Depp did not come running—or even urgently sauntering—after me, but Justine picked me up that night in her cherry-red Mercedes Benz. We ended up having the best time, and Justine ended up letting me crash on her couch, after all.

Three days in, I had to say things were going pretty well in L.A.: I was technically homeless but no longer entirely friendless, Johnny Depp had admired my body, sort of, and I was not yet a prostitute.

That first night, Justine and I were on fire: we hit the Sky Bar and immediately met Dean Factor, the handsome great-grandson of the legendary Max Factor. Dean, who had just launched a cosmetics line called SmashBox, was a hot bachelor about town. The music executive he was with that night took an instant shine to Justine, and Dean became like a big brother to me. All four of us would frequently hang out at the Sky Bar. Justine and I made friends with the bartender and the doorman, a giant Aussie (yes, really) named Stewart, who slipped us past the velvet rope after that whenever we wanted, even when Dean wasn't with us, sweetly ignoring the fact that we didn't meet the criteria of being either VIPs or hotel guests.

The Sky Bar became our fantastically hip *Cheers*. I was forever trying to sidle my way up to the perimeter of the Beverly Hills 90210 circle and work my way into the center where Jason Priestley, Shannen Doherty, and Tori Spelling reigned. I got close enough: I caught the eye of a guy who had a guest starring role on the show, and we went out a few times. One night, he invited me to go to an after, after, after-party at a place called the Mousetrap. It turned out to be this tiny, derelict house in a shady neighborhood off Pico Boulevard. A scary-looking guy let us in. The kitchen had been turned into a bar, and people were sitting around in circles in the little bedrooms off the hallway. I didn't recognize anyone famous.

"Follow me," my date said, pulling me by the hand into a

room where seven people sat on chairs in a circle. As soon as we sat down, this totally beat-up looking woman with gold teeth and weird hair came in with a tray. "Sorry to keep y'all waiting," the waitress apologized. "I have your order." Oh good, I was starving and hoping they were serving something good like cheeseburgers or tacos.

I was the closest one to her, and the first served. She offered me a little bag full of white powder. I'd never been around cocaine before, but I knew instinctively that that had to be what it was. *Omigod, what do I do? Pretend to take it?*

"Go ahead, grab one," my 9021-blow date urged me.

"Um, you know, I'm going to pass tonight!" I said uneasily. I got up to leave. He followed me.

"I'm sorry, I don't do coke," I told him.

"I thought you said you partied?" he said.

"Well, yeah. I do like *dancing*," I explained. That was what I thought partying was—going to a club and dancing, just having fun.

"You know what? It's cool," he said. "Want me to drive you home?" I did, and after he dropped me off, we never saw each other again. I still have notoriously bad drug radar. One time, I came out of an E! interview all excited because the celeb had been so lively and seemed to just take to me. We had been like instant BFFs.

"That was the best interview ever!" I told my producer. The star and I were probably going to become lifelong friends. He looked at me and shook his head.

"Did you not see the residue of white powder in one of her nostrils?" he asked drolly. I hadn't, nor had I seen it years before when 90210 boy was asking me to party, which I foolishly interpreted as dancing on tables. But who needs prime-time actors when I was about to come face to face with the hottest young movie star in the world?

chapter six

As a new arrival to Hollywood, I quickly fell into the familiar groove of most young hopefuls, patching together enough money from working in restaurants or retail to sublet a room. Mine was in a creepy old house in the Hollywood Hills that my sister's college roommate held the lease on. I had my car put on a train from Maryland to L.A., only to have the steering wheel lock one day on the 405 freeway. I got over to the side safely, but the Lexus and I were through, and I gladly let go of my last tie to Richard D. I was able to trade in the Lexus for a cheap Jetta that didn't even have power windows, a hugely embarrassing inconvenience when I pulled up next to any cute guys who wanted to flirt at a stoplight.

I landed my first job in "the industry" as assistant to a small talent manager who worked out of her living room in Venice and tried to get commercial auditions or little plays for clients hoping to break into acting. I spent my day stuffing envelopes for $250 a week. It was an hourlong commute each way, and by the time I paid for rent, gasoline, and the four-dollar coffees my boss made me fetch but never reimbursed me for, I was pretty much broke.

I used to spend all of my free time with Justine, sitting at the Coffee Bean on Sunset, waiting to be discovered, along with a similarly luckless assortment of hopeful actors and models yearning to be in front of the cameras. We would go through the trade papers, network with people we'd met at the Sky Bar ("Hi, did you say something about an independent film you heard was casting?"), and scour the ads for useful classes to take.

I'd been in California for eighteen months when I heard that an upstart talent agency was hiring. Mike Ovitz, once described by the media as the Most Powerful Man in Hollywood, had left his job running Disney to launch a one-stop talent agency called Artist Management Group. AMG proceeded to lure marquis clients like Leonardo DiCaprio, Cameron Diaz, and Samuel L. Jackson from established powerhouse agencies. When I dropped off my résumé, the AMG recruiter asked me what position I thought I might fill. I suggested I could be a junior manager.

"You gotta be an assistant first," I was told.

"Okay," I agreed. "I'm happy to do that first."

"No, before you can be an assistant, you have to work in the mailroom."

"I have a master's degree!"

My objection was met with a smirk and a shrug.

"You'll be in good company. Some people down there have their PhDs."

I was hired to work twelve-hour shifts, five days a week, for minimum wage with no overtime. There were nine of us in the pool, and our job was to deliver scripts all over town. The worst were the Valley runs. It was always boiling hot, and the Jetta's air-conditioning snuffled and wheezed and drooled like some asthmatic bulldog. Plus, no superstars lived in the Valley. Those were usually studio runs.

I quickly established myself as AMG's best runner: I was fast and reliable, and had a great sense of direction, which, in L.A., is like having a second brain. I showed up for work in hand-me-down Ann Taylor suits from my sister and demure flats, but in my car, I always kept heels and a backup outfit for the Naughty Librarian in a Van Halen video, because you just never knew, right? When I got tapped to become the personal mail runner for Mike Ovitz himself, I was excited by the near guarantee of face time with some major players in Hollywood. Martin Scorsese. Matthew McConaughey. Maybe a reunion with Johnny Depp.

Right off the bat, I was handed an envelope to deliver for Mr. Ovitz with very strict instructions to handle it with care and be extremely discreet. I glanced at the name: Morty Weinstein. *This blows*, I thought. Who the hell was Morty Weinstein? Probably some paunchy bald accountant auditing the junior managers' expense accounts. And of course, Morty had to be somewhere in the friggin' Hollywood Hills on a smoggy, sweltering day where the temperature was already in the triple digits before noon. To make matters even worse, I couldn't find his address for the life of me. Keep in mind, this was long before the luxury of iPhones and GPS. I relied on a Thomas Bros. map book hundreds of pages thick to get me from point A to point B. Searching for Morty Weinstein, I kept looping through a canyon, up and down the same winding roads, until I finally decided to ask for help. I was starving to death, so I went back down the hill and pulled into a 7-Eleven to get a snack and a better map. I was looking at the candy bars when I noticed the greasy hot dogs riding that weird little hot-dog Ferris wheel that only 7-Elevens have, and I thought, implausibly, *Those hot dogs look really good.* I got one with relish, sauerkraut, mustard—everything. I hit the road again. After eating a few bites of my hot dog, I felt infinitely better by the time I found Morty Freakin' Weinstein's address and buzzed the gate. I wolfed down the last of the hot dog in the driveway. The house looked really nice. Really, really nice. *Maybe I should take off my blazer and put on the Van Halen heels,* I thought. *Nah, who cares what Morty Weinstein thinks, anyway?* I rang the doorbell and smiled perkily into the camera I knew would be watching me. The door swung open.

Leonardo DiCaprio answered.

"Hi," I said. *Act cool.*

We stood there, just looking at each other like goofy lovesick seventh-graders at the school dance. *He's going to invite me in, and we're going to go out on the balcony and have champagne.*

I stared at him expectantly. Flashed a big pageant smile.

Leonardo started to laugh, then checked himself. The kismet was throwing him off balance, too. He reached for the envelope.

"Thank you," he said. Another awkward pause. "See you later."

He shut the door.

On me.

On us.

I get it, I told myself, climbing back into the hot Jetta, which now smelled like boiled sauerkraut, *he's trying to play it cool. He's going to call the agency demanding to get my number.*

Driving back, I worked myself into a prenuptial delirium. *Omigod, I'm going to start dating Leonardo DiCaprio. I wonder if I was blushing? Did he see me blushing?* I pulled the visor down to check the mirror and see how badly I was blushing, but it wasn't my pink cheeks that were noticeable. It was my green front tooth, where a giant piece of hot-dog relish was lodged! No wonder Leo was stifling a laugh.

Leo would come to the agency now and then, and I'd spot

him in the hallway. He was always nice to the staff, and would wave or nod and say hello to everyone. But any hopes I had that he might remember some special spark with me were doused the first time I interviewed him as an E! reporter.

"I used to work at AMG and delivered your mail," I confessed.

"You're kidding! Yeah, you look familiar," Leo said. I waited for the thousand-watt lightbulb to go off in his head, and for him to say, *The girl in the crappy Jetta, right?* I would even have settled for *The gorgeous mystery girl with relish on her tooth, right?*

Nada.

He more than made up for it at one of my first times to cover the Screen Actors Guild awards ceremony. Where reporters are stationed along the red carpet at these events isn't random, or first-come-first-serve. The prime spot, or first position, is standing at the start of the red carpet. I was in last position, the spot where stars quickly pass just before they enter the building. Everyone's in a hurry by then to get inside and get to their seats. On this particular occasion, Leo, who was up for Best Actor for his role in *The Aviator*, was running late. He hurried down the red carpet without giving any interviews, apologizing along the way as everyone called his name, trying to snag his attention. But when he caught sight of me, he grinned and said, "Hey!" and jumped over the rope to come talk for a second. "Sorry, I'm not doing interviews because they are rushing me inside," he said. "But I just wanted to say 'hi.'" I was able to get a quick sound bite from him about how excited he was, and felt like Barbara Walters as I heard the other reporters frantically telling their producers, "No, we don't have Leo! Only Giuliana got him."

After paying my mailroom dues at AMG, I got promoted to assistant. The manager I was assisting was named Pam Kohl, a no-nonsense boss who wouldn't even make eye contact with me, so deep was her contempt. I did nothing to change her low opinion of me. Running a day planner was never my strong suit. The Sunday night before my second week on the job, I called her up.

"Obviously you hate me," I said, "so I'll just quit."

"No, you won't," she said. "You're going to come in tomorrow."

Pam was only four years older than I was, and little by little, she began to open up and we forged a tentative friendship. I was still terrible at my job (again with the phone messages— seriously, people, they'll call back eventually), but she kept thinking I would get better with experience. I'd been with her a year when she called me in one morning to go over her schedule.

"Giuliana, who am I meeting with at one?"

"That agent and his client?"

"Okay, and what time is my Kaye Popofsky meeting?"

"One o'clock."

"Okay, you see the problem?"

My penance for the double booking was to entertain Kaye Popofsky while Pam finished the first meeting. Kaye was a former agent friend of Pam's who was part of a new startup called LOAD Media. When Kaye arrived, I went out to greet her, apologized profusely, got her some coffee, and stayed to chat. She couldn't have been more gracious about my scheduling blunder, and we ended up having a great conversation. She asked me all about myself, what brought me to L.A., what my aspirations were. It turned out that LOAD had an entertainment division. After Kaye had her meeting with Pam and had left, I went into Pam's office.

"Kaye said I could audition for a reporter gig at her new company," I told her. "I know it's really hard to find a good assistant," I apologized, "but I'm not a good assistant."

LOAD was my cool dream job—a hip, fun start-up using the Internet to compete with the likes of *Entertainment Tonight* and *Access Hollywood*. I would do press junkets, premieres, and set visits to interview celebs. People could then download the segments on their home computers to watch whenever they liked, avoiding the hassles of streaming. It was a brilliant idea, but ahead of its time—the software kept crashing users' computers. My own parents ordered me to stop sending them my videos. I didn't care: I was having the time of my life, standing next to *Access Hollywood* and *Entertainment Tonight* reporters with my big, funky-ass microphone to thrust in famous faces at red-carpet events.

At the premiere of *Gone in 60 Seconds*, a forgettable thriller starring Nicolas Cage and Angelina Jolie, I snagged great interviews with Angie and Billy Bob Thornton. In those days, they were wearing vials of each other's blood around their necks and were all over each other making out. The segment got tons of attention, and I felt like I was maybe starting to make a small name for myself. I kept sending my résumé, headshot, and samples of my work to the big leagues, waiting to be discovered. I was getting a ton of practical experience, working with real editors, writing my own segments, and honing my interview skills.

I'd been at LOAD for six months when I showed up one morning at nine o'clock and got word that there was going to be a staff meeting at ten. I couldn't put my finger on it, but my radar was definitely picking up a weird vibe, and after Angelina and Billy Bob, that bar was pretty high. *Something's off, get your tapes*, the shrewd voice inside my head commanded. The tapes technically belonged to the company, not the individual reporters. I spent the next hour surreptitiously packing mine up and sneaking them out to hide in my car. My delinquent teenage years had given me balls of steel when it came to bending or breaking rules, and there's a good chance I wouldn't be where I am today if I hadn't known when and how to go rogue. When the appointed meeting time rolled around, we were taken into rooms ten at a time and summarily fired. LOAD was in its death throes, and only twenty of the 120 employees remained at the end of the hour. We were told that we would be allowed to go back to our desks to collect our personal belongings only—under supervision—before being escorted out of the building. If I hadn't taken my tapes, I would have had nothing to show any prospective employer. All my hard-won experience would have evaporated forever right along with LOAD itself.

I didn't have time to sit there and congratulate myself for fore-sight, though: I spent what little savings I had on an editing session to turn my LOAD work into a demo reel. I was ecstatic when MTV called.

"Do you have a very wide knowledge of music?" I was asked.

"Oh, yes. Vast knowledge," I said. I'd grown up with Kurt Loder and Downtown Julie Brown. My musical taste ran from Madonna to Beastie Boys to Frank Sinatra to New Kids on the Block and everything in between. I was a natural for MTV! These were my peeps. I was ecstatic when I was invited in for an interview.

I appeared before two interviewers, who held out a bag and told me I had forty-five seconds to go through it, pull out a CD, and succinctly describe what it meant to the world of music.

First up: Madonna. "Madonna is known for constantly rein-venting her image, but with this album, she is also reinventing her sound."

Michael Jackson: "How do you top *Thriller*, the best-selling album of all time? Well, it's not easy, but if anyone can do it, the record breaker himself can and this album in my hands may be the ticket."

P. Diddy: "Having started out in the biz as a talent direc-tor before founding his über-successful label Bad Boy Records, Diddy is a force to be reckoned with in the industry and this latest album proves just that."

Jennifer Lopez: "J. Lo recently debuted her first studio album, *On the 6*, after achieving success as an actress . . . In fact, she was recently the first Latina actress to get paid over one million dollars for a role in the hit *Out of Sight*, opposite George Clooney."

I was on a roll. I could be writing liner notes. Then I pulled out Daft Punk. Instead of just admitting that I knew absolutely nothing about them, I decided I could bullshit my way through it, so I just started making up all kinds of lies about how they were reinventing punk music and bringing huge numbers of new fans to the genre because of their creative genius, etc., etc. The interviewers looked at me blankly. Because, I discovered later, Daft Punk had nothing to do with punk music whatsoever.

"Okay, thank you. Uh huh. Bye-bye."

I squeaked by on savings for a few months. Then, as luck would have it, my best friend, Colet Abedi (we'd met while giving each other Bitchy Resting Face over the copying machine as low-level associate producers for a late-night syndicated gossip show that instantly tanked), got a job casting for ABC's *The Bachelor*, and she brought me on board as a casting assistant for an upcoming project. We were going on the best girls' trip ever—an all-expenses-paid weekend in Minneapolis to find hot guys to be potential cast mates for the show. We went out partying our first night, and all but forgot our mission when a waitress walked by our table and said "Weezer" under her breath. I looked over and spotted the band hanging out.

"I get the lead singer," I told Colet, who had no idea who Weezer was, anyway.

"Fine, who's the lead guitarist?" she agreed.

"Tall dude with the tats."

Weezer seemed delighted to see us, and we proceeded to spend the whole night hanging out with them, taking it from drinks to dinner to clubbing. We were on our way to party more back at our hotel when the topic of tattoos came up, and the lead singer (mine) said his friend (Colet's lead guitarist) had done the ink we were all admiring. I was impressed. "He sings and is a tattoo artist? Is there anything this guy can't do?" I said out loud. All of my date's bandmates started laughing and saying stuff like, "Sing? Have you ever heard John sing? He is the worst!" I thought it was all band humor until one of the other guys said, "Come to think of it, none of us have good voices. Good thing we're great tattoo artists!"

"Wait, you guys aren't Weezer?" I asked. They looked at each other and laughed some more.

"Why would you think that?" my almost-boyfriend wondered.

"Well, because I think the waitress mentioned it when you sat down at the restaurant." Had we misheard? Or been set up?

More laughter, accompanied by high-fives and drunken keeling-over glee. Colet and I turned away without a word and walked away, pissed that we had just wasted our whole night with a bunch of drunk Minneapolis tattoo artists. I wanted to tattoo the word *asshole* on my forehead.

"Bitches!" the spurned tattoo artists called after us.

"Screw you, non-Weezers!" I shot back.

The next day, we slapped some flyers in a few gyms and waited around for hot glistening men to come flex for us and beg to be on our show. It didn't happen. We were perplexed. This was Minnesota. Shouldn't it be swarming with second-generation Scandinavian studs? It was the July Fourth weekend, and we decided that the quality hot guys must be on the water, so off we headed to Lake Minnetonka. Because, yeah, everyone knows it is nationally acclaimed as the Lake o' Ripped Bachelors. Right? Our plan was to wangle our way on to someone's fancy boat. Once there, the flaw in our thinking became obvious: The fancy boats were in the middle of the water. We would need a boat of our own to get to Gatsby's yacht. Or Sven's party pontoon. Whatever. We just needed some not-ugly men in their twenties with a pulse and all their teeth at this point.

"We'd like a pontoon," we told the boat rental place.

"No, we're all out."

"Um. Okay, do you have a cigarette boat?" Clearly I had been watching way too much *Miami Vice*.

"No."

"A Scarab?"

"Nope."

"Okay, what do you have that we can drive?"

We ended up with a little motorboat that we couldn't manage to steer in anything resembling a straight line. Or even a lazy zigzag. We just kept spinning in circles. We'd come up to some fancy boat and pirouette in front of it like some overexcited Pomeranian about to pee on the fancy people. Nobody invited us aboard. Finally, we headed for Lord Fletcher's Old Lake Lodge, renowned for its lively bar scene on the shores of Minnetonka. We pulled up to Lord Fletcher's berth and crashed into it. We tried but failed to act cool as we hoisted ourselves out of our toy boat and went inside to recruit gorgeous Norwegian American bachelors. Lord Fletcher's has six bars and something like nine dining areas, and still we struck out. Minnesota, we were forced to conclude, had a serious lack of desperate people willing to humiliate themselves on a reality show. We went back without a single candidate.

Back in L.A., Colet and I were driving down Beverly Boulevard one Friday afternoon, talking about our career hopes like we often did, when I felt this sense of despair swamp me.

I'd been in L.A. for four years, and nothing was happening. I had no money. No one was hiring me. Everything was falling through. The few opportunities I had fizzled quickly. I had gotten on television exactly one time, and that was only because the ship was going down and the producer had nothing to lose: I had been a lowly associate producer for a late-night *National Enquirer* syndicated gossip show, and on the brink of cancellation, my boss told me I could report a piece about the eighties making a tiny comeback. I went all out, dressing like Madonna and roller-skating down the boardwalk of Venice Beach with a boombox on my shoulder, making an absolute idiot of myself as I called out to gawkers, "Hey, the eighties are back, didn't you hear?" The cute spoof was all I had to show for my on-air aspirations. I was a total loser, and my world felt small and pathetic.

"I'm done," I told Colet. "I'm never going to make it here."

Colet was having none of it. If I wanted a pity party, she was not going to RVSP.

"Giuliana, you can't give up hope! What're you going to do?"

"Maybe go home?" I ventured.

"And marry Richard?" she scoffed. I shook my head. It wasn't as if Johnny Depp, Leonardo DiCaprio, or any real Weezers were going to carry me off on a white horse.

"I need a sign," I declared. Colet was deeply spiritual. She was into crystals and oils and energies and all sorts of weird shit I don't understand. A sign was something she could relate to. My spirituality was more traditional, but I had my superstitions, too. Bizarre as it sounds, my phone rang as if on cue, interrupting our contemplation of my future. I glanced at the number but didn't recognize it.

"Get it," Colet suddenly urged.

"Nah, I don't know the number. I don't mess with unknown numbers."

"You have to answer it!"

I picked up the call and heard a woman's voice.

"Giuliana?" she asked. "This is Gina Merrill."

"OH MY GOD, *the* GINA MERRILL?" I shouted back. "I've been sending you tapes for years, did you get them?"

Gina was a talent recruiter at E! Entertainment. Surprised by my fangirl reaction, she couldn't immediately confirm that she'd gotten my previous six thousand pieces of mail, but she had gotten the latest tape, with my LOAD work and the goofy eighties-is-back piece.

"Can you come in on Monday to audition for a week?" she wanted to know.

I stayed calm long enough to get a time and place, then hung up so Colet and I could scream with excitement.

"I know this is it," I said. The turning point.

The first thing I did was trade in my Jetta for a Jeep Cherokee, taking out a loan to pay for it. I was that sure that my fortunes were about to shift.

I was supposed to report to E! on the Miracle Mile at 6:30 on Monday morning. I showed up fifteen minutes early, carting a big suitcase full of clothes and shoes, curling irons, and my Miss Maryland Caboodles case full of makeup. The office building was all high ceilings and marble floors, silent and empty. No one was there, and a sign said they didn't open until eight a.m. After some confusion and calling around, I discovered I was at the wrong reception area. The executive producer, Peggy Jo Abraham, came to fetch me. She looked surprised by my suitcase.

"What's all this stuff?" she asked.

"My hair and makeup and clothes," I replied.

"We have hair and makeup and wardrobe," Peggy explained. *Whoa.*

It got even better as I walked through the newsroom and caught sight of popular anchors Jules Asner and Steve Kmetko, and was ushered into a cubicle and given a temporary password.

I soon learned from a friendly assignment editor named Maureen that I was the thirty-ninth person to try out for the job. *And the last*, I silently vowed.

Nowadays, when you see a segment of a host interviewing a celebrity, he's most likely reading questions that a producer writes. A small hive of broadcast worker bees perform all the vital tasks and make the necessary decisions that go into each segment. Back in 2001, though, it was all on the reporter. We were expected to come up with questions, log the tape, find the best moments, do our own research, write our own scripts, and choose the clips to go with them—all before the show went live at 4:00 p.m. Pacific time.

My first day on the job, I was assigned to report on that night's premiere of *Summer Catch*, a movie starring Freddie Prinze Jr. and Jessica Biel. In the movie, a character played by Wilmer Valderrama has an affair with his friend's mom, played by Beverly D'Angelo. When Wilmer came up to me on the red carpet at the premiere, I thought it was a stroke of genius to ask him:

"So, do you like moms in real life?"

"I don't know what you mean," Wilmer said playfully.

"You know," I went on, "do you *do* moms in real life?"

"I don't know what you mean!" Wilmer coyly insisted. We both laughed it off, and he moved on.

The next day, I was sitting with my editor, Don, when the moms riff came up. Don swiveled in his chair and fixed me with a hard look.

"You can't put that in there."

"Yes, I can!" I objected. It was a great bit. No way was I losing it.

"No," he insisted. "You'll get fired and so will I, and I don't want to lose my job over this."

"I got it approved," I countered. Don was dubious.

"No way. Who approved it?"

"Peggy."

"Peggy approved this."

"Yes!" Technically, this was true: Peggy read all of our scripts before they went on air and signed off on them. I had submitted this one to her. With ellipses where the words "do moms" would have been. Even as a cub reporter, I knew full well that the sly innuendo was too racy for most networks, E! included.

That afternoon, I was almost bursting with excitement, waiting for my piece to come on. I was already rehearsing humble thank-yous in my head for all the kudos I was going to get. In the newsroom, everyone was watching the monitors as usual when that afternoon's show went live. My segment came on, Wilmer and I had our little exchange, and it was over. I glanced around expectantly. No one congratulated me. The newsroom, in fact, was briefly, weirdly silent.

"Told you," said Don, before walking away.

Phones started ringing all over the place, including back in my cubicle. Peggy summoned me to her office. The managing editor, Eddie Delbridge, was waiting there with her.

"What was that?" Eddie demanded. "What did we just see?"

"That was the premiere of *Summer Catch*!" I answered brightly. Sometimes if you pretend nothing is wrong, nothing is. Okay, it almost never really works like that, but it's worth believing for the one time in 42 million that it does. I needed it to be that time.

"I did *not* approve that!" Peggy said.

"Can I have my script again?" I asked, stalling for time.

"I have your script," Peggy said. "It says 'Do you . . . in real life.'"

"Mmmm, yes," I said, trying to sound preoccupied and reporter-like. "In fairness, Peggy, I meant to go write it out. Thank you so much for catching that!"

Eddie cut in.

"Thank *you* so much, but you can get your stuff and go now."

"Oh," I said, still all innocence and bafflement. "I don't have a few days left? It's only Tuesday."

I didn't have any days left. My E! audition was officially over. Candidate number thirty-nine was going down in flames. I went outside, got into my most-likely-to-be-repossessed Jeep, and started crying. I called Colet.

"I screwed up," I wailed. "It's over. E! is the only place I can work. It's exactly what I do."

Colet lined up another gig, casting this time for a cheesier, raunchier *Bachelor*-like show, with a small budget to hire an assistant. We were in business again, and another scouting trip was on the horizon. This time, we knew we had to rethink our strategy. Then it came to us.

Miami. Why hadn't we thought of that before? If ever there's a place outside of L.A. to find attractive, shallow, desperate, vain people, it's Miami! We booked ourselves a room at one of the cool hotels and announced open calls at Crunch Fitness. If the guys passed our audition there, they could come to our hotel room for an interview. First, everyone had to fill out our questionnaire: Did you ever contract an STD? How do you feel about threesomes? Foursomes?

Howard Stern had nothing on us. Colet and I tried not to look at each other and fall into giggling fits during the interviews, but we weren't entirely successful.

"Okay, Joseph, I see your first sexual encounter was at thirteen. Can you tell us about that?"

Colet and I were sharing the king-size bed back in our hotel room, and one morning I woke up to the ringing phone. Colet answered. "What? What?" I heard her say. She sounded panicked. "Jules, turn on the TV!"

I hit the remote, and the screen filled with the terrifying image of the second World Trade tower collapsing in smoke and dust.

Colet and I sat in bed that entire day, watching it all unfold. We couldn't go home; flights were grounded. My parents had told me the day before that they were going up to New York to see Monica and her year-old daughter, Alexa. I tried calling but couldn't get through. I was freaking out, watching TV, thinking New York was about to be bombed into oblivion at any moment, that my sister, niece, and parents would all perish. After several hours of frantically trying everyone's cell phone, I finally reached Monica. She was hysterical. She was holding her baby, safe in her apartment uptown, while the sky filled with smoke and the chaos unfolded on the streets below. Mama and Babbo were with her, petrified and in tears, too. Once we were able to get a plane back to California, I spent the entire flight digging my nails into Colet's arm, convinced that everyone on board was a terrorist.

I spent the next few months moping around. My sister and her husband had moved to L.A., and my brother-in-law, Bryan, paid me to run errands, wash the car, and babysit. I knew it was pity money, not a paycheck, but I couldn't afford to not accept their help. The whole country was still mourning the 9/11 attacks and I was as angry as the next person. I came up with what I thought was a good idea. I tapped into the little savings I had and spent $300 creating bumper stickers that read FUCK THE TERRORISTS. Every afternoon I would stand on various corners of Ventura Boulevard in the sweltering hot San Fernando Valley and wave my stickers in the air while yelling "FUCK THE TERRORISTS!" "JUST THREE DOLLARS!" I got hundreds of honking horns in support but very few takers. Careful not to stray from my original plan, I kept sending out my portfolio and answering cattle calls for auditions. I went to one for a crappy TV show and said my one line, "Hey, put your gun down," so convincingly, I got a callback. Maybe I had acting talent! I hadn't even been trying all that hard. I was Meryl Streep! On the way to the callback, I wondered how many years the series would run and if I would have to hire a bodyguard to keep the fans and paparazzi at bay. I was called into a room with eight people—all producers and writers—waiting to hear me read again. I choked. I never got another callback for any acting or modeling job. Now I had not only blown my shot at my dream E! job, but I had used up the last of my beginner's luck, too.

My parents kept telling me I could always come home.

"Get a job here," Mama suggested.

I was about ready to do that when Gina Merrill called me out of the blue right after the holidays. That moment with Wilmer Valderrama had generated a lot of buzz. Good or bad, people had been talking about it. I thought to myself, *Wow, it's true what they say, any press is good press.* This time, she wasn't offering me an audition. She was offering me a job.

When I think back to my very first official day at E!, I remember walking into the hair and makeup room and sitting down, when suddenly Joan Rivers walked in with her team. Actually, it's misleading to say Joan walked into any room; Joan touched down, like a tornado. She crackled with energy and was always mid-monologue. I sat in my makeup chair in awe as she settled in next to me.

"Are you the new girl on *E! News*?" she asked.

"Yes, I'm Giuliana."

"How do you say your name?"

"Ju-lee-AH-na with a G," I said, starting, idiotically, to spell it for her, like she was going to write me a check or something. "I'm Italian, we don't have J in our alphabet," I blathered on.

"Have you signed a contract yet?" Joan demanded.

"I think my agent is still working on it," I said. Great, I had so underwhelmed Joan Rivers that she was trying to find a loophole for the network to dump me before my first show.

"Have you signed anything?" Joan asked again.

"No," I admitted.

"Whatever they're paying you, get them to agree to more. And then get your agent to get them to ten percent more," she said. "Get a monthly allowance for hair and makeup, and I don't mean to pay the hair and makeup people here. They take care of that. I mean an allowance to cover highlights and haircuts, facials, manicures, pedicures, waxing, whatever you need to do to look beautiful. From here on out, you're not doing it for yourself, you're doing it for your job, which means it's all covered. Oh, and health and medical coverage, you need that but that goes without saying. Also, don't let them walk all over you."

I nodded. Everyone in the room had fallen quiet and was listening as Joan went on.

"Don't be exclusive to just the network, make sure you have an out clause in your contract to be able to do shows on other networks and also a clause that allows you to be a spokesperson for products and big brands," she said. "While you're at it, make sure you have photo approval, that's probably more important than health insurance." She was only half joking about the last one. The whole room erupted in laughter.

I had taken out a notebook and was madly scribbling this all down.

"Okay, you got that?" she said. "Call your agent. Make them put that all in. Tell them Joan Rivers told you. No, I'm not kidding. Drop my name."

Joan left in another personal tornado, and I sat there in disbelief. Had that really just happened? Had the queen of comedy just given me invaluable advice, and basically said she had my back? A soft, appreciative *whoa* from my glam squad brought me back down to earth.

"Yeah," I agreed. "That was pretty badass."

The fairy tale I felt like I was now living in just kept getting more fantastic. The morning of my first Academy Awards as an E! correspondent, I was thrilled to find myself assigned to what the network refers to as the E! Sky Box, perched like a bird over the most famous red carpet in the world. Joan and her daughter, Melissa, hit the airwaves about an hour before going live on the red carpet to do a little pregame commentary. Just before they came on, I was in the Sky Box telling viewers who they could expect to see on the red carpet that day. I then tossed to a commercial break and when we came back, the cameras were live on Joan and Melissa for the first time that day in another area of the red carpet. The mother-daughter team was on fire, cracking jokes with one another and giving viewers the inside scoop on the celebs that would soon be interviewed by the most irreverent woman in Hollywood.

I was watching the whole exchange on my monitor, giddy with the idea that I was on the same channel and on at the same time as Joan Rivers. It was pretty cool. As I watched, I literally forgot I wasn't in my living room like the year before and jumped to high alert when a producer yelled in my ear that Joan was about to toss to me live. Joan was finishing her bit, and as I watched the prompter, I saw my name come up. I nervously got ready for Joan to toss the ball up to me. "Okay now, let's go up to the Sky Box with Guh, um, Gooey . . ."

I peeked at my monitor and immediately recognized the perplexed look on her face. It was the exact expression that would cross the brow of every single teacher coming across my weirdly spelled name for the first time on an attendance roll. I learned early on to cut them off with a frantic "just call me Julie!" before the class broke into hysterics over some butchered pronunciation and spent the rest of the year calling me Googly or Gooiana. I hadn't run into Joan since our makeup chair tutorial in advanced Hollywood economics, but I knew she was famous for botching unusual names—even on *Fashion Police* years later, she could never say "Rihanna," it was always "Rowena" or "Rwanda"—and now she was massacring mine live.

"Mom, it's Joo-liana, not Goo-liana," I heard Melissa coach her mother.

"What're you doing up there, Hooliana?" Joan sang out.

"JOO-liana," Melissa tried again.

"Wooliana, Wooliana, is that you?" Joan called.

"Yes, Joan, it's me, Wooliana," I answered. "I should be upset that you just mangled my name, but you can call me whatever you want, I'm just honored to be here hosting with you."

Joan cracked up. She liked my recovery so much, she began asking me to come on her other *Fashion Police* specials throughout the year. When the popular show became a weekly series, she gave me a permanent seat as moderator, the "everyday woman" foil to the sharp-tongued repartee of Joan and fellow panelists Kelly Osbourne and stylist George Kotsiopoulos. Joan was a talented writer and had her own killer team of joke writers to help out with the enormous amount of content on each show, and, of course, she could ad-lib zingers like nobody's business. But the rest of us, I was alarmed to discover, were on our own trying to be funny, a kazoo orchestra under the baton of the great Leonard Bernstein.

Every week, an intern would deliver fat binders full of photos for the next show, a fashion gallery of hits and misses running the gamut from Miley Cyrus in a raunchy onesie with her tongue hanging out to Sofia Vergara in a designer gown and a million dollars' worth of Chopard borrowed jewels. At first, I would spend hours and hours doing research before an episode, thinking I needed to sound authoritative when I talked about a bias cut or a dress that had been deconstructed. But that wasn't what impressed producers and Joan. It was all about the funny.

I would try to prepare clever remarks or jokes, and it would all go out the window on set, because the vibe would be off. The show was too organic for canned responses, no matter how smart or funny they sounded back in my dressing room when I was saying them to myself. I discovered it was much funnier if

I just saw the photos for the first time during the show and said whatever popped into my head. It was fun to voice my opinion and let loose, especially coming from the tightly produced format of *E! News* at the time. I found the less I prepared jokes and gave my real, authentic reaction to a photo, the more laughs I got. I even pushed a guest into practically sexually molesting Joan in front of our live studio audience (and the cameras).

"She's got boobs I'd kill to motorboat!" I exclaimed about Halle Berry during a Rate the Rack segment in season two. I then dared our guest panelist, comedian Adam Pally, to motorboat Joan, and led the studio audience in a chant of "Mo-tor-BOAT! Mo-tor-BOAT!" Joan gestured to her chest. "C'mon," she invited the cornered Pally, who pressed his face between Joan's knockers and waggled his head with the appropriate "vvvvvvvvrrrrr" sound of a motorboat while everyone, including Joan, fell over laughing. It was the funniest thing ever, and the producers loved it.

As moderator, it was my job to keep the show moving. Dead air or people talking over each other are the quickest ways to ruin a show like *Fashion Police*. The second-to-last thing you want to do in this format is step on a comedian's lines; the last thing you wanted to do was step on one of Joan's, because the audience would miss out on the kind of world-class humor you can't really re-create if you try to go back and retape it. One of the greatest compliments I ever got at E! was the time word got back to me that Joan had asked a producer after taping one day, "Is someone writing Giuliana's jokes?"

"No," she was told. "Giuliana does her own writing."

"I don't believe it. Does she really?" Joan pressed.

"No, really, it's all her!"

"God, she's gotten funny," Joan said.

Not everyone was always amused. Most celebrities are secure enough or mature enough to take the occasional slicing-and-dicing by *Fashion Police* in stride as entertainment. Lord knows Helena Bonham Carter must have the thickest skin and best sense of humor on earth given how often she appears in something that makes no sense. I've even speculated on air whether the British actress had discharged herself from a psych ward to go shopping in her hospital jammies. When I trashed Tina Fey's flouncy Golden Globes dress by Zac Posen and cracked, "Little Bo Peep has lost her chic," I thought nothing of it. Until the following week, when I was covering the SAG Awards and I spotted Tina coming my way, looking gorgeous in a sleek black gown. She did not look happy to see me standing in first position on the red carpet, impossible to avoid.

Oh, fuck, I thought, as I announced maybe a little too enthusiastically, "Hi, here's Tina Fey joining us!"

"Um, excuse me," Tina replied icily, "weren't you one of the people who took a hot, steaming dump on my dress last week?"

I looked at her with my smile pasted on and my mind reeling: *Just lie! Tell her it was George who said it!* Tina waited expectantly for me to respond. She obviously knew I was the guilty party.

"Ummmm . . . Yes," I finally admitted. "Yes, it was me." She started to storm off. "Tina, hold on!" I implored. "Tonight, you look amazing. Last week, that dress did not do you any favors." Tina returned.

"I know," she said sweetly. "I was just messing with you."

In the poor sport category, the worst I've encountered would have to be a certain B list star. I was at an Italian restaurant having a romantic dinner with Jerry O'Connell when the bitch marched right up to the table and interrupted us. At first, I thought it was some stalker fan about to go off the deep end because Jerry was on a date with me, not her, but Jerry vaguely recognized the intruder as someone he'd worked with or met before. "Oh, hey," he started to say, ignoring her rudeness. But she was staring at me, not him. Her face was twisted with rage.

"You talked shit about my outfit on *Fashion Police*," she said. "What the fuck do you know? That wasn't cool."

"I was just talking about the fashion, it was nothing personal," I assured her.

"It *is* personal," she said. "Don't you ever fucking talk about me again." She walked away and I swore to never say anything about her again (good or bad) on television, because with hideous manners like that, she wasn't worth a second of my time. I saw her almost an entire decade later when she was a guest on *Fashion Police* (wait, didn't she loathe our show?), and I barely looked her way or said two words to her, even though she was sitting five inches to my left. All I could think was what a hypocrite she was.

I've been on Worst Dressed lists myself. I think it's funny. Who cares? At the Golden Globes a few years ago, I wore a sleeveless black gown with a weird lace garter circling my throat, like I'd just come from a bachelorette party for Goths. When I make a red-carpet mistake, I'm not blessedly there and gone in thirty seconds like the stars sweeping into the awards show: I'm standing out there on display in my bad choice, broadcasting for hours and to over one hundred countries. Sometimes there are heaters blasting away at my feet so viewers won't see goose bumps on my arms when I'm wearing some skimpy dress in forty-five-degree weather, or a big fan to keep from getting sweat stains on my gown when it's ninety degrees and I'm standing in the blazing sun for three hours.

On *Fashion Police*, we're all put together by the stylists before we come on set, with hair, makeup, and jewelry carefully chosen to create a specific look. You can't have second thoughts about the dress with batwing sleeves, tell everyone to hang on for fifteen minutes, and run back to the dressing room to put on something else. Since there's no turning back, we always tell each other how fabulous we look as we settle in to tape the show.

My all-time worst might have been the day I strutted on set looking like Snooki's cheesy cousin. Actually, Snooki doesn't have a cousin as tacky as I was this day so let's say I looked like Snooki's cheesy cousin's ex-boyfriend's new video ho. I came out in a tight leopard dress with a fresh orange spray tan and thick clip-on bangs—yes, *clip-on bangs*—to match my long, straight blonde extensions. Somewhere back in time, a caveman was looking for his missing escort. Meanwhile, I thought I was hot shit. I walked onto the set the way Nicki Minaj must crawl into bed with a new man: feeling sexy, sultry, and seductive. About ten minutes into the show, I caught a glimpse of myself in the monitor and thought, *Who's that scary-looking girl on set with the nasty bangs? Is she from a Lil Jon video?* I realized it was me. What's amazing is that I had the nerve to play my favorite segment, Starlet or Streetwalker, on that episode and actually laugh and call other people streetwalkers. When I got home that night, Bill said I should fire my stylist and my hair and makeup team.

"While you're at it, fire yourself from *Fashion Police* for allowing that," he added.

(I did tell them I was pissed, and, for the record, I happen to have a whole new team now.)

Withering as she was on air—she once lamented Billy Joel's weight gain by saying he'd eaten the Dixie Chicks—Joan was the ultimate diplomat in real life. She always waited until I was leaving before casually asking me about what I had worn that day.

"Bye, Joan!" I'd say, giving her a hug and kiss and wishing her a safe trip back to New York.

"By the way, Giuliana," she would begin, "is this outfit yours or Wardrobe's?"

If I said it was mine, she would go, "Oh. It's nice!" If I said it came from Wardrobe, she offered one of two comments:

"Give it back," if she hated it.

And if she loved it?

"Steal it."

Joan herself could be wearing a pink feather boa with a black beaded top and a statement necklace, along with several chunky bracelets and a couple of golf ball rings, but none of us ever would have criticized her fashion choices. She could carry off over-the-top beautifully because she *was* over-the-top.

The designers whose creations sometimes get shredded by *Fashion Police* have never complained that I know of. In fact, they see me on the red carpet each year at the Met Gala, which is the fashion industry's version of the Super Bowl, and they run to me to say how much they love watching *Fashion Police*. And not just little-known designers: I've had Tom Ford and Valentino make a beeline to me to tell me they watch, as well as newer designers like Prabal Gurung.

It still sometimes amazes me what we can get away with on air. Sometimes I wish the producers had stopped us. Kelly and I once went off on the longest gross-out tangent describing just how disgusting we found the shade of yellow reality star La La Anthony was wearing one week. On and on we went, from bad to worse, until it got to some revolting STD reference. As a general rule, Kelly, George, and I were limited in the number of swear words we could use, because Joan would rack up so many bleeps. As moderator, I had to maintain some semblance of control.

The dirty jokes, the freewheeling guests, the risqué games we play, and the side-splitting laughter are all reminders to me of how lucky I am to call this work. My favorite part of the show, though, was always Joan's greeting. She made up a new silly term of endearment for me every episode. I was her chickie-poo, her captivatingly cool cucumber, her gentle giantess of journalism, her beautiful baller of broadcasting, her tall tamale of truth. One time, I was her bug-eyed beaver. "Do I have bug eyes?" I asked the camera, while flipping Joan my middle finger. She coined the word *slassy* for Rihanna, explaining that the singer always managed to look slutty but in a classy way, "like you, Giuliana."

I looked at the camera and mouthed the word *bitch*, but admitted out loud, "Only Joan can say that and warm my heart." And that's the truth. Only Joan. Which makes it all that much harder to imagine the show going on without our beloved Joan. When Joan passed away, my first inclination regarding the future of the show was that there was no future. That the show would go away. When producers first reached out to tell me that Melissa had given her blessing for the show to continue with a new host, I was shocked. Melissa and I went to dinner, and she explained that her mom, the consummate professional and hardest-working woman in show business, would have wanted the show to go on. She told me that Joan wouldn't want any of us to miss a beat, and I believed her. After having known Joan so many years, I knew what Melissa was telling me was the truth. The question was, what would *Fashion Police* look like and who could ever replace Joan Rivers?

There were months of conversations among the executive producers of the show, Melissa, Lisa Bacon, and Gary Snegaroff, and the network head honchos. All sorts of names were making headlines as possible replacements, but the one that was mentioned in every article was Kathy Griffin. From the minute her name came up, I was not-so-secretly rooting for her. I have been a fan of her stand-up for years and loved that she would always credit Joan for paving the way for female comedians like herself, something she made sure to mention in interviews long before Joan passed away. To me, it came down to respect, and I liked that Kathy respected Joan in life and in death.

When the official announcement came out that Kathy was joining the panel, I was ecstatic and shot her an e-mail that said "Amen! Welcome to the family." She responded by inviting me to her house for dinner and late-night karaoke. My kind of girl.

chapter seven

y love life and my professional life never seemed to fall into sync, and I started my dream job without any dream lover at my side. I wasn't exactly burning up the gossip columns as the new "It Girl" in town. By the time I got to E!, I'd been in L.A. for nearly five years, and all of my close encounters with any bona fide stars fell into one of two categories: disastrous or ludicrous.

My losing streak had begun, of course, at the Sky Bar. Even before I met the 90210 actor who took me on a date to a skeezy drug house, I had landed an invitation one night to the home of someone I'll call Mr. Prime Time. It was only a few weeks post-Depp, and I had wriggled into a tight black tube dress with sky-high hooker heels in hopes of finding him again back at the Mondrian. I had come with Justine, but she was off somewhere with her music executive when a good-looking guy with chiseled cheekbones and great dimples struck up a conversation with me. He wasn't anybody I recognized, but he was nice to talk to and look at, so I decided to give him a chance and finesse my woman-of-mystery skills until Johnny Depp reclaimed me.

"So, what do you do?" I asked.

"I'm an actor," he said. Standard answer at the Sky Bar. I may have raised an eyebrow or smirked ever so slightly.

"Yeah, cool. Are you on a show?" I asked. I didn't get an advanced journalism degree for nothing.

"Yup," he said. He named a show, and I told him I'd never heard of it, in an airy tone that suggested I had better things to do with my fabulous, mysterious life than watch no-name cable channels at three a.m. My dismissal of his acting claims hit a nerve.

"Do you want me to prove it?" he challenged me.

Now I was curious. What was he going to do, recite the soliloquy from *Hamlet*? Big deal, so could I, and that didn't make me Judi Dench.

"Turn around," he instructed. I did, and there he was, smoldering from a giant billboard above Sunset Boulevard. He was the sexy new face of a major retailer. Not only was his TV show a hit drama that everyone in America except me apparently watched, but Mr. Prime Time was the show's resident hunk. Oh, and it was on a major network, not cable. I still didn't know the show, but I loved the brand he was modeling for on the billboard, and I liked that he could handle some attitude.

We had a few more drinks and he invited me back to his place, which turned out to be a dreamy apartment in West Hollywood. The living room had tall windows dressed in gorgeous white drapes, and the whole apartment had this beautiful, chic European feel to it—an aesthetic weirdly disrupted by a bowl full of Blow Pops on the coffee table. I promptly unwrapped one and popped it in my mouth. Subtle. Mr. Prime Time and I settled on the couch, and as we sat there talking, he fell into this dark funk over his ex and his kid, and started confiding how conflicted he was. We were both pretty buzzed by then. I listened with an intense concentration that had more to do with getting to the bubble-gum center of my Blow Pop than to the bottom of his psyche. Here I was, a tipsy twenty-three-year-old, offering relationship advice to a man more than ten years my senior, when all I really wanted was to have my first actor make-out session. Finally, we started fooling around, and, moving to the bedroom, I asked if he had anything more comfortable I could slip into. He pulled out a gently worn T-shirt and boxers from the same retailer that he was the face for on the billboard. Smooth.

Long before Patti Stanger made the line the catchphrase for her *Millionaire Matchmaker* reality show, I had a strict no-sex-without-monogamy rule. I planned on being famous someday, and I didn't want some parade of past conquests coming out of the woodwork.

"Okay," Mr. Prime Time said, "I like you. You're smart. So, in the morning, I'm going to have cereal. Do you like cereal?"

"I do," I said.

"I have Cap'n Crunch," he said in a somber way that made me think it was code for something kinky that I didn't understand and quite possibly did not want to. Pirate games? Wrong girl, matey. Get a parrot.

Six in the morning came with sun pouring through the tall windows, and I felt a dead weight pinning down my arm. He was asleep on it. I opened one eye and immediately thought, *Omigod, I hafta get outta here, even if it means pulling a coyote and chewing my arm off.* I needed to be gone before he woke up, to leave him wondering where I went and who I really was and when he might see me again. Women of mystery did not stay for breakfast. I carefully extricated my arm and crept out of bed.

There were two cereal bowls neatly laid out and a box of Cap'n Crunch on the table. I scribbled a note to leave on his pillow: "Had to run, busy day. Raincheck on cereal? My # . . . Giuliana." Breezy with a hint of interest, damn, I was good. I was totally channeling La Femme Nikita.

Dressing for my great escape posed something of a dilemma: my choices were a black hooker dress and heels or a pair of boxers and wrinkled T-shirt. I put on the dress but stole his clothes anyway. I wanted a souvenir, and I needed proof to show my girlfriends. (How a plain tee and boxers would prove I spent the night with OMG DON'T YOU KNOW WHO THAT IS?! I wasn't sure, short of DNA testing, but they seemed like important evidence at the time.) I tiptoed out his front door, into the gated pool area. I went to let myself out, only to discover that I needed a key. I was trapped. Again. I considered my options: Throw rocks at his window and yell up, "Maybe I will have that cereal?" Too embarrassing. Or throw my bag and heels over the fence, put the boxers and T-shirt in my mouth, scale the fence in a tube dress, and then drop eight feet to the ground on the other side, twisting my ankle in the process? Yes, that's the ticket, Giuliana, because it's so much *less* embarrassing to hobble barefoot down Sunset Boulevard at the start of rush hour in smeared makeup, tangled long blond hair, and a hooker dress, carrying a man's boxer shorts and T-shirt along with the stilettos my rapidly swelling ankle could not fit into.

I eventually made it home without attracting the attention of vice cops, and promptly rented every movie I could find featuring Mr. Prime Time while waiting for him to call, which didn't happen. After a week had passed, my friend Justine insisted I call him and stop playing so hard to get.

"Hey, it's me, Giuliana!" I said.

"Who?"

I reminded him.

"Oh yeah, the girl who stood me up for our cereal date. What's up?"

We ended up going for dinner in West Hollywood, and there was no connection whatsoever. Zero, zip, not even a flicker. He went on to become an award-winning director. Eight or nine years after our hook-up, I walked into my sister's kitchen, and there he sat. It turned out that he had recently met my brother-in-law, Bryan, a film producer, while discussing a project.

"Hey," I said.

"Hey, are you Monica's sister?" he asked.

"I'm *Giuliana*," I said a bit testily.

"Nice to meet you!" he said. He clearly did not recognize me.

After I left, he turned to Bryan, who later relayed his request to me: "Your sister-in-law is hot. Think she'd go out with me?" I told my brother-in-law I wasn't interested. Every time I went over to my sister's house, though, it seemed like I was seeing Mr. Prime Time, who would then proceed to hit on me. It was the bad-date version of *Groundhog Day*. Was I that unmemorable? One day, after he had said, "We should go out sometime" for about the tenth time, I finally told him we already had.

"You offered me Cap'n Crunch!" I reminded him. He looked sheepish.

"So we hooked up?" he asked. "I don't remember that at all. How could I not remember you? I was drinking back then, maybe that explains it."

Which means we never would've gone anywhere, anyway: guys who drink too much are high on my list of turnoffs. At the top are guys with no real ambition: I don't count being in a band and having no long-term goal as ambition. Next would have to be mama's boys, especially the ones who ask their mothers for advice about you, and then actually take it, even when they know it's wrong. I also rule out guys who dance too well, ones who know nothing about handling finances, men who are disloyal and think cheating is okay in the "right" situation, guys who watch porn and go to strip clubs, guys who have mandatory guy nights and guy weekends, serial confessors who reveal their deepest, darkest secrets by the end of the first date, and cheesy men who drive flashy cars. (Thank you for curing me of that forever, Richard D.) Oh, and beefy guys with too much muscle, like Joe Manganiello and Chris Hemsworth. Some women think of them as beef cakes; I think of them as Lumbersexuals.

My list of turn-ons is short but nonnegotiable: men who are elusive, smart with their money, family oriented (must be good to their mothers), loyal, and morally sound. Puppy dog eyes don't hurt, either.

I had matured enough since Lance and Richard to add the most important quality of all: kindness. I wasn't in the market for any more dysfunctional relationships with men who belittled me in any way.

Since the whole dating thing wasn't working out so well in L.A., I shifted gears when I got my job at Artist Management Group and became a stalker, instead. Not a professional, pop-out-of-your-closet-with-a-butcher-knife kind. I was purely a recreational stalker, and I had just one lone quarry. He was the first person I met at AMG, a tall, gorgeous man who stepped into the elevator with me. Aquiline nose, green eyes, dressed to the nines.

"What floor?" he asked.

"Six," I said.

"Me too. AMG?"

I nodded. "I start today. I'm in the mailroom."

"Oh, that's on four," he said. The elevator stopped and I had no choice but to get out. I waved like a dork as the door closed on my very own Mr. Big.

Pushing my little mail cart around the offices, I spotted him again soon enough. His name was Jordan, and he was a talent manager. Matthew McConaughey was among the stars he represented, and they were tight enough that McConaughey dropped by on practically a daily basis. Most women at AMG silently willed McConaughey to linger in the agency's offices, but I silently heckled him to go home already so I could go in and schmooze with Jordan on a real or fake mail errand. Whenever he spotted me, Jordan would wave me into his office or stop in the hallway to chat awhile. He was slightly flirtatious but never inappropriate, a sexy mentor who treated me like an amusing and promising protégé. He called me "Talent," and I was a love-sick schoolgirl who spent hours deconstructing and analyzing every tiny gesture or casual greeting, hoping to ferret out the hidden valentine. After work, I would tail Jordan and park outside his house, waiting to see if a woman's silhouette appeared in his window. If he went back out again, I followed to see if he was meeting a date at a restaurant. I didn't have any specific plan; I just wanted to know about his life because I could never actually be *in* his life. He was way out of my mailroom girl league.

My sister, Colet, Colet's sister, and all my other friends got wrapped up into my love fest with Jordan. I was their one-person telenovela. When I got promoted to assistant and my boss, Pam, became a friend, I sucked her into my infatuation, and she would join me on my nighttime Jordan vigils. Pam and I usually finished work at eight, then we'd get dinner and drinks somewhere, then we'd go stalk Jordan till eleven. We'd hide in my car and wait for him to pull up to his house, then watch his living room light come on, then the bedroom. Then he'd pull the shades, and we'd debate whether there might be some slut who didn't deserve Jordan waiting in bed for him. We were just bored, when it came right down to it. It was entertaining at the time.

Pam did her best to find me a better date than Jordan, who had no idea we were, in my mind at least, meant for each other. When the 2001 Academy Awards rolled around, Pam happened to be dating Benicio Del Toro's manager, and she invited me along for a dazzling night of Oscar parties. When we came out of the Awards ceremony, the streets were backed up like crazy, of course, so she told me to wait at a gas station on Sunset Boulevard, and she would pick me up. I was standing there in a gown and fur vest with high, high heels when a limo pulled up and I got in and sat next to Benicio Del Toro holding an Oscar. He had just won Supporting Actor for his role in *Traffic*. "Hi," he said. We all went to the *Vanity Fair* party, and I tried to stay as close to Benicio as I could, shadowing him and pretending to rub his arm so the paparazzi on the way in would think I was his girlfriend. "Hey, everyone!" I sang on my way in, doing my pageant wave. Inside, every star on the A-list was coming up to congratulate Benicio—Tom Cruise, Angelina Jolie—and I just latched on and rode Benicio's coattails the whole night. They were the best coattails ever. Benicio was having the time of his life and didn't seem to mind. We even danced together in a group.

On my last day at AMG, Pam was watching me pack up my stuff and being all supportive, telling me how much she hoped my dreams would come true, and so on. Then Jordan walked by, and Pam called after him.

"Hey, Jordan!"

"Pam, no, don't you fucking dare, please, oh God, no no no, dammit!" I warned her under my breath. I sensed epic humiliation about to unfold. Jordan had stopped and turned around.

"Yeah?"

"Come back here! Giuliana wants to tell you something!"

Epic. Humiliation.

Jordan came up and flashed his Mr. Big smile at me expectantly. I smiled back, and Pam jumped right in.

"She wanted to tell you that she thinks you're God's gift to women," she explained oh-so-helpfully. When it came to reckless disregard for my well-being, nonexistent Australian bungee jumpers had nothing on Pam. I tried to laugh it off so Jordan would see that this was all just some dumb joke. Pam's dumb joke. We could laugh together at Pam and her lame-ass joke. The three of us stood there smiling sort of maniacally.

"You're very sweet, but Pam said it," I pointed out.

Jordan looked straight at, and through, me. He cocked his head and walked away.

"Well, I wish *you* did," he called back over his shoulder.

So ended our entirely imaginary, one-sided affair.

It's funny, given how focused and ambitious I was about my career, that I never even noticed how my love life was following a similar trajectory, save for a few minor detours: When I was blowing off school and doing nothing to prepare for my future, I sought out abusive loser-boys who underscored my unworthiness. Then, when I started getting serious in college, I graduated to starter men, like Richard. Now, I finally had gotten the big break that would shape me as a broadcaster. I was eager to be molded into star material. Romantically, that same hunger for affirmation catapulted me straight into the arms of a master manipulator.

It was January of 2003, and the San Diego Chargers were hosting the Super Bowl. For the first time since starting at E!, I didn't have to work a weekend. Some friends had invited me to drive down to San Diego with them for the game, but I politely declined. I'd been working nonstop, and I was looking forward to just staying home, ordering in, and vegging out. When Saturday rolled around, L.A. was a ghost town, and I was suddenly restless. I just felt something pulling me to San Diego. I didn't even want to go to the game, and didn't have a ticket, but I felt compelled to just go. I drove down by myself, figuring I could catch up with friends and enjoy some party-hopping. When I pulled into San Diego, the city was jam-packed and jumping. My friends were at a street festival downtown, where we met up for a while before I headed by myself over to the W Hotel, planning to join my friend Pete Yorn and his bandmates. They always threw the best parties. As I walked through the W's buzzing lobby, I heard a deep male voice boom out:

"Oh my God, it's like an angel from heaven just walked into my house!"

I turned around, assuming Halle Berry or Charlize Theron had made an entrance.

"You!" the voice said. I found myself looking into the grinning face of actor Jerry O'Connell. Jerry is one of those actors you feel like you see everywhere, but can't quite place. He had basically grown up on screen, from his starring role as the fat kid in the movie *Stand by Me* to a string of film credits as an adult. By the time I laid eyes on him in the W lobby, he was costarring in the popular TV crime drama *Crossing Jordan*. He was as entrenched in Hollywood as I was green.

"Oh my God, I just think you're the cutest thing ever!" he gushed. From that night on, Jerry was the most incredibly loving, hilarious, amazing boyfriend I had ever had. He was my biggest cheerleader and best friend. Over the next two years, we spent only one night apart, when he went out of town with his dad for a football game (and spent most of the time on the phone with me). We spent nearly every weekend in Palm Springs, where the manager of the La Quinta resort would save us our favorite bungalow with a private pool. My parents adored Jerry, and his warmly welcomed me into their close-knit clan, too, inviting me along on their Hawaiian vacation and to their beach place in Montauk. When Jerry and I were in New York, we'd stay at his folks' townhouse in Chelsea and play Boggle with them all night. The O'Connells loved word games and were killer at them. I always lost.

In L.A., Jerry and I spent our free time indulging a mutual passion for karaoke. We discovered all these private hole-in-the-wall Japanese and Korean karaoke clubs where you could rent a little room and they'd provide the music catalog and serve you drinks and you could belt out Bon Jovi to your heart's content. Jerry and I would slip in at eleven at night and spend hours singing to each other, or performing sappy duets like "Endless Love." We were no Lionel Richie and Diana Ross, but we were pretty good. Jerry insisted in the most heartfelt, convincing manner that my solo of "Don't Know Why" was better than Norah Jones's. More cynical types might think that should have been the red flag for the silky-smooth lies to come from Jerry, but I must say, I have been known to hit those high notes better than Norah. (I actually auditioned for *Rent* and got a callback, but that was as close to Broadway as I got without a ticket.) Occasionally, Jerry and I would lasso friends into going to karaoke with us, but they'd gradually peel away because we always came with our well-rehearsed songs and were totally obnoxious.

When Jerry landed a role in a movie called *Fat Slags,* I went with him on location to London, where we had a fabulous mini-vacation while he got settled for a four-month shoot. We were crazy in love, and the thought of being away from each other was unbearable. I promised to visit again, despite my deep fear of flying, and Jerry would pop back to L.A. as soon as he got a break. When he dropped me off at the airport, we swore we would speak a hundred times a day and never let the eight-hour time difference get in the way as we wiped away tears and hugged till the last second. I hadn't been back long when Ken Baker, a correspondent for *Us* magazine who frequently appeared on air for E!, stopped by my desk.

"Hey, how're things with Jerry?" he asked me. "Are you guys still together?"

I knew Ken well enough to know that he wasn't asking because he cared about the state of our relationship. The journalist in me knew instantly that he had to be asking because he had something on Jerry. I needed to think fast and quash whatever ugly rumor was about to surface. I decided that being vague and uncertain was the safest route to go.

"Well, he's been in London and we've been figuring things out lately, so . . ." I hedged.

"Oh, good," Ken broke in, "so this won't come as a shock to you." He handed me copies of some photos *Us* was planning to run of Jerry with Geri Halliwell, a former Spice Girl who was his costar on *Fat Slags*. "Whatever you do, don't go on the Internet," Ken added cryptically as he walked away.

Which, of course, I did the instant he left. Up popped pictures of Jerry coming out of a London restaurant, arms locked with the former Ginger Spice. The caption said they were a hot item. When Jerry and I had gone to set the first day of shooting the (huge flop) movie, Geri was being a diva over something unrelated to us and refused to come out of her dressing room to meet Jerry. Seeing pictures of her flaunting him as her latest conquest was shocking. My heart fell to my feet, and I felt as if the wind had gotten knocked out of me. What the hell was going on? She hadn't even been top Spice! I was being two-timed for one of the lesser Spices? I kept Googling. There were more pictures, more hand-holding. Picture after picture showed them coming out of or going into her London house, going to work in the morning with bedhead and bleary eyes, coming "home" after a night on the town. Disbelief turned to fury. How could Jerry talk about what we were going to name our children, constantly tell me how we were meant to be together forever, tell everyone he knew how obsessed he was with me, and then cheat on me as soon as my flight took off? I would have emasculated the scumbag, but the online photo gallery indicated that Bitchy Spice had beaten me to that: now Jerry was holding her hand, carrying her tote bag, and clutching her little dog. Jerry *hated* little dogs. The faint scar above his lip was from a childhood bite. I hit speed dial in a hurt and tearful rage.

"Are you fucking kidding me?" I screamed when he answered. "Are you *dating* that little *puttana*?"

Jerry was nonchalant.

"Yeah, I know. I'm so sorry. I don't know what happened." He had as much emotion as the customer service representative who tells you your bag missed the flight.

"You don't know what happened?" What happened was, he put fleeting gratification ahead of lifelong commitment, lust ahead of love. He screwed his cast mate and he betrayed his lover. What happened was this: He destroyed me.

I hung up and bawled my eyes out. I had been completely blindsided. This was the love of my life, and now he had been taken from me just like that. There had been no dramatic quarrel, not even discussion of a breakup. *We were happy.* And now, I assumed, he was going to marry this amoral bitch and carry her stupid dog forever. I wasn't some random starlet he'd dated and left behind in America; I was his partner of two years. Pictures of us together and stories identifying us as a couple (including many that erroneously described me as his fiancée) would pop up if you Googled his name. I had been right there on set with him when Carrymypurse Spice was too indisposed to come out of her trailer and act like she had proper manners that first day.

In no time at all, the tabloids and gossip columnists were all asking me about Jerry's affair with the former pop star. Trying to preserve some dignity, I told everyone that Jerry and I were on a break while he was in London. Total lie, but no one doubted it, since Jerry was acting like it, anyway.

A month later, I was walking into my condo building when Jerry appeared out of nowhere. I couldn't believe my eyes. I didn't even know he was back in L.A. I wanted to strangle him and hug him at the same time. I resisted the urge to do either, and pushed him aside.

"Get out of here, Jerry!" I said.

He kept insisting he just needed to speak to me, and tried to block me as I headed for the elevator. He followed me inside, and we didn't say a word the whole ride up. I stared at the numbers . . . two . . . ten . . . fifteen. I was fuming, and Jerry was just staring at me.

When I unlocked my apartment door, he barged in. He kept begging me again to talk to him, and I kept trying to walk away. I felt trapped and upset. I went out to the balcony to escape him. He followed, then dropped down to his knees.

"I love you, I made the biggest mistake of my life, and you've got to take me back!" he blubbered.

I urged him to stop, to get up and get out. Jerry was literally begging me to forgive him, saying he couldn't live without me. I had no idea if he was being overdramatic or not, but I half worried that if he did anything crazy, he would take me with him. I started crying and Jerry came back in, and we both cried and cried all night, and by morning, I had taken him back. I believed he really was in love with me, had made a terrible mistake, and was genuinely contrite. I still loved him. Nothing like this would ever happen again, and this whole drama only proved that we were meant to be together.

I can't remember why, but we later ended up in London again for a quick trip. We were back to normal, and it felt like our love had survived a test. I forgave Jerry, and his love felt all-encompassing again. We even hit a karaoke bar in Soho and ridiculed Disposable Spice with a side-splitting version of her former group's hit, "Wannabe."

So tell me what you want, what you really really want,
I'll tell you what I want, what I really really want

Forgiving and forgetting aren't the same thing, though, and when we were taking a romantic stroll through the city and Jerry mused aloud about getting engaged, I stopped him short.

"If you're even thinking about proposing in London, please don't," I cautioned. "This city has a lot of negative connotations for me, and I don't want to get engaged here."

It wasn't that I would refuse him—Jerry knew that. I just wasn't going to say yes in London.

Jerry backed off but told me months later that he had been genuinely upset, "because a proposal is a proposal, it shouldn't matter where."

When I made the *Maxim* list of 100 Hottest Women in 2004, Jerry and I went to Vegas that June for the magazine's big party for the honorees. I was number ninety-four—"That's bullshit!" Jerry had proclaimed—but still flattered to be included. Jessica Simpson was number one that year, and model turned *X-Men* actress Rebecca Romijn was also on the list. E! actually has the footage of Jerry and me being interviewed on the red carpet by my field producer, Lee. "Behind us!" Jerry suddenly murmured, alerting both Lee and me to a star sighting. I turned around to see Rebecca in all her cartoon villainess glory. "We should wrap up," Jerry said, urging Lee to go interview Rebecca. We were all, "Oh, boy, big star here, okay, bye, Lee!"

Inside the party, while I was doing interviews and taking pictures, Jerry wandered off to mingle. Little did I know he was in the VIP area talking up Rebecca. As a prelude to feeling up Rebecca.

A week later, when we were back in L.A., Jerry announced out of the blue that he had to go to Vegas for some guys' weekend. One night turned into two nights, then three. On the phone, he seemed in a hurry to say he loved me and hang up. Next thing I knew, radio silence. I kept calling and calling, but he wouldn't answer. That childhood sense of evening-news dread overtook me, convincing me that the worst must have happened, that Jerry had been in an accident, that he was hurt, or dead. I left one more message, saying I was worried and calling the police. Finally he called.

"Oh my God, you're blowing up my phone!" he complained. "I'm back. I'm fine!" He told me he had to go, and hung up again.

I was confused. Why hadn't he told me he was home, or come by? I headed over to his condo. I rang the bell but got no response. I could see his lights were on. I started yelling up at his second-floor window, like Brando in *A Streetcar Named Desire*.

"Jerrrrrrrrry! Jerrrrrry! Are you up there?"

He came out on the balcony.

"Jerry! Can you please buzz me in?"

He laid his arms across the railing and casually leaned on them, peering down at me.

"You should go," he said.

"Jerry, what's going on? Just let me in!"

He shook his head.

"Nope. Sorry, homegirl."

"Jerry! What's *wrong* with you?" I was sobbing by now. It was pretty obvious why he didn't want me to come inside.

"Yeah," Jerry sighed. "I dunno. Things change, but you take care, okay?" He went back inside and shut the door.

I don't remember how I even made it home, I was so distraught. I literally wanted to die. It was over. I knew it was over, but a lifetime of never allowing myself to feel pain, of avoiding it at every cost, all caught up to me that night. I couldn't believe this was happening. There had been no sign of trouble. One day he loved me; the next day, nothing was there. I had never suspected that the man I loved had a Dr. Jekyll and Mr. Hyde switch until he flipped it on me. Jerry left me with the same intensity that he had loved me. I sank into a depression.

The only thing that made me feel better was dessert. I've always had a sweet tooth, but sugar became my drug, and I went on a binge every single night. I would call three or four different friends a night to meet me for dessert. I'd polish off a piece of Oreo cheesecake at the Cheesecake Factory with one girlfriend, then say good-bye and call another friend from the car to come meet me at the House of Pies. I'd practically bury my face in a slice of banana cream pie, leave, and drive through McDonald's on the way home for a hot fudge sundae. In the morning, I would look at myself in the mirror and start crying. My skin was breaking out, my hair was lifeless and dull, and my whole body felt like I was constantly fighting a low-grade flu. I slept fitfully and cried constantly. I gained eighteen pounds and couldn't fit the sample sizes at work. It was so embarrassing, because my stylist at the time kept letting out seams and saying, "Is your mom in town? Are you eating a ton of pasta, because girl, you are not fitting my clothes!" I started bringing in my own wardrobe. Even the manicurist I had gone to and loved for years started giggling and speaking Vietnamese with her coworkers when I dragged myself into the salon one day. It had been a while since I'd been in. After much tittering and discussion back and forth, she finally blurted out what was on their minds: "We wanna know why you so fat now?"

"I had a breakup and I'm very sad," I replied, wondering as the words left my mouth why I was explaining myself to these mean-ass bitches.

"You look younger now," she said in a lame attempt at recovery. "Just fat."

I left her a big tip, which said a lot about my feelings of unworthiness. But I also flipped the bird at them all from the parking lot, which said maybe there was hope for me yet.

The sugar binge lasted for the better part of a year. Finally, I went to see a nutritionist for help breaking the addiction. She gave me a journal and told me to religiously write down whatever I ate.

"At night, when it's time to have dessert, you can have any fruit," she instructed me. "Have as much as you want. Just document it."

I went to the grocery store and loaded my cart with all kinds of fresh fruit. *This is great*, I thought, *I like fruit, I can do this!*

That night, when the sugar craving hit, instead of heading out on my dessert prowl, I had an apple. Then some berries. Then some watermelon. Then pineapple. I had eight, nine, ten servings of fruit in all before I finally finished gorging and went to bed.

The next morning, I woke up without a headache and thought, *Omigod, that's the first time I haven't had dessert in a year!*

I was so excited, I ate healthy all day, happily entering my cottage cheese, salmon, and salad into the journal. Then I ate twelve pieces of fruit.

The next day, I started over again, and that night I was down to ten pieces of fruit. Each night, the servings of fruit dwindled. Would I have rather had banana cream pie at the House of Pies than a fresh banana at home? Hell, yeah. But I also knew that this was an addiction, and I couldn't go there thinking "What if they give me just a small slice of carrot cake?" because I knew I would need more. I was like a crackhead who meets her dealer under the bridge. You don't grab some drugs, say thanks, and save some for tomorrow. You get that shit and you're going to smoke it there because you're a fucking crackhead. House of Pies was my bridge. Fruit was my methadone. I enjoyed my cantaloupe or pint of strawberries or bunch of grapes and re-claimed my life. Once I regained control of my body and choices, I started feeling better and became happier. I had the energy to start running again, and the excess pounds started disappearing.

A month into the sugar-busting plan, I met Bill Rancic.

Life itself was about to become sweeter than I ever imagined.

chapter **eight**

By the time I met Bill, I had been at E! for four years, and had made it across the minefield of network politics intact to become anchor, despite my embarrassing tic of hitting on George Clooney at every opportunity. He is taller than you think. The first time I met George, at a press junket for his movie *Solaris*, I blurted out a marriage proposal in front of a room full of people and two cameras recording my every breath. A girl's gotta take her shot when the sexiest bachelor in the known galaxy is standing right in front of her, right? Before I even got the second syllable of "marry" out, he rejected me and broke into a sweat, like I was a horny cavewoman about to club him and drag him off to my dressing room. Hurtful. But not a deterrent. I've asked several times since, and the answer is still "get away from me, you psycho stalker," or something to that effect. At least that's what he is probably thinking, though George is way too polite to ever say anything like that. Instead, he breaks the awkward moment by making a funny joke and gives me that perfect Clooney smile complete with dimples.

I'm a flirt by nature. I flirt with everyone. I'll flirt with straight men, gay men, old men. I flirt with women, with babies, even dogs. In cases of actual infatuation, however, I do my research first. When I came to work one day and noticed that E! was sending a reporter to cover Bill Rancic, who was doing volunteer work at the Boys and Girls Club of Santa Monica, California, I snatched the assignment for myself, claiming I wanted to get out in the field more and raise my charity profile. No one bought it. I had been a major fangirl ever since Rancic had won season one of Donald Trump's reality game show *The Apprentice*. My BFF Colet and I were obsessed with Bill, and I would watch the NBC show and tell Colet that I needed to marry him. I was dating Jerry at the time, and ironically, Jerry is the one who first introduced me to my future husband. We were at an NBC party in New York City for Jerry's show *Crossing Jordan*, and Bill was one of the guests. Jerry spotted him first. "You are going to freak out, homegirl! *The Apprentice* is here! Your favorite!" He dragged me over to meet Bill while I begged him not to. "Jerry, you're gonna embarrass me. Please don't embarrass me!" I hissed. He said, "I won't. I just want him to know what a big fan you are and that you were rooting for him every week." When we reached Bill, Jerry introduced himself, and the two men got caught up in a guy convo about sports and stuff, leaving me just standing off to the side. Finally I nudged Jerry.

"Oh, yeah," he said. "Bill, I would introduce you to my girlfriend, but I'm afraid the two of you would run off together." We said hello, shook hands, and then Bill said it was nice to meet the two of us and walked away. Two years had gone by, and I was eager to continue the conversation. I hurried back to my desk to do some hard-hitting journalistic research before heading out for my interview. I did what any good reporter would do and Googled the words "Bill Rancic girlfriend." (If Google had been around when Barbara Walters started out, I'm sure she would have done the same thing.) Up popped a name. Bill Rancic had a girlfriend! I immediately went to the producers to try to wiggle my way out of the assignment, but it was too late to get someone else to cover. I was pissed, but Bill was more handsome (and taller) in person than he'd looked on *The Apprentice*, and it was a battle not to go full-flirt ahead. Instead, I crossed my arms tightly against my chest and tried to seem as disinterested and unattracted to him as possible.

"Do you have a girlfriend?" I asked him. He looked taken aback by the question.

"Well, not at the moment," he replied.

"Wait, what?" I wasn't sure I had heard right.

"Not at the moment, we broke up a couple months ago," he repeated. This was starting to get a little awkward. Didn't I want to know more about the charity he was out there to support? Charity, schmarity. The arms came unfolded, I did the old hair flip, moved in a few inches closer, and rested a sympathetic yet shameless hand on his broad shoulder.

"*Really?*" I said. This interview was getting better by the second.

"Yeah," he repeated. "I'm holding out."

"For what?" I said.

"I'm holding out for you," he answered, throwing an arm around me.

"He *so* knew I wanted him to say that!" I laughed to the camera.

We ended up talking in the parking lot for forty-five minutes after the cameras were gone. He mentioned how he liked to go running along the shores of Lake Michigan back home in Chicago. I said something about how I enjoyed running by the water, too. As I turned to go to my car, I could tell he was going to ask me out on a date. "By the way," he called after me, "would you like to go for a run sometime?" *Oooh, Spandex and no makeup at nine a.m. Not happening! I need dim lighting, heels, sushi, and a drink.*

"Or we could go out for dinner," I quickly suggested. We made plans for the following night, and by our second date, we were mapping out our future together. The thing is, when we began dating, Bill liked me because *I* liked me. I was funny and confident. But he wouldn't have met that person thirty days earlier, when I was burying my grief—and my face—beneath a mountain of sugar. I put off a totally different vibe and energy then, morose and full of self-loathing. I would have been distracted and anxious instead of quick-witted and fun. I would have cut dinner short so I could go get my second and third desserts of the night. Bill never would have felt a spark. There wasn't one *to* feel, until I kicked the sugar habit.

Once I got the sugar out of my system, it was as if I had hit the reboot button on my emotions, too: the fog and depression lifted, and I realized that it wasn't the loss of Jerry that had been causing most of my misery—it was how I had dealt with the shock. I could have spared myself months of feeling like crap! In hindsight, though, I get that I had to experience a Jerry in my life so I could evolve enough emotionally to fully appreciate everything I have in Bill. And I have to give the devil his due: Jerry was the first person who taught me it was okay in a relationship to tell someone they're amazing. I used to cling to that old-fashioned belief that you should leave them guessing so they would want more; I was always holding back. And just the fact that a famous actor who could have had his pick of desirable women had fallen in love with me boosted my self-confidence. I stopped aiming low.

Professionally, I never held back. My seize-the-moment philosophy about reporting is what put me on a fast track at *E!*

News. When I first got hired, back after the whole Wilmer do-you-do-moms Valderrama incident, the executive in charge of *E! News* made a big deal of presenting me to the newsroom as the embodiment of a whole new style of reporting that was going to revitalize the show. The reason I was brought on board, they said, was because I was irreverent.

Irreverent? As I looked around at the faces in the meeting, I acted like I was owning the word, but in truth my Italian brain didn't have a clue what it meant. Was it a good thing? I had no idea what it was I was, and I needed to find out, so I could keep being it. Whatever it was. So I snuck off to my computer and Googled it.

I soon discovered that news directors and editors saying they wanted ballsy did not necessarily translate into them actually being ballsy. I stomped in one morning at six a.m., still fuming from a red-carpet interview with Russell Crowe at the premiere of *A Beautiful Mind* the night before. Crowe had been a nasty piece of work, and I had the footage to show the world that fame had not only gone to his head, it had fermented.

"Russell Crowe! Are you excited to be here tonight for your big movie premiere?" I had asked the star on his way into the theater.

"I'm contractually obligated to be here," he snarled. "Next question."

I kept smiling, determined to keep it light. I'd heard he could be surly, and there were more gracious stars I could buttonhole, so no need to draw this one out.

"Is it wonderful seeing all your fans?" I asked. It wasn't a soft-ball question; it was a marshmallow. Crowe gave me a withering look, which admittedly was hard to distinguish from his normal look. Boyfriend has some serious Bitchy Resting Face.

"That's your second question?" he sneered. "One, two, you're through." He turned his back on me and walked away.

Three, four, you're a boor, I wish I'd said. Next time, I would have to remember that what viewers really longed to hear were Russell Crowe's thoughts on climate control or the Kosovo crisis.

Back in the newsroom, I gave my editors a heads-up about the blockbuster story I had for that day's show: "Russell Crowe is such a jerk! I've got a piece all about how he was pissed to be at the premiere and was contractually obligated to be there. We've got footage! Let's expose what an asshole he is!"

I was swiftly shot down. "No," I was schooled. "We want to *celebrate* celebrities!"

(I would interview Russell Crowe again years later, and he couldn't have been lovelier. Not in the same warm, down-to-earth league as Clooney or Sandra Bullock, but few are.)

One of my first big interviews at E! was with Sean Penn, who was promoting his movie *I Am Sam.* All I really wanted to talk about was *Shanghai Surprise* and Madonna and their volatile relationship, and what more could he tell me about my obsession, Madonna. I was dying to blurt out something about her. But Sean Penn is as intimidating as they get. He's so serious and intense, it's easier to ask an esteemed senator a stupid question. I couldn't get anything cute or funny out of him, and gave up quickly. I asked him only lame-o questions. *What's your movie about? How did you like working with this director?* I remember looking at my producer and asking how many minutes we had left. Dreadful as it was, my one-on-one with Sean Penn was a good lesson for a beginner: Read someone's vibe and follow that, even if it means aborting your plan for the interview.

My first year with *E! News*—called *E! News Live* back then—was a sleepless blur. I would be up by five in the morning to start the day, heading into the office to put together all my material gathered from the previous evening's events or premieres and turn them into polished reports before the broadcast went live that afternoon. The newsroom would turn into a crazy hive of people shouting, tapes flying, and correspondents rushing to get their segments on the air. After we wrapped at five p.m., I'd turn around, put a new outfit on, and spend all night at parties or red-carpet events to get interviews for the next day's show. Then I'd go out afterwards to unwind with friends, and finally collapse around one in the morning to grab a few hours' sleep before starting the cycle all over again.

Sometimes I wonder if I ended up getting cancer because of that whole period of my life. I would go to bed stressed and wake up stressed. I was running too hard, and never stopping to catch my breath. A full day off, let alone an actual vacation, wasn't on my calendar. Weekends were never free: too much celebrity news happened then, with premieres, weddings, funerals, gala events, and so on. And in the competitive world of broadcasting, if you're not out there front and center every day, someone else will be. Other than casual dates here and there, relationships took a backseat to work, and I was fine with that. I genuinely loved what I was doing, exhausting as it was, and I brought my own sense of fun to even the routine, grab-a-quote assignments. Entertainment news, I believed and still do, should be entertaining. I became the go-to girl once the producers realized that I was game for just about anything, whether it was letting Hulk Hogan pick me up and spin me around or challenging Neil Patrick Harris to an impromptu juggling contest at the SAG awards. (NPH won, but I'm self-taught and he obviously received professional training at an elite clown college or something.)

I had been at E! for a little over a year when both news anchors, Jules Asner and Steve Kmetko, moved on, and management launched a search for new talent. Correspondents in the running for the coveted spots would be rotated to the desk to fill in for a couple of weeks. When my turn came, I wasn't rotated off, but different guys from both inside and outside E! were brought in to test with me. As week after week passed with me still in the anchor chair, there was a general assumption that I had one of the coveted spots locked down. In the newsroom, I was getting great reviews and encouragement from my supervisors and colleagues, and judging from the feedback we got, viewers also seemed to like me. But Mindy Herman, midway through her brief reign of scandalous terror as network CEO, was not as pleased, and issued this directive from the executive suite: *Giuliana is dominating the man. She should be more subservient.* I tried to take the note to heart, but they kept pairing me with a bunch of Ron Burgundy types whose only skill was to read from a teleprompter and not have a thought of their own. Was I supposed to just sit back and watch the show fall apart each episode? I couldn't. So I would jump in and save each chitchat or interview we would be doing. I considered it professional. Mindy saw it as overpowering. In the words of Ron Burgundy, agree to disagree. But I was right for the most part, and everyone told me they agreed with me.

Then I came to work one day to discover that Mindy had announced that two outsiders who hadn't even done a test run had been hired to anchor *E! News.* John Burke was an actor with gray hair and chiseled features. Alisha Davis was a young CNN cultural correspondent with a fresh, pretty face and a head full of luxurious braids. They were perfectly nice people but couldn't have made an odder on-air pairing, and they had zero chemistry together.

I was unceremoniously booted back to correspondent, a humiliating move, especially after viewers had come to assume I was an anchor. (I was made weekend anchor, but that was a joke. Maybe ten people watched.) I was devastated and angry. My old boss-turned-friend Pam Kohl, by then my manager, called E! to read them the riot act, and the official press release the network put out announcing John and Alisha's new jobs included a paragraph extolling my talent and contributions to E! over the years,

The big baby at six months old.

Taking a poop standing up while everyone waits for me to blow out my candle.

My cousin and me and my old man shoes.

No, that's not my grandmother in the 1800s. That's me in Naples in 1976. Mom, did you want to update your camera?

Left: My family at a friend's wedding in Naples, Italy. Monica (in the center) was the flower girl. I'm the blonde on the right. *Right:* Hanging with Curly #2 in the last few months of cuteness before puberty.

New York Fashion Week, here I come! *©Eduardo DePandi*

Obviously our entry fee for the Miss Maryland Pageant didn't go to wardrobe. *©Anna DePandi*

Left: One of my first home photo shoots. Nice hair. . . and shoes!

Right: Photo shoot number two. I stole that belt from my sister's closet.

My scoliosis in full effect. I'm standing up straight here.

My brother Pasquale's photo shoot at fifteen with his Porsche. Baller.

©*Stone Photography*

Liz and me during senior year of high school. Are these the faces of thugs about to commit Grand Theft Auto?

In the DJ booth at St. Mary's College. This is the week before I got fired. I should have stuck to Travolta sound tracks instead of 2 Live Crew.

With my sister, Monica. Our birthdays are three days (and five years) apart. Even as adults my mom went for the two-for-one birthday party.

I stole this Versace dress from my sister's closet to wear to the Italian ambassador's home. I had a conservative pantsuit on, but my dad insisted I dress more fashionably so I wore this hot number.

Richard and one of his many fancy cars.

Graduating from the University of Maryland at College Park. My parents are holding me up to help ease the pain of surgery.

With my first L.A. roommate, Justine. She was beautiful and reminded me of Charlize Theron.

My desk at AMG next to my friend Corey. Miserable assistants at work.

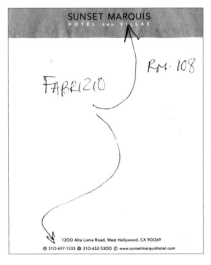

First Avenue w/ KURT + STEVE
July 2002 Minneapolis

SUNSET MARQUIS
HOTEL and VILLAS

FABRIZIO   RM. 108

1200 Alta Loma Road, West Hollywood, CA 90069
℗ 310-657-1333 ℗ 310-652-5300 ℗ www.sunsetmarquishotel.com

Left: Oh, just a random invite to a famous musician's room sometime around 2001. *Right:* With Colet and fake Weezer in Minnesota.

Left: On the set of *Fashion Police* in 2011. And I have the balls to critique people's outfits looking like this? ©*E! Entertainment Right:* In London with Jerry. I should have known he was up to no good by the look on his face.

Anna Nicole Smith asked to do our interview surrounded by all of her stuffed animals. I can't make up this stuff. ©*E! Entertainment*

Top: I don't know if I'm happier that we just got engaged or that we survived the helicopter ride on a windy night in Chicago. *Left:* Bill catching a marlin in Mexico (Bill insisted I put this photo in the book).

Bill looking hot in Mexico (*I* insisted I put this photo in the book).

Left: Giving Duke his bottle right after he was born. Bill and I are so happy here. *©Karen Soenen* *Right:* You are never too young to be a Chicago Bears fan.

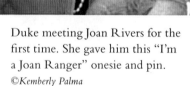

Duke meeting Joan Rivers for the first time. She gave him this "I'm a Joan Ranger" onesie and pin. *©Kemberly Palma*

After interviewing Clooney for thirteen years, gotta keep it fresh. #tequila *©Monica Rose*

with a vague reference to a prime-time show being developed just for me. That was news to me, and nothing materialized. *They treat you like shit!* All my friends kept urging me to quit. "Water finds its own level," I would reply. I had a feeling this wasn't over yet.

Within six months, the show had gone from being merely mediocre to being the lowest rated on the network, and Mindy, for entirely unrelated reasons and amid widespread staff jubilation, was ousted. Her departure came after an internal investigation into accusations that she had abused her power by throwing two over-the-top baby showers for herself, including one at E! headquarters, at E!'s expense. For weeks beforehand, staff-wide e-mail updates from Mindy's assistant would land in our in-boxes, reminding employees—who were making zilch—where millionaire Mindy had registered for her luxury baby gifts. Disloyal and embittered underlings warned us that Mindy was privately demanding her own regular updates on who *hadn't* sent a present.

I was assigned, on Mindy's orders, of course, to go cover the more exclusive shower she had for a few dozen friends at an oceanfront restaurant in Malibu. Mindy personally directed what the cameras should film. Our first order of business was to report on the gift bags she had waiting for her guests, with me pulling out each item to ooh and ahh over and identify by brand name. (Mindy had a thing for swag bags—the *Los Angeles Times* later reported that she once jacked costly Grammy goodies intended for two entertainment reporters.) I can only presume that my enforced infomercial at her shower had to do with Mindy hitting vendors up for free "gifts" in exchange for product placement and mentions on air. She was also keen for viewers to see E! stars paying homage to her. "Where's the gift Joan and Melissa sent?" she barked. "Be sure you get that on camera when I open it!"

But where is a rich executive pirate supposed to stash so much glorious loot? Mindy had just the answer to that . . . hypothetical . . . question: in a new nursery decorated for free by one of Style network's home makeover programs, minus the two-thousand-dollar budget restriction the decorators usually had to work under. Compared to all this, it wasn't even shocking when the CEO made gossip headlines herself after reportedly getting into a brawl with another woman in the parking lot of a hot Hollywood club where the launch party was held for the network's new reality show starring Anna Nicole Smith. I was there but missed the fisticuffs. The reason I was there was because I had to be anywhere Anna Nicole was. The voluptuous former Playmate's show was Mindy's brainchild, and she envisioned Anna Nicole virtually rebranding E! across the board. To that end, I was temporarily pulled off *E! News* to do nothing but follow Anna Nicole for two weeks to film promotional footage. I was supposed to go to her house in the Valley every morning and just hang out to conduct mini-interviews with her practically every waking hour of her day. The waking hours were tricky to come by.

That first day, we showed up and were let in by Anna Nicole's purple-haired assistant (who, at Anna Nicole's urging, got a large tattoo of Anna Nicole's face on her arm). Anna Nicole was in her bedroom, so I had the crew set up their equipment out on her balcony. It was a clear, sunny Southern California day in the nineties, and the gorgeous view would make the perfect backdrop. An hour later, Anna Nicole came out and greeted me politely.

"Where are we going to do this interview?" she asked.

"Right out here," I said, leading her to the balcony. She stopped at the door and shuddered.

"Ohhhh, can we not do it outside?" she pleaded in her babyish Texas twang. "It's so *cold*!"

Wha'? Okay, maybe she hadn't been out yet and didn't follow

the weather forecast. Or notice that really large bright ball of fire in the sky.

"I'm sorry—cold?" I tried again.

"Ohhh," she shivered again. "Soooo cold!"

"No, sweetie, here, why don't you just check and see? Give me your arm, let's just put it outside and I'll show you!" I tugged her arm through the open door and she yanked it back in alarm.

"Ooooh! I have *goose bumps*!! Please, can't we do it somewhere else?"

We spent twenty minutes resetting the cameras in front of the marble fireplace, and I went to fetch Anna Nicole again.

"Okay, so we'll just stand here with the mantel behind us, how about that?" I chirped. My smile was starting to hurt.

"Uh, no," she pouted. "I don't wanna stand that long."

Okay, so ninety degrees was cold, and ten minutes was an eternity. We had some perception challenges to overcome here. But E! was banking on this childlike woman with boobs that probably each needed a channel of their own, and I had been handpicked to babysit her. I was stuck, and I had no choice but to humor her. "We can just stand there for a couple of minutes, then walk around and talk," I offered. With diplomatic skills like these, I really belonged in Geneva, not the San Fernando Valley.

"Ohhh," she sighed, making what I understood to be another objection. "Do we hafta walk?"

How lazy can someone be? You just slept twenty hours, and you can't fucking walk across the living room? I kept the thought to myself and poured extra syrup over my words before asking her, "Where would *you* like to do the interview?"

"Can we do it on the floor of my bedroom with my stuffed animals?" she suggested.

WTF? Acting like her request was a totally normal one, my crew and I followed her upstairs and went into her bedroom, which by the way was very heavy on Hello Kitty. Very heavy.

Hello Kitty clocks, Hello Kitty pillows, Hello Kitty towels. There were also stuffed animals piled everywhere, more than a hundred of them, easily. We sat on the floor while Anna Nicole and her assistant decided which stuffed animals could sit with us. Only fifty made the cut. I clutched a teddy bear and stroked its stuffed head so Anna Nicole would feel reassured. I just wanted to come down to her level of insanity. I started asking questions: Why did she want to do a reality show, what was going to be in it, was there any romance, did she have a boyfriend? All of a sudden, in the middle of answering a question, Anna Nicole started screaming. Really screaming—like, full-throated, horror-movie chainsaw murder screaming. I thought she was having some kind of seizure or maybe an acid flashback.

"THERE'S A SPIDER ON MEEEEE!" she cried. She was flailing around, looking at her chest in sheer terror.

"Anna, no, no, no! Honey, that's a microphone!" I shouted over her. She stopped screaming.

"Oh. I thought that was a tarantula. That scared the behooties outta me."

Riding in the back of the van with the cameras on the way home, the crew was still cracking up.

"That woman was high as a kite!" one of them crowed.

"No, she wasn't," I insisted. Drugs have never been my scene, and I pretty much need a lab report to tell me whether someone is using any. "Guys, it was an honest mistake. The microphone *does* sort of look like a spider!"

My two weeks with Anna Nicole were like a bizarre mini–reality show within a reality show. The highlights: Anna sitting on the couch in her living room under Hello Kitty blankets, yelling for someone to get her a Yoo-hoo; Anna drinking Yoo-hoos; Anna "remodeling" her bathroom. The latter announcement had me all excited, until we discovered that the renovation involved Anna moving her Hello Kitty clock from the bedroom to the sink, placing a pink sponge in the tub, and adjusting a Hello Kitty bathmat on the floor. Move over, Nate Berkus. It had more empty calories than my year's residency at House of Pies, but *The Anna Nicole Show* was E!'s biggest reality hit ever. There are entire episodes where Anna herself appears barely coherent. I ended up on the "Anna Nicole beat" at E! for years, covering the legal battle over the fortune left to her by the eighty-nine-year-old oil tycoon she had married at the age of twenty-six, and later reporting on the disputed paternity of her daughter, Dannielynn.

When I heard in 2007 that Anna Nicole had died of an over-dose in a Florida hotel room, I felt sad for her. There are some people who can handle sudden fame and fortune and others, like those lottery winners you hear about, whose unexpected riches destroy them. Anna was a really sweet person, just living a life she was never meant to live, and she couldn't do it. She just couldn't.

The callousness of Hollywood and its false beauty have always offended Bill's Midwestern values, and he made me promise at the outset of our relationship that any life we built together would play out on a kinder stage. If we ended up having children together someday, Bill said, I had to agree right then and there to raise them in Chicago. "I don't want to live in L.A.," he said. "If we ever get engaged, the deal is one year there, then we're out." I happily accepted his terms. I'm not a California person either. Chicago and I clicked just as naturally as Bill and I did. I love that city and feel instantly at home whenever I'm there. I figured I could just commute when the day came, and maybe do more segments out of New York, which would cut my white-knuckle time on a plane in half.

A month after we began dating, Bill invited me to come

visit him in Chicago for the Memorial Day weekend. My work schedule had become a lot more predictable since Mindy blew away in her reported $20 million golden parachute. She had been replaced as CEO of E! by veteran broadcast executive Ted Harbert, whose affable style and amazing track record of bringing hit shows to the air (*The Wonder Years, NYPD Blue, My So-Called Life*, to name a few) promised to boost both morale and ratings at E! My contract was coming up a few months after he arrived, and I still intended to leave. His first day on the job, Ted wanted to meet all the hosts. This was new. I had never set foot in Mindy's office. As soon as I launched into my background with E!, Ted interrupted.

"Why aren't you the anchor?" he wanted to know.

"Don't ask me," I responded. "Your guess is as good as mine. I used to ask myself the same question, but I don't anymore. My time here overall has honestly been an amazing experience and I'm fine with it for now."

"Okay, here's the deal," Ted said. "The *E! News* ratings are terrible, and I'm getting rid of the anchors. Effective immediately, you are going to be made anchor. We'll be announcing it tomorrow."

I left the room and didn't breathe a word to anyone, for fear I would jinx it.

At a full staff meeting of the newsroom the next day, our boss relayed the news from Ted: "John and Alisha have left. The second bit of news is that Giuliana will be the new anchor." Everyone was shocked. Someone raised a hand and asked who the male anchor was going to be.

"Actually, there is no male anchor. Giuliana will be the sole anchor."

Now I was shocked.

"That, I did not know," I murmured.

There was something else I didn't know, and wouldn't find

out for years to come: They were planning on canceling *E! News* in two weeks, and my promotion was just a magnanimous gesture on Ted's part to make up for my having been treated like shit. I was going to be the last anchor of *E! News*. There was nothing to lose by giving me my moment in the sun before they pulled the plug.

That night I found Ted in a cluster of executives at a party the network was throwing for a new E! show. I walked up to them. "I just wanted to say thanks for believing in me," I said. "And, Ted, I just want you to know, I've dreamed of anchoring *E! News* since high school, and want to thank you from the bottom of my heart! And mark my word, I'm going to get those numbers up and make this a great show!" I had somehow been teleported back to the Miss Maryland pageant and was finally giving my killer speech. I topped it off with a toothy pageant smile.

"Giuliana, don't put that pressure on yourself," Ted said. "Just have fun. Don't worry about numbers and ratings. Promise?"

"Yeah, but I need one thing. I need to be managing editor. I need to change the content and line of vision. I argue every day with the producers. You're going to give me the power to change the show." Pageant girl on a testosterone rush, this was new. Go big or go home.

"Okay," Ted agreed.

I was elated. Every morning, I would get into screaming matches with the executive producer, Peggy Jo Abraham, and the line producer over what the story lineup should be. It was a battle between Old Hollywood and Young Hollywood.

"No one cares about Harrison Ford!" I would rail. "Lead with Britney Spears!"

Now that the reins were in my hands, I fully intended to make *E! News* the cool, fun broadcast for and about Young Hollywood.

"I think we should lead with Paris Hilton shopping on

Robertson Boulevard," I declared my first morning as managing editor. Paris was a club-hopping heiress about town who starred with her friend Nicole Richie in *The Simple Life*, a reality show Fox had picked up where the two young socialites tried to do manual labor.

"Are you crazy?" Peggy shouted. "We have Harrison Ford!"

"No one gives a shit about that space odyssey movie, Peggy! I want to lead with Paris Hilton. She's the new 'It girl.'"

"You should never lead a news program with a photo of nothing happening!" Peggy countered. But I did. Young Hollywood was about fashion, beauty, hot designers, and young socialites who got out of limos drunk with no underwear on. I changed our tagline to "We're your hookup to young Hollywood," and let our competitors at *Entertainment Tonight* and *Access Hollywood* have Old Hollywood. (Except for Clooney. I will always give Clooney a pass.)

Our ratings shot up 10 percent in one week.

Two more weeks were tacked onto our cancellation date. The numbers kept climbing. The network brass quietly gave the program a stay of execution, carefully tracking our numbers in case this was a fluke. A year after I took over as anchor and managing editor, Ted Harbert surprised me with a full-page ad in *Variety* with my picture, thanking me for making the show number one. The whole building posted it all over, from elevator banks to reception, to every wall in the newsroom. It was awesome, and I finally felt recognized and appreciated.

Nothing, though, could ever match the thrill I felt when I spent that Memorial Day weekend in Chicago with Bill. Next to the day our son was born, it still ranks as the absolute happiest time of my life, because it was when I knew with soul-deep certainty that I had found the person I was meant to be with forever. Bill and I had known each other for less than two months, but the long-distance relationship limited the time we got to spend together. Away from L.A. and its demands, Memorial Day belonged entirely to us. Beforehand, I went to visit my nutritionist again. Bill, like me, has a major sweet tooth, and I had told him I was "on a no-dessert kick" for a couple of months, but I hadn't gone into detail about being a sugar junkie in recovery. One of his favorite things about Chicago, he had told me, was a killer chocolate layer cake from one of his favorite restaurants. There was no way he wouldn't want to share that with me.

"I think you can do it," the nutritionist said. I'd been sugar-free for nearly three months. I went ahead and indulged in Chicago—it was every bit as decadent and delicious as Bill had promised—then I jumped right back on the wagon that Monday. I waited anxiously to see if the sugar cravings were going to kick in again, but night came and I felt no magnetic force drawing me to the Cheesecake Factory. I took this as the best of omens: with Bill, I actually could have my cake and eat it, too.

Bill would later tell me that he knew I was the one that weekend, too. We had gone for a motorcycle ride along the North Shore and got caught in a torrential downpour on the way back. We pulled over in a little mall that happened to have a Crate and Barrel. "Let's go buy some towels," Bill suggested. We went inside and he randomly pulled a couple of thick, plush towels off the shelf. I examined them more closely. "Whoa, whoa! Too expensive!" I objected. I had another idea.

"Just start drying off and fold them up and put them back," I said.

"Oh, Jesus," he said as we rubbed ourselves dry and I stuffed the sodden towels back on the shelf. "We better buy those."

"Are you kidding? We're not going to spend a hundred dollars on towels! Let's get out of here!" We jumped on the getaway bike and sped off. Bill thought he'd met the frugal girl of his dreams. Most women he'd known would have gone for the towels, added a couple of robes, and kept shopping.

Our first big fight happened that August, just as I was about to *not* turn thirty. When we first met, and age came up in casual conversation, I fibbed. I was still twentysomething in my head and not ready to put a "three" in front of my age. "Oh, good," Bill said when I claimed I was twenty-nine. He admitted that he had this rule against dating women over thirty, because he felt they were "in a hurry." He had just turned thirty-five himself. As my birthday approached, Bill grew worried and then angry that no one was reaching out to set anything in motion to celebrate my big three-oh. *Man, her friends are horrible!* he thought, racking it up to the inherent self-centeredness of L.A. Obviously he was going to have to arrange a surprise party himself. He got in touch with Monica. She played it cool but called me with a heads-up. When we all went out to dinner and my approaching "big day" came up again, Monica had had enough. She fixed me with a hard look.

"If you don't tell him, I'm going to," she warned.

I confessed to Bill that twenty-nine was my "Hollywood age." I was actually about to turn thirty-two.

He was livid, and refused to see anything funny about it.

"Oh, c'mon," I said. "What's the big deal? Everyone has their Hollywood age!"

But to Mr. Salt of the Earth Midwest, this was a major moral transgression. Even worse, it called my entire character into question. If I was going to tell white lies, Bill argued, then how could he trust me about anything?

I didn't think a woman claiming to be twenty-nine instead of thirty-one, especially in the entertainment industry, was tantamount to torturing small animals or instructing people to wire their life savings to a Nigerian bank account because my passport had been stolen, but my Bill was not cutting me any slack.

"Either we're going to be honest or we're not going to be together," he said.

I swore I would never lie to him again. (Occasional misleading for the greater good doesn't count, for the record. The time I blindfolded him and took him for a birthday surprise that he thought was going to be a Cubs game and turned out to be an appointment for Botox injections, for example, was not dishonest because he's the one who jumped to a false conclusion. And then wouldn't get the Botox. Big baby. I thought it was the perfect gift, because he had been moaning and groaning about getting old.)

Our next falling-out happened when I was the one who felt deceived. We were taking our first big trip together, to Hawaii, and Bill started out on a sulky note when I discovered that the upgraded seats I'd gotten us weren't together.

"Forget first class," I snapped. "Let's trade these seats for a couple in coach."

"I'm six foot four, I'm not going to sit in coach," he said.

When we got to Maui, we rented a Jeep to drive around the island. I had tried to wax my lip with a homemade wax kit the night before, and had this huge, painful welt on my mouth as a result. Of course, I couldn't admit to waxing my lip, so I made up some bullshit excuse about how I burned my lip drinking hot cocoa the night before. Thankfully, he bought it, but being unkissable does not make for a romantic vacation. Truth is, I was really expecting Bill to propose to me on this trip. I thought I might jump-start that with a little conversation.

"So where do you see us in six months?" I asked.

"Maybe we'll be engaged," Bill answered.

Maybe? WTF? What aren't you sure about?

I silently fumed. For ten hours, I refused to speak to him. My lip hurt, anyway. I finally cooled down enough to tell him how I felt: "We've been mapping out our future together since we met, and now I'm feeling like maybe you're not serious. Do you not see us going somewhere?"

"Of course I do," Bill said. We were still learning about each other, and Hawaii was an important lesson for me. Bill likes surprises. He's the type of person who doesn't want you to tell him what to get you for Christmas. He likes to give it thought and plan every little detail without someone else stage-managing everything. I had trusted Bill absolutely from the moment I met him—you *know* when you're with someone worthy of that—but I still needed to learn how to let go. He wasn't about to tell me then that he wanted to pop the question someplace more special than the front seat of a rental Jeep.

We spent our first Thanksgiving together with my parents, and Bill pulled my father aside when I was out of earshot and asked for permission to marry me. Babbo gave his blessing, and Bill began planning an elaborate engagement. He began scouting for perfect diamonds to design my ring. Jewelers would FedEx him bags of diamonds, and he would sort through them with his mother and sister Karen, handpicking only the flawless ones. "I'm not looking for the biggest ones," he told them. "Size isn't what's important; they just have to be perfect."

The second weekend in December, I was supposed to come visit him in Chicago. Bill said he would be getting in later from a business trip, and would send a limo to pick me up. When I landed, the limo was waiting, but it wasn't our usual driver, and he wasn't taking the usual route. On top of that, he weighed about three hundred pounds and looked like a guy straight out of *The Sopranos*. When he suddenly pulled into a deserted field, I convinced myself I was being whacked and started freaking out. *What if he's kidnapping me? Will Bill just pay the outrageous ransom or refuse to negotiate with thugs? Who's going to do* Fashion Police *for me?* The limo stopped and the back door opened. Expecting to see a gun aimed at my head, I was beyond relieved to see Bill on the other side with a huge grin on his face and his hand extended to help me out of the death car. He led me to a waiting helicopter. We climbed inside and put on the giant headphones as the chopper lifted off the ground. I am absolutely terrified of helicopters, but as we swooped over Lake Michigan, the spectacular view of Chicago and all its Christmas lights glittering beneath us made me forget that I was going to die any second. Bill had deep-dish pizza and champagne for us, and he set his glass by his feet and unstrapped his seat belt. He got down on one knee, accidentally smashing the champagne flute in the process. Unhurt, he went on.

"Will you marry me?" he asked.

I pretended I couldn't hear him over the whir of the helicopter's propeller, but really I just wanted to hear him say it again. And again.

"Yes!" I finally answered. He slipped a ring onto my finger.

When the chopper landed, Bill led me back to his place, where a path of rose petals led to a whole chocolate cake from Bill's favorite spot. We were in heaven.

Later, when I went to the bathroom, Bill heard a sudden yelp. *"Holy crap!"*

"Honey, what's wrong?" he called.

"This ring is *innnnsannnnnne!*" I shouted back. I hadn't looked at it in the light yet. The five-carat cushion-cut diamond was clear as ice, throwing off sparkles in every direction.

We planned a September wedding and decided to have it in Capri, where I had spent my childhood summers. It would be a small, elegant ceremony with a full, traditional Mass in both Italian and English. Like any woman, I had been working on the details since I was a little girl. We were surprised when the Style network asked to film our wedding, but thought why not? Great way to save the cost of a videographer.

I had been in awe of Monique Lhuillier dresses ever since I had first seen her exquisite creations. She had jumped into the international spotlight when she designed Britney Spears's wedding gown, and her evening wear frequently appeared on A-listers walking the red carpet. When I reached out to the boutique for an appointment to look at wedding gowns, I was shocked when I got a call back the next day telling me that Monique happened to be a big fan of mine and would like to meet with me herself. She wanted to personally design the perfect dress for me. I freaked! It was a dream come true! Just like marrying Clooney. I mean Bill.

I went in to meet Monique and she was the kindest, sweetest woman. She showed me around the showroom, and we picked apart the different silhouettes to get a feel for what I gravitated to and what felt right for me. Was it a strapless princess gown with a big, full tulle skirt? Or a long-sleeved, lace-embroidered sleek and super-elegant gown with a straight skirt? I had always admired Grace Kelly's iconic wedding gown of silk tulle and taffeta, with a bodice of antique Valenciennes rose point lace with seed pearl buttons. Created by MGM costume designer Helen Rose, it was a masterpiece that managed to be regal yet understated. I pictured mine to be very similar. Long lace sleeves, cinched waist, full skirt, dramatic and long veil. Monique gently brought me back down to earth when she reminded me that my wedding was in the hottest month in southern Italy. Was the church air-conditioned, she wondered.

"Great question," I said. I called the Santa Sofia Church in Ana Capri and shouldn't have been shocked to learn that a church built in the late 1400s did not have AC. Crap, *there goes Grace Kelly part deux!* I said to myself, not to the nun who presumably answered the phone. Instead, I settled on a gorgeous satin strapless ivory gown with ruching on the skirt and a pretty bow wrapped around the waist. I still got the dramatic veil, à la Grace, since one of the most moving parts of the ceremony I always envisioned is when the bride reaches the altar and her father tenderly lifts the veil to reveal her face. I didn't give a shit how hot it was, AC or not, I was not willing to give up that moment!

I got to know the creator of BCBG, Max Azria, and his stunning and fabulous wife, Lubov, when I first started at E! and often wore their pieces on air. When these longtime friends heard I was getting married, Lubov, the designer of the line, offered to design my bridesmaids' gowns. This whole wedding planning thing was turning out to be a lot more fab than I expected. I should get married every year, I thought. Errr . . . maybe not.

Anyway, I went to her showroom on Sunset Boulevard in West Hollywood, and the choices seemed endless. Together, we then came up with a flowy chiffon floor-length dress that was lightweight but still elegant. "I can do this dress in any color," Lubov told me. I considered all the possibilities. Black? Too harsh for summer. Blue? Never been a fan of blue. Then I literally closed my eyes for a few seconds and thought of Capri. The tastes, the smells, the yellow lemon trees. Yellow!!! That was it! I decided on canary yellow for the four bridesmaids—Bill's sister Karen, Pam, Colet, and my friend Bobbi Thomas. Monica was maid of honor, of course, but I wanted her to stand out. Her dress needed to be different, not matchy matchy with the other girls in the wedding party.

"I know the perfect dress," Monica announced. She would precede me down the aisle in a stunning yellow Oscar de la Renta with black embroidery throughout. The dress was one of the most coveted pieces from Oscar's most recent runway show. I recall a friend of mine asking if I was cool with my sister wearing such a statement dress at my wedding, not to mention it having close to the same price tag as the bridal gown.

"Heck no, I think it's fabulous," I quickly responded. My sister is a baller. Always has been, always will be. She added so much glamour and high fashion to my wedding day. I will never forget that dress. I may have to relive our teen years and sneak into her closet someday to steal it. I burglarized her closet so often when we were younger that she's probably upgraded her security system and has guard dogs living in there now.

The bridesmaid dresses came with a sash, and Lubov once again offered limitless color options. I decided on black. Yellow and black looked cool together, and it was really the only color that would work with the embroidery in Monica's dress. When I called my mom on the way home to tell her, she freaked.

"A black sash? On your wedding day? You-*a* crazy or what? Is this your wedding or a funeral? No black sash, Giuliana! No black sash!!!"

Here's the thing: I could either argue with a superstitious Italian woman that a black sash at an Italian wedding does not signify death, or I could just let it be. A matching yellow sash it was.

Bill and I made a reconnaissance trip to Italy a month before the wedding. For a control freak like me, having to do it long-distance had been unnerving. And not without disaster. For the reception, we booked the historic five-star Grand Hotel Quisisana, nestled on one of Capri's sunniest bluffs. Conversations with the catering and special events staff about my very specific requests tended to end in typical Italian fashion, with a noncommittal "Don't worry, we take-*a* care of it!"

"Yes, but will you be able to get enough red roses for each centerpiece?"

"Ah, roses!"

"How many can you get?"

"Enough."

"Let's do two dozen."

"Okay, no problem, you going to like it."

"No, can you do the centerpiece like the picture we sent you?"

"Don't-*a* worry!"

When they faxed a photo of the centerpiece they had put

together, it bore no resemblance to what I had ordered. The menu was having similar ad-lib issues. Everything fell into place once we were in Italy and I could be hands on, with backup from Mama DePandi and my personal assistant turned wedding planner, who kept banging his forehead against the wall and whimpering, "I don't speak Italian!"

Then Mama threw a curveball.

Only native Italians were allowed to actually get married in the Catholic Church on Capri, she informed us. Ummmm, had she thought to break this little bit of news to us before we had put down a $25,000 deposit on the hotel and sent out two hundred invitations to people, of whom 190 had RSVP'd "yes" and booked their nonrefundable travel to Europe? Presumably this "natives only" rule was set in place to prevent foreign tourists from booking up the church and forcing the locals to live indefinitely in sin, but I wasn't foreign, strictly speaking, and as practicing Catholics, Bill and I didn't want just a pretty destination ceremony. We wanted the church wedding. Mama consulted with her old parish priest in Naples and assured us she had a solution. We just had to do what she said. That alone should have made us nervous, but we were stressed enough already, so we just felt relieved and grateful. She told us we'd have to go to the government office in Naples and take some test.

Once we were there, a sour little bureaucrat handed us some forms in Italian.

"*Si, si, brava!*" Bill said, pretty much using up his entire Italian vocabulary. The bureaucrat eyed us suspiciously and turned his back to run off some copies at the Xerox machine. Mama had told him we were all Italian. Scanning the documents, I assumed this was the Italian equivalent of filing for a marriage license, but judging from Mama's cues, you had to be an Italian citizen to get one.

We're screwed, I thought. There was no way Mr. Si Si Brava could pass as a native son now that he had opened his big Croatian American mouth. Mama sidled up next to Bill to help with his forms while the official's back was still turned. The bureaucrat watched us leave with his arms folded and a scowl on his face. We made it out of the government office without getting arrested for wedding fraud and assumed the coast was clear.

Mama pulled me aside. "Giuliana, I know you're leaving, but you have to fill out some important paperwork tomorrow in Naples. They said you have to do this before you can have the ceremony in Capri." It was just a few forms, she said, and it didn't mean anything. We hadn't come to Italy planning to have the equivalent of a civil ceremony, and a legal wedding date a month before the one we had chosen, without our friends there to bear witness and help celebrate.

The next morning, there was a knock on our door. Bill opened it, and all my local relatives were standing there, holding plates of cookies and bouquets of flowers dyed green, for some superstitious Italian reason. They had been tipped off by Mama that we were getting legally married that morning, even though the supposed bride and groom had no idea at this point. I told Bill that the family just wanted us all to go to church together and that we needed to fill out some paperwork before our wedding in Capri. We set off, with Bill wearing shorts and me in jeans. A dozen Italian relatives surrounded us, and the uncles and male cousins tugged at Bill's arm, trying to peel him away. I attempted to get between them, like one of those wildebeests on a *National Geographic* special who try to protect the most vulnerable ones when lions move in to separate them from the herd. It didn't work, and Bill was carried away. Pretty soon, he called out.

"Jule, c'mere!" He understands Italian way better than he can speak it, and what he'd been able to put together from the uncles' chattering alarmed him.

"Why do people keep saying 'You're getting married!' and congratulating me?" he asked.

"Don't listen to them! We're just going to church!" I insisted.

Once inside the church, though, they suddenly split us up, and Bill had to go in the back. The priest was there with all these forms in Italian, and Mama was yelling at him to go. He returned with someone from the Italian consulate. Bill had to prove he could read and speak Italian. The guy spoke to me first, and Bill heard him say, "and William Rancica" so he said, "Mmm hmmm, *si signor.*"

We left the church, with the relatives congratulating Bill again and saying, "Let's go celebrate and eat!"

Bill turned to me with a confused look.

"Did I just get married? I'm not understanding what happened."

"I have no idea," I said. "I'll ask my mom later."

Her explanation never did make sense to me, in Italian or English, but technically, we may have gotten legally married in shorts and jeans with a ragtag bridal party holding green flowers more than a month before our planned wedding date of September 1, 2007.

Bill bitterly refers to the incident as his "ambush wedding."

When the real wedding weekend arrived, I was at the hair salon in Capri the afternoon before the rehearsal dinner when I overheard one of the customers say, "Finally, it's raining!" I almost snapped my neck looking out the window and couldn't believe my eyes. It was drizzling. "Four months without a drop of rain, and tonight we finally get rain. Amen!" the receptionist chimed in. Everyone was happy and smiling, but my eyes welled with tears and I raced back to the hotel to grab Bill.

I was still panting from the run when I grabbed him.

"It's raining, Bill! It's raining on our wedding weekend, and tonight the entire dinner is outdoors and it's going to be ruined!"

Bill ran to the window, surveyed the sky, and put his hands on my shoulders.

"I promise you, the sky will part and the sun will come out. There will be no rain at the rehearsal dinner." Lo and behold, he was right! At dinner, we watched great swaths of blazing violet and orange paint the sky as the sun slipped into the Mediterranean Sea. It was the most spectacular sunset I'd ever seen. A sneak preview, it turned out, of the gorgeous wedding day I woke up to.

There are moments every bride cherishes on the day she becomes a wife. For me, it was my first glimpse of Bill, waiting for me at the altar, so tall and handsome in a tuxedo my father the master tailor had made for him, his eyes filled with a love that I knew God had meant only for me.

Looking into those eyes, I began reciting my vows. It's a bit eerie now when I watch our wedding tape and see the exact moment when it hit me how real this commitment was, how eternal this bond. Tears I couldn't stop began streaming down my face as I spoke aloud those five simple words:

In sickness, and in health . . .

chapter nine

Barely a month after our wedding, Ted Harbert, the E! Networks president who had made me anchor, approached Bill and me with the proposition that sparked our first philosophical disagreement as husband and wife. Our wedding special had drawn over three million viewers, a one-episode blockbuster that was Style's highest-rated special ever. And that was before it re-aired domestically and aired internationally for five years following our wedding. Now my bosses wanted us to do a reality show. Bill, the practical one, was mortified. I was intrigued.

"Why would we even consider it?" Bill wanted to know. "What's the upside?"

"Bill, why does there always have to be an upside?" I teased. "Do something just because it's fun and an adventure!" I honestly thought it would be a lighthearted romp through the park. It appealed to my impulsive nature and tendency to live life out loud, anyway.

Looking at it, as was his nature, from a business perspective, I had to admit it didn't make sense, though. Or dollars. The only reality stars who get rich exposing their lives for the world to dissect are the ones ambitious enough to use the show and their newfound celebrity as a branding opportunity for an already viable business venture. Bethenny Frankel had managed to parlay her three-season *Real Housewives of New York* platform into a multimillion-dollar Skinnygirl Cocktail empire, but any number of Bravolebrities who'd stuck around for much longer runs on air worked their asses off to hawk makeup, jewelry, or accessory lines with very modest, if any, success. Far more have ended up in financial straits, not to mention divorce court, jail, or all of the above. The desire to be on TV can quickly turn aspirational people into desperate attention whores who will stoop to just about anything to stay on TV. I've seen them try to fake fights, affairs, and scandals to get on the cover of the weekly magazines in the hopes of keeping their ratings up and their shows renewed. It's so pathetic.

Even celebrities who were accustomed to being in front of the camera have ended up feeling the pressure of public scrutiny and private manipulation and watched their marriages fall victim to the "reality show curse"—Jessica Simpson and Nick Lachey, Tori Spelling and Dean McDermott, Bruce and Kris Jenner. In my years at E!, I had probably interviewed every big reality star at some point or another, though, and I felt like I had a unique perspective on this weird corner of pop culture. My belief is that reality shows accelerate your marriage forward in whatever lane it happens to be in. If you're headed for divorce, you'll get there faster. But part of me wondered whether the opposite could be equally true: If you're solid and happy to begin with, would putting yourselves in a glass bowl make that bond even stronger?

"Let's make marriage look cool," I urged Bill. "What harm can come from that?"

Besides, I pointed out, he had already been on a reality show when he competed in and won the first season of *The Apprentice*.

"That was all about business," Bill objected. "They didn't follow me into my bathroom and bedroom!"

I had no such qualms. Culturally, I was predisposed not to have any expectation of privacy whatsoever, thanks to my crazy Italian family. Case in point: my first period. I was thirteen, and it came in the middle of a big Fourth of July barbecue we were having, with all the Italian aunts, uncles, and cousins over. I was all freaked out, but Mama was busy with all the guests, so I went outside to sit on the brick wall lining our driveway and wait for Monica to come home. She was in the eleventh grade and would know what to do. My sister pulled up in her white Rabbit convertible with her cool friends.

"What's up, loser?" she greeted me.

"I think I got my period," I confided.

"What?!" She and her bitchy friends immediately ran to the backyard, and I chased after, hoping she wasn't about to do exactly what she did:

"Mom, everyone!" I heard her crow. "Giuliana got her period!"

Everyone started applauding, the cousins started hooting, all the aunties and mothers dabbed at tears, and I was hoisted up onto a table. Uncles started handing me hundred-dollar bills. I ran inside crying.

It was even worse my second cycle, when we were in Italy for our annual August vacation. This time, it was ninety degrees outside and oppressively humid, and we were walking everywhere to say hello to all the relatives and old friends. I wasn't allowed to wear tampons ("You're Italian, you don't wear tampons!" Mama had decreed) because they would steal my virginity (and then what? I would be forced into a shotgun marriage with a box of Tampax?). Unfortunately, I had a really heavy flow, and I had to use four pads at a time, fashioning them into a bulky Kotex diaper that anyone around me could hear squishing as I walked. As we toured the town with me in my period pants, hot and miserable and crampy, I would look for the nearest place to sit down when we ducked inside the hair salon, bakery, or wherever Mama, the grand marshal of our little parade, decided to stop. When we went inside our family friend Maurizio's clothing store, everyone was greeting each other while I sat off in a corner with my eyes half closed, mouth-breathing over my braces, my bad perm sticking out in ten different directions, and I overheard Maurizio suddenly ask, "But where is Giuliana?"

"Giuliana? She's right over there!" my parents exclaimed, pointing to me like a zoo specimen.

"*That's* Giuliana?" Maurizio said, remembering the little blond angel who had left Naples six years earlier. His voice dropped lower, but I could still hear him. "What's wrong with her? Is she . . ." Political correctness hadn't made it to Italy yet, and my eyes flew open at the Italian word. ". . . A mongoloido?" My parents seemed shocked and swiftly set the record straight:

"No, she just has her period!!"

Worried that I might leave the wrong impression elsewhere as I traipsed through Naples in my period pants, my family made it a point to inform anyone and everyone from then on that Giuliana was menstruating.

So there was no possible way I could end up embarrassed on a reality show. It's pretty much impossible to offend me. I've been immunized for life.

"We can use it for good instead of evil," I urged Bill. Honestly, we didn't have any big issues to reveal, and we were both so committed to maintaining integrity and authenticity that the only way we would sign an agreement was if we were allowed to produce the show ourselves rather than handing the steering wheel over to someone else. Granted, that would give us the power to refuse to air footage if we chose, but that wasn't our motive and we never exercised that option: We wanted an iron-clad guarantee that what viewers saw was our unaltered reality. No ginned-up story lines, and no major cast members except us. Friends we'd never met would not suddenly materialize to go on vacation and fight with us. Bill agreed to give it a go.

When we went to the semiannual Television Critics Association press tour in Pasadena, California, where networks present their new lineup of shows to over two hundred columnists, critics, and reporters at once, the very first question out of the pack was one we'd asked ourselves:

"Why would anyone watch the two of you?"

I said something along the lines of us feeling that people were hungry for something more positive, that this was just the beginning of a new trend, a whole wave of reality shows that were more down to earth and that people could relate to. "We want to inspire people, not disgust them," I explained. The critics' reaction seemed to waver between total disinterest and open hostility. When we walked off stage, Bill looked at me with something just short of terror in his eyes. "Maybe this is not such a great idea," he said.

Back on stage, the press was gobbling up another new E! reality offering: *Leave It to Lamas*, featuring Lorenzo Lamas's multi-divorced family and a story line revolving around his grown daughter's attempts to reconcile Lorenzo and the son who no longer spoke to him. Mike Fleiss, who produced *The Bachelor* and was behind the Lamas show, was going on and on about the drama and scandal this family had to offer when a reporter jumped in and said, "The Rancics were just out here, and they said people are tired of that sort of thing and are craving positive reality shows." Mike gave him a sardonic smile and replied,

"That show won't last one season." Funny thing is, the Lamases were gone in four episodes; we've aired over eighty. When it came to real-time drama, we would turn out to have more than enough to spare.

On the first day of filming, we were expecting two cameras, an audio guy, and a producer to show up. Instead, we opened the door of my one-bedroom Wilshire Boulevard condo to a traveling circus of fifteen people, including two executive producers, a network executive, and a director. Two trucks were blocking valet parking, people were loitering in the hallway because they couldn't all fit into our living room, and building management was freaking out and telling us we needed various permits. We needed more than that. Some Valium, for example: Bill was ready to pop my head off my body. Our supposedly low-key little glimpse inside the life of two newlywed lovebirds was suddenly a Spielberg movie. Our little kitchen was overtaken by the day's catered spread for the crew, while the rest of the condo was busy getting an unwelcome makeover. Big paper globe lanterns known as China balls were permanently affixed to the ceilings of our bedroom, kitchen, living room, bathroom, and closet. Filters were put over all the can lights in our ceiling, and our windows were coated with a dark tint. Sloppily, it turned out; Bill was super pissed when he saw all the bubbles left behind. It felt like we'd signed the wrong contract and had accidentally agreed to let moles flip our house.

"Um, so you take this all down at the end of the day and put it back again next time, right?" I said brightly.

"Oh, no, we're going to leave it here for several months," the producer replied. "We're shooting ten episodes."

After they called it a wrap that afternoon, Bill surveyed the muddy footprints, half-eaten sandwiches, empty toilet-paper rolls, and other assorted debris left behind.

"This is so invasive," he complained.

It didn't get any better, but I kept trying to make excuses until I ran out.

"Maybe we could live somewhere else and just come here to film," I suggested. Bill looked at me with a mixture of disbelief and disgust.

"That's not reality, honey," he said. Integrity is one of Bill's sexiest qualities, but it can also be one of the most frustrating when he feels like he has to examine everything so carefully under his personal microscope. Sometimes you just have to live life ad-lib. From the get-go, *Giuliana and Bill* was a major bone of contention between us, and we argued about it constantly. But you can't break that invisible "fourth wall" on TV and talk about being on TV while you're on it. So the very subject that was dominating our lives and causing the most friction was taboo when the cameras were around. Instead, we'd have to pretend we weren't pissed off when the crews arrived, and sit and talk about our day.

External Me: "So how was your day, honey?"

Internal Me: Just be nice for the fucking cameras, Bill, is that too much to ask?

External Bill: "Good! How was yours?"

Internal Bill: Actually, I'm terrible, because I had no idea I was marrying a camera whore!

External Me: "Good, I just found out I'm interviewing Angelina Jolie next week!"

Internal Me: It's not my fault you come across as such a stick-in-the-mud.

External Bill: "That's great, honey! So, I went to check out a new building I'm thinking of buying today."

Internal Bill: And maybe after I kill you for getting us into this, I'll bury your body in the foundation.

External Me: "Really? That sounds exciting!"

Internal Me: Maybe I should've just held out for George Clooney, after all.

Every scene that first season, we'd watch and then second-guess afterwards. Did we say too much? Not show enough? Bill thought I was being too candid; I thought he was being too uptight.

"This isn't going to work if you won't open up!" I lectured him.

"Well, you're acting like an over-exaggerated version of yourself!" he shot back. When we gave our separate on-air interviews—the ones they call "confessionals"—we would sometimes end up surprised by the other person's take on whatever had just happened. Watching later, we would look at each other: "Really? *That's* what you thought?" Bill would be surprised when I dissed some friend of his he thought I liked; I would be pissed when the camera caught him being curt with my mother and rolling his eyes behind her back when she was bugging him while he was trying to work.

"Why do you want to do this so bad?" Bill was getting exasperated. He kept issuing dire predictions about *Giuliana and Bill* hurting our marriage; I kept insisting that our marriage was stronger and bigger than our reality show. *Giuliana and Bill* were like some passive-aggressive clone couple whose sole purpose was to aggravate us to death so they could take over our life. It's true that I was getting most of the attention. Reality shows tend to favor women more than men—shopping, lunching, and gossipy spa days are always good fodder for the cameras. Women make up the majority of the viewers, and they're not interested in watching guys sit around and talk about Sunday's big game or how the market is doing. There's a much finer line for men to walk on reality TV: guys who participate too much will draw resentment and ridicule for being wannabe *Housewives* (witness

Slade Smiley from Orange County and Simon van Kempen from New York), but the ones who balk and just lurk in the background can end up vilified as selfish jerks or just plain shady. Producers loved it when they got me in some funny, relatable predicament like buying an oversized, overpriced sofa behind Bill's back, but then Bill would end up the killjoy talking on camera about budgeting and finances. The straight guy never gets credit.

"You can't have Lucy without Desi, honey," I'd try to appease him.

It would have been easy enough for him to sneak out and buy some piece of furniture he really wanted, or stage something else to "get even" with me on the show, but that wouldn't be Bill in real life, and he wasn't going to sacrifice authenticity for Q scores. He stuck to his guns and played it real, and the tables actually turned: men started tuning in because they liked the way Bill thought and had been in situations like his in their own relationships; women started scolding me on social media for spending too much on the stupid couch. Bill still felt aggrieved. Adding insult to injury, I would show up looking glamorous because I was coming home from shooting *E! News* or *Fashion Police*, or hosting some red-carpet event, which meant I had the benefit of professional hair, makeup, and wardrobe people, while Bill was stuck with whatever was clean in his own closet and whatever hair gel was in our bathroom. (Reality stars have to provide their own glam squads and wardrobes.) When we added all the aggravations up, the show was more of an effort than it was worth in the beginning. The only reason we didn't walk away mid-season was because of my separate relationship with the network, and the fact it would be my boss we were letting down.

"You know what?" I told Bill. "Let's just do one season, and we're done. One and done, okay?"

That first season was pretty dreadful, both on air and off. One entire episode was spent picking out lanterns for our brownstone on Chicago's Gold Coast. Should we go bigger or smaller? This shape, or that one? *Who would want to watch thirty minutes of that?* I wondered later. At one point, I had even tried to convince Bill that lanterns were "like choosing your earrings with a little black dress—they're what makes the dress pop!" Next thing we knew, people were quoting that line all over the place. It was a good reminder that what our audience wanted to see was every-day life.

Even though being on the show was stressful, watching it was actually having the opposite effect: It was like free therapy. I would see myself incessantly taunting Bill about a cheesy piece of art an ex-girlfriend had given him depicting a sax player with his cheeks puffed out and think, *Am I really that annoying?* Bill, on the other hand, was troubled by his own seriousness. That reluctance he still had to just let go when the cameras were around was detracting from how funny—and fun—he really is. Watching himself, he gradually became more relaxed and pa-tient. ("You're right, honey. I was too tough on you. It looks great and we use it all the time," Bill conceded when he saw the infamous sofa episode.) I worked on turning myself down a notch or two: when you have the luxury of seeing yourself played back on TV after the fact, you realize that you never sound or look exactly the way you think you do. Learning to compromise and not be right all the time is a big lesson for any couple, especially when you've already been independent for so long before you married. *Giuliana and Bill* showed us what we were doing wrong, and probably saved us thousands of dollars we would have spent having a marriage counselor tell us the same thing. Watching our best and worst behaviors playing out on the screen, we saw how we bonded, and how we drove each other away. We could cor-rect course as we went. The reality show kept us in check.

That first summer after our wedding, Bill and I decided to "pull the goalie from net," as he likes to put it, and start trying to have a baby. Growing up in close-knit clans had made both of us yearn for a big family of our own, and with me at thirty-five and Bill at thirty-eight, we didn't have time to waste. When I still hadn't conceived by Christmastime, I consulted my ob-gyn. He suggested we try artificial insemination to turbo-boost my aging eggs.

"What about him?" I demanded, shooting Bill an accusatory look. "He has old sperm!"

"Excuse me?" Bill objected. "I do not have old sperm. My sperm is amazing! You have old eggs!"

From that point on, our pet nicknames for each other became Old Eggs and Old Sperm, or just OE and OS. People were horrified, especially when Bill called me Old Eggs on air, but hey, I was going on thirty-six and my eggs *were* old. It may have been lame, but that stupid private joke made us laugh, and we were going to need that.

I would have to give myself shots in my belly for the week leading up to insemination. The first two days, I was too nervous and went to the doctor's office to have them do it. The third day, I did it myself with the nurse coaching me. By the fourth needle, I was okay with doing it myself. We would come to the doctor's office right when I ovulated, and a market-fresh sample of Bill's sperm would be washed and concentrated into a team of top candidates, which would then be inserted into my uterus via catheter. It was relatively quick, minimally invasive, and even though it didn't have as high a success rate as in vitro fertilization, where the sperm and egg are fertilized in a petri dish and then transferred to the mother's uterus, it was worth trying.

The production crew trundled into the doctor's office with us and commandeered a nurse's station to set up their equipment and lay out their catering for the day. "No way in hell," Bill said when the cameras tried to follow him down the hallway as he carried his little plastic cup to a private room. We also barred cameras from filming the procedure itself, but we let them come into the room afterward, when I was supposed to just lie on my back with the table slightly inverted, and stay as still as possible for thirty minutes. It was awkward. At home, or running around doing stuff together, Bill and I had gradually learned to ignore the cameras and forget that we were miked. You're never *not* aware that they're there; you just stop caring that they are. But this was so intimate. I was supposed to keep quiet, Bill was holding my hand, and everyone hovering in that exam room was basically waiting for my egg to invite some passing sperm to stick around for Cap'n Crunch. Were we expecting some sound effect to confirm it so the news could be relayed to the production command center in the nurse's station? ("We have contact, copy that . . .")

Afterwards, Bill was upset. "That was *so* intrusive," he remarked. That was another one of our hot buttons about the show: Bill was the "No" guy, more likely to ban the cameras than I was; knowing this, the producers naturally tried to pull end runs around him and ask me first. "I'm the one everyone hates for always saying no, and you're always saying yes," he grumbled. Getting on the same page 100 percent of the time was never going to happen, given our different natures, and we never really knew how far we were willing to go until we were in the actual situation. We agreed wholeheartedly about sharing our struggle to have children, but the boundaries shifted as unpredictably as our life did; we had fully expected a quick, happy ending. Infertility hadn't touched either of our families— both my sister, Monica, and Bill's sister, Karen, had beautiful children and no problems conceiving. I was otherwise healthy and fit, with no history of endometriosis or other conditions that might impact my ability to get pregnant. Bill was perfectly healthy, too. We were one of the countless unlucky couples diagnosed with "unexplained infertility."

Artificial insemination carries a high risk of multiple birth, because you don't know how many of the eggs will be fertilized. *Oh my God, I'm going to be the next Octomom*, I thought. We would have to convert a tour bus for all the car seats. I would have to get some kind of industrial breast pump, maybe a milking machine from a dairy or something. When I calmed down, I settled into the happy certainty that we were going to have twins. I was certain of it, and Bill eagerly bought into what I believed to be my woman's intuition, too.

A month later, we learned that I wasn't even carrying one baby. I felt disappointed, but we decided to try another round of IUI. Still no baby. After a third attempt with no results, my gynecologist told us it was time to consult a fertility specialist. We did some research and made an appointment to start this tougher journey.

The question was: Should we take a few million strangers along with us, or was it time to ditch *Giuliana and Bill* and face reality alone?

As we tried to educate ourselves as much as possible, we were shocked to discover that one in four American couples experiences issues with infertility. That's a staggering number, and even sadder when you look around your own circle of friends, family, coworkers, and acquaintances and consider statistically how many might be suffering in silence.

"You know how many people we can help?" I urged Bill as we considered whether to cancel the show. "We finally have our purpose." He agreed. Maybe we could all draw hope from one another. In February of 2009, we began in vitro fertilization with a team of specialists in Chicago. Dr. Brian Kaplan was a handsome South African with a sexy accent. I prefer ugly doctors, especially if they're going to be exploring the promised land while I'm in stirrups. IVF has a higher success rate than IUI, and I was optimistic about getting pregnant after the first round. For two weeks, I would have to get two shots daily, one in the stomach and one in the butt. There were a lot more side effects than before. I had to stop working out, and any physical movement became painful as my ovaries enlarged according to plan. I was bloated and a little hormonal, too. I started feeling resentful that I was doing all the work, and Bill didn't have to do anything. "If I could do this, I would," he told me, and I knew he would in a heartbeat.

I was put under for surgery so my doctor could retrieve the eggs, and I woke up to good news: fifteen had been harvested. Five days later, I went back to have three fertilized ones transferred. Two others had also become embryos and were frozen in case we needed to use them later. Dr. Kaplan phoned us with the news: I was officially pregnant. *Very* pregnant, it seemed: my follicle-stimulating hormone level was extremely high, which often indicates twins. Bill and I immediately started discussing whether the babies should have separate bedrooms or share one. I went out and bought a baby book.

A week later, we went in for an ultrasound to see how many I was carrying.

"It's a singleton," Dr. Kaplan said, pointing to the single little embryonic sac on the monitor. Our son or daughter.

Later, we got to hear the tiny heartbeat. We were overjoyed, hugging each other, eyes glued to the monitor.

Even when we were dating, Bill and I would fantasize about the family we would have together. Now we felt within sight of those rollicking backyard barbecues in the summer and snowy Christmas mornings with our kids laughing and playing with all their little cousins while the house filled with wonderful smells from the kitchen. We decided we would put our urban Gold

Coast townhouse on the market and start looking for a house in the suburbs of Chicago. Bill was keen to find the perfect fixer-upper to showcase all the construction and design expertise he had amassed during his years of flipping investment properties. A place he could turn into our unique dream house. He began the search for a mansion in need of TLC in Hinsdale, a community with both a charming downtown and the beautiful, leafy streets we both loved.

When I went in for a checkup at nine weeks, the nurse furrowed her brow and squinted at the monitor as she ran the wand over my belly. The sac came into view, but was silent. "Huh, let me try this," she would say, and then, when we asked if everything was okay, we knew the answer already when she hedged. "I don't know if the equipment is working right. Let me get the doctor." She left the room.

"Bill, hand me the fucking wand, I'll find the baby!" I snapped. I felt outraged by the nurse's incompetence. I was pregnant. I was the mother, I would be able to summon that small heartbeat, know where it was hiding. I swiped the wand quickly over my stomach, then pressed it into Bill's hand. "Here, you do it!"

Dr. Kaplan came in and sat down in front of the monitor.

"I don't hear a heartbeat," he said as he guided the wand to the spot where the empty sac hung. "Huh. Okay. I'm sorry, but I don't know if this one is viable."

The baby was gone.

On the way home, we stopped to eat pancakes, picking sadly at the comfort food that would never fill such a void.

Bill, in the meantime, had found our house: a twelve-thousand-square-foot Hinsdale mansion that had been abandoned mid-construction and was so dilapidated that he had to help me up a wooden gangplank over the debris just to get to the front door. He was so excited when he discovered the place and couldn't stop telling me how he knew instantly when he stepped inside that it was home. When he opened the door with a flourish to lead me inside, I had a very different gut reaction: *Oh, hell no!* It was a mess, and impossible for me to envision as anything but an expensive heap of rubble. Bill was passionate, though, and I never questioned his talent, so we became surburbanites on paper, at least. "It'll just take a few months," Bill assured me.

In retrospect, I think that Hinsdale house was the marker we were placing on an emotional bet: a self-fulfilling prophecy with six bedrooms. Our parental field of dreams.

Devastating as the miscarriage was, it did establish that I could become pregnant, and once we'd given ourselves a chance to recover, we decided to brave another grueling cycle of IVF. It was late summer, and the camera crews were with us as I went to have eggs retrieved yet again. All the way home, I kept saying I wanted a big fluffy omelet from the Pancake House, with spinach, mushrooms, onion, and tomatoes. Bill fetched me one, and as I stood there eating it in the kitchen, I suddenly felt something hard in my mouth. I spit it out.

"OH MY GOD, it's a finger! There's a fucking fingertip in my omelet!" I started gagging. Bill rushed to my side.

"What is it?" he asked as I dry-heaved.

"Look at it!" I choked. "The chef's fucking finger is in my omelet!"

Bill examined the hard, white evidence.

"It's not a finger," he assured me. I was still gagging. "It's a fingernail."

I kept gagging. Bill reconsidered.

"No, wait, it's a tooth!"

"The chef's TOOTH is in my omelet?" I shrieked before retching anew. "Call the Pancake House, I'm going to sue!"

"That's crazy," Bill said. "How can the chef's tooth be in your omelet?" He pondered this mystery while I continued with the retching and swearing. "Hey, wait a second. Open your mouth, honey."

I opened, assuming he was looking for more discarded chef's teeth.

"Honey, it's your tooth," he said with some relief. "You have a hole in your mouth. *Your* tooth fell out."

Great. Now I was going to have to have my eggs retrieved and a crown put on in the same day. More than I could deal with. Between the meds from the egg retrieval and the false alarm over random chef body parts in my omelet, I was exhausted. And not feeling very well. "I'm going to go lie down," I told my husband. After a while, he came in to check on me and gently laid a hand on my stomach. "Ow!" I screamed. It felt like an electric shock. "Oh my God, Bill, something is wrong with me!" I cried. The pain was excruciating. "Something is going on with my body! Oh, God, there's so much pain!" The *Giuliana and Bill* crew was in the living room, breaking down their equipment and getting ready to leave, a little sulky that they'd decided not to follow me into the kitchen earlier because eating an omelet sounded too boring. Now Bill came charging out of the bedroom.

"Get out of here!" he yelled. "Turn off the cameras! This is serious!"

As soon as they'd cleared out, he carried me out to the car, and we raced to the ER.

"I think I'm overstimulated," I told the young doctors trying to figure out what was wrong. I knew that was a risk with IVF, and that overstimulated ovaries could swell and push against the abdominal wall. They took my vitals and started running tests. My suspicions were confirmed. They gave me painkillers and we waited. Bill was dozing in a chair around three in the morning when one of the doctors came back into the room and told me my hemoglobin levels were dangerously low, and they needed to do a blood transfusion.

"Okay," I groggily agreed.

Fortunately, Bill snapped awake.

"Blood transfusion?" he asked. "No blood transfusion! How long can we hold off?"

"A few hours," the doctor said.

"Okay, let's wait till six a.m. and call our ob-gyn," Bill said. If Dr. Sabbagha confirmed that such drastic measures were needed, then we'd go ahead with the transfusion. At six, Dr. Sabbagha came in, examined me, saw that my numbers were starting to improve, and decided to hold off for two hours to see what happened. By eight, I was out of the woods.

I had never challenged a doctor's decision before. Bill's insistence on a second opinion—one we trusted implicitly—spared me an unnecessary and potentially risky transfusion. It was the first time I truly realized that doctors aren't gods, that they're human and fallible just like the rest of us. That knowledge was both scary and empowering.

I went to cover Fashion Week in New York City at the beginning of September with my belly grotesquely distended. I looked seven months pregnant, and hid it with long scarves and coats. I was in excruciating pain. Only my personal assistant and hair and makeup people knew it was because my ovaries were swollen to the size of grapefruits. They choreographed themselves like a precision dance team to body block any paparazzi shots so no one would notice my belly and report that I was pregnant. After Fashion Week, I went back to Chicago utterly exhausted. Dr. Kaplan told us I needed to let my body heal for four months before we continued. Then I would have to start the meds all over again.

True to his word, Bill somehow managed to rehab the Hinsdale mansion and get us moved in just in the nick of time before I would try to get pregnant again. It was beautiful. I had my big, white dream kitchen, and Bill had his Scotch and cigar room, painted navy blue to show off a built-in bar with white marble top. The huge yard reminded me of Tuscany with its planters of purple salvia, herbs, and a gorgeous tulip tree. There was even a bocce court for my Italian relatives. When we moved in, neighbor kids welcomed us with homemade cookies. We hosted a big Thanksgiving for our families in that house, Mama and Bill cooking together in the kitchen.

Despite the hellacious near-death ordeal of the overstimulation, lots of eggs had been retrieved during that round of IVF, and two "A-plus" embryos were finally transferred after the holidays. I was pretty sure they had implanted. My body just read "pregnant." The reality cameras captured the anticipation shining in our eyes when Dr. Kaplan called to tell us the results.

"Well guys, I don't know what to tell you," he said. "You're not pregnant."

"Wait? What?" I repeated dumbly. "Not pregnant! That's impossible!" My head was spinning. I thought I was going to faint.

We must have asked the doctor to repeat himself five times. How could this be happening? We had been told that the number and quality of our eggs were above average; we were in perfect physical condition; we had followed the shot regimen to a tee. To be told now that it hadn't worked was a sucker punch. The doctor couldn't give us much of an explanation. He, too, sounded perplexed and deflated. Bill pushed the "End" button, and the two of us just looked at each other in shock. Tears streamed down my face, and I fell into Bill's arms. Our dream was once again shattered.

About three hours later, the familiar sorrow made a crash landing at our dinner table as just the two of us sat quietly eating at a table for eight.

"Do you hear that?" I asked Bill.

"What?" he said.

"Do you hear our echoes?"

His face fell. "Yeah."

At first, I chose my words carefully—words I was sure Bill would not want to hear after pouring his heart and soul into building our dream home. "I'm sorry honey, but I think we have to move," I began. "We have to sell this house. I can't stay here."

Then the deeper truth came tumbling out: "And I can never go through IVF again." Bill didn't argue. Not with my plea to move, or with the revelation that I was giving up on having a baby. We would make L.A. our primary residence—I'd sold my little condo and we had a lovely house there now. We would just stay at the Trump hotel when we commuted to Chicago.

Bill quietly sold the house, no questions asked, no pleas for me to reconsider. But he didn't let go of his dream of fatherhood as easily.

Whenever he would tentatively broach the subject of trying for kids again, I would shoot him down. "Stop asking!" I implored. I couldn't imagine enduring another round of fertility treatments—the daily shots in the stomach, the raging hormones, the pain of hyperstimulated ovaries pushing against my insides, the delicate egg retrieval, and ultimately, the risk of another heartbreak. Who were we fooling, thinking we had any control over this? Whatever happened, or didn't, was God's will.

Although I was raised Catholic, and prayed each night as my grandmother had taught me, my relationship with the Church was more casual than Bill's when we first got married. When I was a kid growing up in Bethesda, most of my best friends were Jewish. I went away to Camp Judea with one of them for four weeks one summer and came back able to recite Hebrew prayers so perfectly that a rabbi later asked me at a friend's bat mitzvah what temple I was a member of. "Oh," I said. "Holy Rosary Church."

"How are you Catholic?" he wondered. "I saw you know the prayers!"

Junior high was one long merry string of bar and bat mitzvahs. *This is so dope*, I decided. "I want to be Jewish," I told my mother.

"Shut up. Don't ever say that again," Mama replied. She held Jews in the highest esteem, too, since she considered them very similar to Italians, but she drew the line at letting her youngest daughter convert just so she could have a bat mitzvah. I tried to negotiate the bat mitzvah without the actual conversion, but that plan was nixed, too. I whined about it enough to finally get permission for a big blowout confirmation party. I invited the entire school and everyone was bored out of their mind during Mass, but there was a DJ at the after-party, so I was good.

When I started seeing Bill, I would accompany him to Mass, and praying together was a tender part of our relationship. Over the years, we had both become more devout. But infertility was testing my faith: I remember once being in church with tears running down my face, I was so hurt and angry at God. My sister had three perfect little girls. MTV was full of teen moms who'd rather party than change a diaper. Newborns were found in Dumpsters. How could God put babies in Dumpsters, but not in me? I remember looking up at the sky and literally raging at the God I wasn't sure I believed in anymore. *Why, why? What the hell is this about?*

Bill was hurting, too, but held fast to his conviction that whatever happened to him, to me, to us, was meant to be, and that God had a plan that was still unfolding.

Because of the reality show, our private anguish was public knowledge. We would get cards, letters, and e-mails of support from fans, as well as weird but well-meaning promises from people who swore that crystals or acupuncture or meditation would cure us. Women on Twitter would offer to become my surrogate. It wasn't unusual for sympathetic strangers to approach us on the street or in a restaurant, or for women to share their own fertility stories and offer advice in the checkout lane of the supermarket. But the weirdest thing started happening. Over and over again, I kept hearing women referring me to the same fertility specialist: Dr. Schoolcraft.

One day, I stopped at this random nail salon in Venice Beach to get a mani-pedi. It wasn't one of my usual places, and as I settled into the spa chair, I noticed this one customer stealing glances at me. She was a young, stylish Asian woman. The more she looked at me, the more I racked my brain, wondering if I knew her from somewhere. Maybe she worked for a magazine and we'd met on a shoot? When she got up to pay and leave, she walked up to me. She was hugely pregnant.

"I'm so sorry to bother you, but have you ever heard of Dr. Schoolcraft?" she asked.

"Yes, I have, but I've never gone to him," I said. What was with this Schoolcraft guy?

"We tried everything for years," the woman went on, "and nothing worked. I went to Dr. Schoolcraft, and now I'm pregnant with twins. I'm telling you, you *will* get pregnant with him. Just try." She left, and I went home and Googled the doctor's name. I found out that Dr. William Schoolcraft and his clinic, the Colorado Center for Reproductive Medicine, boasted the highest success rate in the country for live births—70 percent of his patients had babies. They blew the next closest clinic, with 50 percent, out of the water.

"Bill, take a look at this," I said. When he saw that the website I had on my computer screen was a fertility clinic, he looked at me hopefully.

"You think you might wanna go meet with them?" he asked tentatively, feeling me out. "Should we call them and find out more?"

"Yeah, sure," I agreed. "A call doesn't hurt." We made the call and asked about the program. We quickly learned that one of the reasons their success ratio was higher was because they screened their candidates so rigorously: Dr. Schoolcraft only accepted patients he felt certain he could help become pregnant. I appreciated the extra effort being made not to waste the time, and more important, the emotions of couples already at the point of desperation. We made an appointment.

For the first time in my life, I stepped onto a plane filled with excitement instead of dread. Unlike the medical towers we visited in Chicago, the CCRM was a freestanding building in the shadow of the Rocky Mountains outside Denver. Inside, it was airy, clean, and bright, with a beautiful waterfall in the waiting room. Couples from Russia, Germany, and Florida were waiting to take the one-day battery of tests to see if Dr. Schoolcraft would accept them into the program. The workup included blood tests, ultrasounds, and a full medical history and exam. I was nervous. What if he didn't take us?

Bill Schoolcraft turned out to be a quiet, soft-spoken family man with a kind bedside manner. He told us he thought he could help us, and accepted us into the program. Just like that, I knew I was definitely ready to try again. I got my meds and my protocol, and headed home to start the by now familiar but still scary routine. I barely even flinched at the shots anymore, and Bill knew what to expect with my hormonal moods.

It takes a measure of hope to put yourself through IVF, and despite our long, heartbreaking struggle to have a baby, we still embraced that sliver of possibility. I let myself think about nursery colors and names again, about my Nonna Maria teaching me to make the pillowy gnocchi I craved as a child for my own daughter, or about Bill indoctrinating his son into the cult of Cubs fans. We could only hope, and wait to see if it was God's will this time.

Two weeks later, I went to Denver for retrieval, and Dr. Schoolcraft extracted seventeen or eighteen eggs—my best harvest yet. But the memory of my Chicago emergency still frightened me, and I was frankly worried about the next step.

"Dr. Schoolcraft, I cannot overstimulate again," I begged. I knew it rarely happened—less than 5 percent of the time—but since I already belonged to that minority, I figured it could happen again.

"You won't," Dr. Schoolcraft promised. "I can give you a shot that will reduce the risk, but that means we'll have to do frozen instead of a fresh transfer." Usually, the fertilized eggs would be transferred five days after retrieval. Frozen didn't have an expiration date. We opted to go the frozen route so I could take the medication to thwart overstimulation. I went home and felt elated when I got through the first day without any problems. This had to be a good sign.

Before we'd left Denver, Dr. Schoolcraft's nurse had sat me down to go over my charts before we scheduled the embryo transfer. The camera crews were there that day, and I told the producer not to bother setting up the shot. "This is going to be boring," I warned him. "It's just paperwork. You're never going to use the footage."

"Yeah, but we don't really have much else today," he shrugged. They filmed as the nurse read aloud from the list of tests I had to complete before the surgery.

Hemoglobin, *check*.

Blood, *check*.

"You haven't done the mammogram," she noted.

"Oh yeah, I meant to talk to you about that," I said. "I'm

thirty-six. I have no family history of breast cancer, so can't I skip that one?"

"Sorry, it doesn't matter whether you're twenty-six, thirty-six, or forty-six," she said. "Dr. Schoolcraft requires all patients to have one. If there's estrogen-positive breast cancer and you get pregnant, nine months of hormones can fuel the cancer."

I went home to L.A. and got the mammogram the following Monday—the very last day I could do it and make the clinic's deadline if I wanted to keep my implantation date, a week away.

On Tuesday, I got a call from the radiologist to come back and redo the mammogram. The technician had spotted a speck, in all likelihood because I had moved slightly. But then it showed up the second time, too.

"Could be something, or it could be nothing," I was told. "You need to take it to a cancer doctor."

I was sure it was nothing. I was fit and healthy, and women get benign breast cysts all the time, right? It was a speck, not a big mass. I underwent a needle biopsy and was so confident about the results that I went to the follow-up appointment alone. Bill was in Mexico on an Operation Smile charity mission. He had offered to cancel and come with me, but I had scoffed at the idea. "Bill, there's no way I have breast cancer," I insisted.

At Cedars-Sinai, they put me in the doctor's office to wait. And wait. About fifteen minutes into my wait, I started getting a really weird vibe. Something just came over me, and all I could think of was that I had to get out of there. I did something I had never done at the doctor's office before, no matter how long I had been waiting. I opened the door quietly and slipped into the hallway, hiding under my baseball cap and dark glasses. I made it to the elevator and started nervously hitting the "Down" button when a nurse named Jessica intercepted me.

"Where are you going?"

"Hey, you know what? I just got a phone call from work and I have to get to set ASAP," I lied. Badly.

"You need to get back in the office," Jessica firmly ordered.

We argued back and forth until she gently escorted me back to the room. I kept asking her if it was good news or bad news. She kept saying, "The doctor will be right with you, you're going to be okay." I was going to be okay! She said it and she's got the intel, right? I sat back down in the little white room and before I could put my sunglasses back in my bag, I heard the doctor walk in.

"Giuliana, I'm sorry but . . ." That pause will forever be etched in my mind. I remember leaning back, like I was about to get hit in the face, my body language screaming "No, don't do it! Please don't tell me what you are about to say." My mind sent a different urgent message: "This is it. Brace yourself. Your life is about to change for the worse."

". . . you have breast cancer."

I've learned since then that there are two ways women typically react to that news. Some go into shock and become very quiet and analytical. I fell into the other category. I fucking lost it. I lost my mind. My head dropped, and everything went black. I felt the ground fall away. *It's over. This is it.* I didn't know anything about cancer, except you die. You lose your hair and then you die.

The doctor was matter-of-factly saying something about radiation, lumpectomy, chemo, mastectomy. Cancer's slam poetry. The words bounced off the shell that was left of me. I was in hysterics for what seemed like hours but was most likely about five minutes of straight sobbing. I asked the doctor if I could have a moment alone and made the one call I couldn't dial quickly enough. Incoherent and wailing like a baby, I reached Bill. He couldn't believe what he was hearing but managed to stay calm and soothe me through his own shock. He was on the next flight home.

What I did next is something I will never be able to fully explain. I drove to work. How, I don't know. It's a blur. But it didn't dawn on me to go home and burrow beneath the covers in bed, or drive to my big sister's house so I could collapse in her arms and be comforted. I had that day's segment of *E! News* to shoot. I told everyone my eyes were swollen because of allergies. I went to my dressing room, splashed cool water on my face, and shot the peppiest *E! News* I'd ever done. There I was, perky Miss Television Hostess, cracking jokes with Ryan Seacrest and reporting on Beyoncé's baby bump. I was overcompensating so hard. I know I went back to work because I didn't want my life to change. I just wanted to pretend a little longer that it hadn't. After all, E! was my dream job and waking up seemed like an especially bad idea right then.

"Great show!" I said to the crew as usual when it was over. Then I went back to my dressing room, closed the door, fell on the floor, and cried. I checked to make sure the hallways were clear before sneaking out. At every red light on the way home, I put my head on the steering wheel and sobbed some more, not giving a shit if anyone saw me. I pulled into our driveway and sat there. Bill had called to let me know he had landed, and I didn't want to go inside until he got home. At last, he pulled up, got out, and I crumbled into his arms.

Then we unlocked the door and went inside to our different life.

chapter ten

*L*ove Story, Terms of Endearment, The Fault in Our Stars . . . Hollywood has made us all believe in the cinematic Cancer Heroine, who's impossibly smart, funny, brave, selfless, and beautiful even as she stares death in the eyes.

What a bunch of bullshit that is.

Staring down cancer is scary as hell, depressing, and if anything, it makes you even more vulnerable—not brave—because you realize how little control you have over your life, and how crazy-unpredictable it all is.

My instant reaction was that no one could find out. Bill and I kept my diagnosis to ourselves. Each hour we discussed whether to tell our families, and when. My parents knew, of course, that I had been undergoing tests, but there was still so much we didn't know. You know how people say the hardest person to tell is your mother? Well, they're right. She had been trying to reassure me as I waited for answers. *You're fine, Giuliana, you're fine!* Having to tell her that her little girl had cancer was heart-wrenching, the last words she ever wanted to hear. I reached her at Babbo's store.

"No, I can't believe this! *Gesu, Gesu!*" she wailed.

"Mama, get Babbo on the phone," I said before going into all the details. Babbo came on but quickly fell quiet, and I realized he was crying. When they heard the news, Monica and Pasquale were hysterical, barely able to speak. We didn't tell anyone else for several weeks. Everything was happening too quickly, and denial was like some secret fort where we could huddle together. Letting the fear out would only give it life and make it bigger. *Giuliana and Bill* didn't happen to be filming when I went for the mammogram or learned the results, so the people at E! had no idea what was going on. I thanked God for that small favor.

I was something of a legend as a notorious workaholic at E! I didn't take a sick day or vacation for ten years. I didn't set out to be such a martyr; I just loved my job and was completely wrapped up in it and devoted to it. If I wasn't on camera, I was likely out promoting my shows at some event, or giving interviews instead of conducting them. Getting married and struggling to start a family changed that. I had a soul mate to come home to, and we had a life to build together. I didn't hesitate to take the time off I needed for fertility procedures, and because of the reality show, everyone knew exactly where I was and what I was doing. Two days after I found out I had cancer, I was summoned for a meeting in the E! executive offices. I figured maybe they were going to add something else to my on-air duties. When I entered the room, four executives were sitting in a circle—one from each of my shows. I was told to take a seat, and informed that there was a general consensus that I had started to slack off at work.

"We brought you into this meeting because we noticed that you're neglecting your job and have lost interest," the head honcho began. One by one, each of the four producers read from his own list of grievances against me, complaining about what event I had missed or day I was unavailable to anchor *E! News,* or cohost *Fashion Police,* or do interviews for *Live from the Red Carpet.* There were even complaints from the producer of *Giuliana and Bill,* who should have known better than anyone what I had been going through, since his show's ratings were up as a result of me letting the cameras film every hope and heartbreak Bill and I had endured trying to become parents.

I listened to them all, fighting back tears and feeling the flush of indignation turn my neck, my face, even my ears bright pink. In my mind, I railed at them: *Are you all done? I have cancer! Go fuck yourselves!* I swallowed my rage and kept silent. They weren't getting that piece of me, that pain I found too shocking, too raw, too ugly to lay bare. I was the crooked girl all over again, trying to stand just right, so no one would notice my imperfection.

"Maybe you have too much on your plate to handle," the *E! News* guy was blathering on, "and you should scale back. Why don't we take you off *Fashion Police.*" It was more a declaration than a question, but I cut in.

"No! I love *Fashion Police!*"

"Okay, then. The reality show," he said. "Something's got to give."

This was an ongoing war of network politics: *Giuliana and Bill* aired on Style, a sister network to E! My main gig was on *E! News,* that show was alpha dog, and *E! News* and *Fashion Police,* also on E!, would occasionally go for Style's throat if they felt the need to reassert power. Since I worked for both, there was constant bickering about *Giuliana and Bill* and at times even *Fashion Police* interfering with my anchor and managing editor duties at *E! News.* That battle I was used to. But being ambushed by all four and taken prisoner of war was new.

Maybe if I'd been in a tougher state of mind, I would have

stood up for myself and walked out of the room. But that stupid good soldier gene I have kicked in, and instead, I heard my quavering voice asking these heartless pricks to let me work harder.

"You're right," I said. "I've been distracted. Let me have a second chance, and I'll prove myself. I'll be more focused," I promised. They magnanimously agreed. I fled the room and called Bill, who went ballistic when I told him how I had just been raked over the coals.

The Emmys were the following week, and I was determined to "prove" myself to the powers that be. I was wearing a strapless red dress that wouldn't alter properly and kept slipping down. I kept pulling it up, and it would inch down again. I was so paranoid about my boobs, that something must be different, the cancer somehow evident, and I grew increasingly mad as I felt the dress expose more and more of me. I was swearing under my breath, forgetting I was miked, and complaining to my team. "Guys, it's falling down again! You've got to do something! It won't stay up!" They couldn't figure out what my problem was. "It's fine!" they kept insisting. "You're fine!" The raw footage shows me fixated on my breasts, staring down at them with such a sad and angry look on my face. When we would come back from break and that red light would go on, I was overly chirpy and animated, trying to show how interested and engaged I was.

People often ask me why I went public with the diagnosis. We certainly had the option of keeping it secret by not scheduling any shoots when we had cancer-related appointments and avoiding conversation about my illness when we were filming. There are plenty of bigger celebrities who have managed to keep life-threatening diseases completely private. I saw one in the wing at Cedars-Sinai where cancer patients are treated, and we exchanged looks of mutual empathy in the elevator—I never even told my husband who she was. But the pure shock of it—that breast cancer could happen to me, when I had no symptoms or family history, and was so anal about maintaining a healthy lifestyle—made me realize that millions of other women out there could have no idea they were living with this silent killer, too. What if I hadn't gone through IVF, and my new doctor hadn't routinely insisted on a mammogram? I wouldn't have scheduled one until I was forty—four years away. The cancer was so hard to detect and so deep, there's no telling whether I would have felt a lump before then. My TV career gave me an instant platform to warn other women. I couldn't *not* do that. Bill agreed. He was close to his three older sisters, and he had lost his beloved father to cancer a decade earlier. Six weeks after my diagnosis, we approached the *Today* show and said we had something important to share, and we were prepared to talk about it on air. We made plans to appear on the show the morning of October 17, 2011, a Monday.

The week before, I told my bosses at E! They were sad and felt awful, and apologized for having challenged my frequent absences. The night before, I called a handful of my closest friends and some other family members to tell them what was happening. Ryan Seacrest, my *E! News* co-host, picked up his phone with a breezy "What's up, G?" assuming I was calling about something for tomorrow's show.

"Ryan, I have bad news," I plunged right in. "I'm calling to let you know that I'm going on the *Today* show tomorrow to announce that I have breast cancer and I wanted you to hear it first from me."

Ryan, always so unflappable, sounded like he had been kicked in the stomach. "What? Oh my God," he said. "G, oh my God. G, G, I'm so sorry. If there's anything I can do . . ." There wasn't, but as much as I would hear those helpless words from people I knew and ones I'd never met, I never stopped appreciating them, or believing in them. As tough and full of piss as I act at times, in

reality, I harbor an inner Pollyanna who is optimistic no matter
how illogical it seems. Bill often tells me it's one of his favorite
traits in me. At the end of the day, it's not that I fight so hard, but
that I believe so fiercely.

The next morning, I sat on the *Today* set across from Ann
Curry as she somberly told viewers that I was there to share
some very personal news. They retraced our on-air failures to
conceive, from my devastating miscarriage and tearful question-
ing of why God seemed to be punishing us, to the cliffhanger
at the end of our last season of *Giuliana and Bill*, with us happily
waving good-bye as we prepared to enter the Colorado Center
for Reproductive Medicine to undergo my fourth attempt at
IVF. "Cameras off!" I had cheerily commanded. "Bye! Wish us
luck!"

Ann turned to me at the end of the clip.

"Your fans are expecting you to possibly announce that you're
pregnant," she began, "but you have other news."

"I do have other news," I replied. I was physically shaking,
trembling so hard that Ann would remark on it at the close of
our interview. "Through my attempt to get pregnant through
my third time of IVF, we sadly found out that I have early stages
of breast cancer," I said. Bill and I had prepared what I would say,
but I still had trouble getting the words out. "So, um, it's been
a shock, and a lot of people have been asking, 'we saw on the
season finale of your show that you went and got IVF, so what
happened, are you pregnant?' But sadly we've had to put that off
because of the news."

Ann deftly steered the interview to the message I had come
on air to deliver.

"How you found out is important here," she prodded.

"It is," I stressed. "I wasn't prepared to get a mammogram till
I was forty years old, like I'd been told." I recounted the scene

with Dr. Schoolcraft's nurse, and how I had gone "kicking and screaming" to get the test done, at thirty-six, with no history of breast cancer in my immediate family.

"Eighty-five percent of women diagnosed with breast cancer have no prior history," Ann interjected.

"I think a lot of us think we're invincible," I said. "Women these days are busier than ever, we're multitasking, we're taking care of a million people a day and a million things a day. But we have to start putting ourselves on the to-do list. A friend called me yesterday and said, 'I'm so sorry, can I do anything for you?' And I said, 'Honestly, don't feel sorry for me. Instead just call your doctor and make an appointment. *That's* what you can do for me.' I want women out there to know that, if you can just find it early, you could be okay. I will be okay because I found out early."

I vowed to keep trying to become a mother once I had recovered from the lumpectomy I had scheduled the following week and had completed treatment.

"I'm not going to give up. I want that baby, and what's amazing is that baby will have saved my life because I always said there was some master plan of why my IVFs didn't work and I never got pregnant. Now I truly believe God was looking out for me . . . because had I gotten pregnant, a few years down the line, I could be a lot sicker.

"So right now, I'm okay. So this baby will save my life."

It was the toughest six minutes and fifty-five seconds I had ever spent on television, and without a doubt in my heart, the most important.

But my brave public face was just that. When the cameras were off, I was a wreck. Reflecting later on the massive outpouring of public support I got after the *Today* appearance, I wrote in my new journal:

The world kept commending me for my strength and for being so strong and holding it all together but the truth is that was only for the cameras. Behind the scenes, I was sad and angry and vulnerable and a baby at times, literally kicking and screaming and sobbing uncontrollably. . . . It was a daily occurrence at least once a day but typically more like three times a day.

Bill appeared on the *Today* show again via satellite the day of my lumpectomy a week later. "Yeah, it went great!" he said. "We're very optimistic!"

Another forced smile and half-truth so we wouldn't spook the very people who wanted to root for us the most, the survivors and the women who suspected something might be wrong but were too scared to go have themselves checked. In truth, part of the prep for my lumpectomy involved a ninety-minute guided MRI, where the doctor used a needle to pinpoint the precise location of the mass to be removed. Since you're in the machine anyway, they routinely check the other breast as a precaution.

"I see something suspicious in the other breast," the doctor reported. "I'm going to take it out."

"Okay," I agreed. I wasn't at all alarmed; I already had discovered that one of the reasons mammograms are preferred over MRIs to detect breast cancer is because MRIs are *too* precise; they can pick up even a slight shadow that can end up being nothing to worry about, and are notorious for giving false positives for breast cancer.

Three days later, the pathology report came back. The margins were unclear on the small mass that had been removed. That meant it hadn't gone as "great" as we had hoped (and announced to the *Today* show viewers). There was a chance they didn't get it all. But it got even worse: The suspicious spot in my other breast was cancer, too.

Not only was I the complete low-risk anomaly for getting breast cancer in the first place, now I was among the rare minority—less than 5 percent—of women who get it in both breasts.

In the safe cocoon of my marriage, I met the new diagnosis with bitter resignation. My body was supposed to be my sanctuary, my temple, and now it was betraying me. Of course the lump was malignant. Why wouldn't it be? Bad news had been crashing over us like waves for a couple of years now, since my miscarriage, and I could feel us being swept farther and farther from shore. Now, if I got a strange tingle in my arm, or even a headache, I panicked. Bill would try to placate me.

"Honey, it's nothing."

"No, you don't understand. My body is breaking down, it's riddled with disease. Bill! I'm going to die!"

He would hold me and let me cry when I wanted to cry, and allow me to feel whatever I was feeling. The strength and wisdom it took to do that was incredible, an essential part of Bill and one of the reasons I fell in love with him. His own fear and confusion took a backseat as he gave me every ounce of his own emotional energy and unbroken faith. *Bill let me cry when I wanted to cry and let me feel sad*, I wrote in my journal. *You need to feel sadness to appreciate being happy.*

During our whole long journey toward parenthood, when it felt like we were locked in an endless loop of hope-crisis-disappointment, I used to ask Bill, "When's enough enough? Where's the finish line? What is the meaning of all of this?" And he would always give the same answer:

"You can have fear, or you can have faith."

I spent the last three months of 2011 interviewing celebrities on the red carpet for E!, gushing about what they were wearing or who they were dating. I was on camera every day. If I hadn't gone public with my cancer, work might have provided a welcome distraction. But I didn't have any emotional escape hatches, because everyone knew my story now. People would come up to me with sad eyes. I couldn't take sad eyes. I laid down the law with my glam squad right after the cancer diagnosis: "Guys, I just want you to know I'm still shallow," I announced. "Please don't get deep on me. I want to know who's dating who, and all the gossip, and to talk about clothes and lip gloss."

No one knew that I was going home to agonize with Bill over what to do next. The thought of chemotherapy and radiation terrified me. I was still young, and the repercussions of putting my body through that could last a lifetime. During my *Today* appearance, I had mentioned facing six and a half weeks of radiation, but the new cancer discovered during the lumpectomy had changed that. Even if I did chemo and radiation, there was no guarantee the cancer wouldn't come back. I could end up losing my breasts anyway. One afternoon, Bill got out a legal pad as we tried to figure out my next step. Bill regards a legal pad the way some people regard Ouija boards. Just ask, and it will answer. He calls it the ninety-nine-cent solution. It seemed perfectly reasonable to me that what to do about my boobs would come down to me, my husband, and a legal pad. Bill drew a column for pros and one for cons.

I went in for a double mastectomy on December 13, 2011.

The certainty I felt about wanting the cancer just cut away, an enemy vanquished, was coupled with my anxiety as a woman about how losing my breasts could potentially impact my marriage and my career. I was more afraid of what I would look like than Bill was, and Googling "mastectomy" and hitting the "Images" button made it worse. I called a friend who had undergone an elective double mastectomy in her twenties because she had the breast cancer gene, and bombarded her with questions about how disfigured I would be.

"Look, I'll just come over and show you," Lindsay offered, adding, "Bill should be there, too."

The three of us sat in our living room one night, and Lindsay opened her blouse.

"This is what it's like," she said. I was surprised. She looked really good. Surgical techniques had advanced significantly over the years, she explained, and the scars left were nowhere near as bad as they once were. Lots of women even underwent reconstructive surgery at the same time as the mastectomy, she added, and felt more attractive with their perky new boobs than with the ones they had lost. I felt heartened by Lindsay's candor and courage.

As I slipped under the anesthesia, I urged my surgeon to go on TV and tell women to get screened. When I woke up, according to Bill, I was convinced I was in a shopping mall. He captured my groggy explanation on a flip-cam and let that bit air on our show. We had opened something of a Pandora's box with this whole bare-all reality commitment, and it just felt like there was no closing the lid now. My journal captured what the camera never did:

> Before surgery, I started crying and shaking because the needle hurt so bad when they put it in my bony hand and because I was so terrified I wouldn't wake up. I soaked up Bill's image with my eyes and touched his skin, his face and his hair thinking it would be the last time I would ever do that. My parents began crying which only made me cry more. I endured an overwhelming amount of grief and sadness and can't help but tear up when I reflect back on that period in my life. It's still incredibly painful to think about.

Recovery was a bitch. I was no stranger to post-op misery, thanks to my scoliosis. This was almost worse. For ten days after the mastectomy, I had two drains on each side of my chest, pulling at me painfully whenever I moved. I am convinced that the only thing that got me through the pain during that recovery was the phrase "this too shall pass." I would repeat it over and over in my head and it would instantly relax me or at least give me the strength I needed to make it to the next day. I give that tip to women who are recovering from a mastectomy. It helps to know that the pain has a finish line. My mother hovered anxiously—it hurt so much to be putting her through this—and she seemed to hope that a homemade pasta bender would fix everything. She was livid when I told her Bill had taken off to Colorado to go skiing six days after my surgery.

"See, if you had married an Italian guy, that never would happen!" she scolded.

"Really? That's what you told your mom?" Bill protested when he Skyped me that night. He was underwhelmed by my lame cover story. The truth was, he was in Denver for a very different reason: when we got that first suspicious report from my mammogram, we had asked Dr. Schoolcraft what our options were for IVF, and he had ruled out any pregnancy for me because I would likely have to be on the anti-estrogen drug tamoxifen for five years to reduce the risk of recurrence.

By the time I got off tamoxifen, I would be over forty, and who knew if there would still be any chance of harvesting viable eggs?

"There's another possibility," Dr. Schoolcraft suggested. Had we ever considered a gestational surrogate? Surrogacy made me think of another woman having Bill's child and then reneging on the contract and fighting for custody while she collected checks for selling her story to the tabloids. (As I've explained, I watched the news way too much as a kid, and there was, in fact, a landmark court case like that that had played out in New Jersey back when I was in grade school.)

Gestational surrogacy was much less complicated. The baby would be 100 percent ours, biologically and legally. My egg, fertilized by Bill's sperm, would sublet the fertile womb of an unfathomably generous stranger.

Bill and I had, in fact, discussed the possibility of surrogacy long before Dr. Schoolcraft brought it up. Back then, it had been an option we quickly dismissed. We couldn't imagine letting a total stranger babysit our kid for nine months with no supervision. It involved placing too much blind trust in someone who would then hold all the power in this altogether weird, risky relationship. How carefully did agencies actually screen surrogates? What if they lied on their applications so they wouldn't get rejected by the program? You might never know if they had a history of mood disorders, or that suicide was prominent in their family tree. I knew someone whose seemingly sweet surrogate turned into a conniving shakedown artist who "needed" Gucci bags and other expensive "gifts" during her pregnancy. Surrogates are paid, and all their medical expenses covered, of course, but the stipends they receive are a modest fraction of the eighty thousand dollars that a single attempt typically costs. How do you screen someone to see if they test positive for altruism?

Having run out of other options had changed our perspective, though: "Let us go home and think about it," we told Dr. Schoolcraft.

Bill was more hesitant than I was, but we agreed that it wouldn't hurt to at least meet a couple of surrogates to see how we felt. We had frozen embryos stored away from previous retrievals, so we were halfway there already. Schoolcraft's office referred us to a reputable agency they had worked with before—a matchmaker that specialized in screening surrogates and introducing them to interested parents. We figured it would take a while, but through what could only have been God's intervention, we got a call within days: A surrogate who had already gone through the whole vetting process and was primed to go had suddenly become available because the couple she had been matched with had just gotten pregnant on their own. Did Bill and I want to meet her?

Out came the legal pad again. This time, I jotted down all the questions we would need to ask this woman before we decided whether to implant one of our precious embryos inside her. Delphine, we had learned, had come to America from France to be an au pair when she was nineteen. Now thirty-three and married, she was a businesswoman with two little boys of her own. I wrote my little introduction to this open-hearted stranger:

> *We are going to ask you specific questions about diet and such because we are very clean eaters who live a clean lifestyle, not to be annoying. We just want to make sure we choose someone who shares the same habits we do. When I was pregnant, I didn't have a sip of wine or bite of sushi, so we want someone who will conduct themselves like I would if I could be pregnant.*

I know, could I possibly sound more obnoxious?! But how do you cede control over the most precious, important thing in your life? I couldn't be a disinterested bystander to my own child's prenatal care. What if she ate junk food? Or drank coffee? I didn't want our baby sucking that up in the womb! Did she work out? Did she cook at home (as if I did a lot of that)? Was she open to eating only organic food, if we gave her a grocery allowance? Her history indicated asthma. How often did she use her inhaler? Did she eat anything with high-fructose corn syrup or, even worse, aspartame?

"Jeez, you ask thirty questions and never once do you ask if she smokes meth or does crack?" Bill observed, only half joking. He didn't care whether she did Pilates or not, and even though he's a health nut, too, he refused to see the possible correlation I did between gummy bears and brain damage. He was more worried that she was some fugitive French drug lord.

We flew to Colorado and met Delphine, who turned out to be a petite, pretty brunette whose husband accompanied her to our appointment and sat by her side on the sofa across from us while she calmly and graciously answered every question. I felt such an instant connection, I abandoned the interrogation somewhere after she acknowledged that yes, she did enjoy an occasional glass of wine. She was educated and intelligent. She confided that she had learned about surrogacy while she was an au pair, and had always wanted to become one because she thought it would be the most wonderful gift you could ever give someone. She had never heard of *Giuliana and Bill*, but said she would be willing to consider letting herself be filmed. We didn't consider it a deal breaker if she decided not to, of course. We had allowed cameras to record all kinds of intensely private moments—from Bill injecting me with hormones to the two of us learning we had lost the baby when I was pregnant—but we would gladly retreat and draw new boundaries.

We ended up signing the surrogacy contract, and as I recovered from my mastectomy, Bill flew to Denver to be there when our embryo was transferred into Delphine. It would be a couple of weeks before we found out if it took. We decided not to tell anyone, even our families, what we were doing. After signing with Delphine, though, I couldn't resist dropping a few hints to Monica. My sister urged me not to go through with it.

"You need to recover first, Jules. Why put more on your plate?" she said.

"Because it gives me hope," I had replied.

As Christmas neared, my spirits lifted. I was feeling strong enough to go shopping for gifts on the day before Christmas Eve dressed in a cute outfit topped by a jaunty fedora. I snapped a photo and texted it to my girlfriends with the happy update: "G's back!"

Bill and I were driving down Wilshire Boulevard when the phone rang. It was my oncologist with the pathology results from the mastectomy.

"Everything's good, right?" I asked, certain that it was. And then, there it was again. That ominous pause. I told myself I was just being dramatic. The worst was behind us. I had done the mastectomy. There was no bad news left to report . . . right?

"After reading the pathology, I'm going to recommend . . ." the doctor began. My brain raced ahead: *Crap, I'm going to be on tamoxifen for five years.*

". . . chemotherapy," he finished.

"What?" Then I just started screaming. "No, no, no! I'm not doing chemo!"

Bill took the phone from me, the doctor's words competing with my screams.

"She's HER-2 positive and HER-2 is a rare and aggressive form of cancer," the oncologist explained. I was hysterical. Bill finished the call and pulled the car over. I was a mess, pounding the dashboard. Once I regained some semblance of sanity, a second jolt of reality hit: *Oh my God, we might have a baby coming.* And there it was. If there is a way to feel your body mustering every ounce of strength it has, to feel the resolve in your very cells, that was it for me. They say that survival is a matter of fight or flight. Knowing I had even the possibility of a child coming into this world put me into fight mode. It was time to do the brave act again, and I didn't have much time to rehearse: Bill and I were booked to host Nivea's Times Square gala on New Year's Eve, culminating with a "kiss broadcast around the world" at midnight. We were still shell-shocked when we got to New York City.

On New Year's Eve, we slipped out of an interview to take a call from Dr. Schoolcraft. We were waiting to find out whether the embryo transfer with Delphine had been successful. I had no right to be hopeful. Why should I be? I gripped the phone with trembling hands.

"Congratulations, you're having a baby!" Dr. Schoolcraft told us.

Bill and I embraced for what felt like an hour, tears of joy streaming down our faces. When we kissed that New Year's for the world to see, it felt like we truly were starting anew, that 2012 was already blessed. Bill declared it "The Year of the Rancics."

We flew back to Denver for every doctor's visit Delphine had, and were overjoyed when the sonogram revealed that we were expecting a boy. I had always secretly wanted a little boy first. I felt awkward being a part of another woman's obstetrician appointments, and I would try to sit in the chair farthest away from the exam table, to give Delphine as much privacy as possible. I wanted to be involved but not annoying, winner of the Best Expectant Mom Award at the surrogate Emmys. We would spend time just hanging out with Delphine and her family whenever we were in Denver, and a genuine friendship took root. She would call or text me to let me know how the pregnancy was going—*baby's moving a lot today, you have a very active little boy coming!*

Alone, I opened my journal to express, once again, my most private fears:

Sad I can't be the pregnant one. The one to carry my son. What if he doesn't recognize the uterus he's growing in? I keep thinking he will be lonely, confused, scared and cold. Wondering where his mommy is. I find it's easier if I stop picturing him as a growing fetus and instead imagine him as a three-year-old. A gorgeous little towhead with floppy hair, chubby cheeks and irresistible dimples. Olive skin with big brown doe eyes and a button nose. I picture him acting rambunctiously, having a tantrum on an airplane as Bill and I pass him between our laps, and finally calming down after a DVD-player intervention complete with headphones and his favorite cartoon . . . These are the images I focus on to get me through the anticipation and nerves.

It's funny, when I look back at that, how my favorite fantasy of motherhood wasn't the classic image of cooing parents holding a gurgling baby or watching him sleep sweetly in his bassinette. Traveling with a cranky toddler probably rates up there near the top of parental nightmares, but there it was, my dream sequence. Maybe it had something to do with me not just wanting a baby at that point, but wanting to give life—life at full volume, full speed, life in full color. It also shows how I yearned to give back to my child what everyone I loved, and people I didn't even know, had given me so abundantly over the past few years: comfort and compassion.

Back home in L.A., Bill and I settled on a nautical theme for the nursery and painted it pale blue and beige. Bill loves the water, and thought it would be calming. We bought a glider, and a little sofa where we could sit and read stories to our son. We tried out names. I liked Rush, which was the name of a popular street in downtown Chicago. "Rush Rancic?" I tried it out loud. "That sounds like a porn star," Bill said. He was right. I put out a name I'd always liked: Landon. Landon was a private high school in D.C. with a lacrosse team full of hot guys. My girlfriends and I used to go to their practices and yell lewd things.

Wanna piece of public school girls?
NO! GO AWAY!
Yes, you do!
NO, WE SAID NO! GET OFF OUR PROPERTY!

After he pondered Landon Rancic for a few minutes, it dawned on Bill to ask what my deal was with the name. I explained the history. He looked at me with that unique expression he has that so perfectly reflects being dumbfounded and disgusted at the same time.

"Do you really think I'm going to name our child after a hot private school whose students you sexually harassed?"

We moved on. Another name we both loved was Luke, who was the middle son of Bill's sister Karen. Luke was the cool nephew who always liked hanging with us and appreciated my frankness when I helped the boys with their homework: "Okay, you'll never use this in your life, so just skip it. You do need to know how to spell. Math—just addition and subtraction. Anything else, fractions and shit, use the calculator. Or use your phone. They're tricking you guys, just like they fooled me." Our pet name for him was Luke the Duke.

"How about Duke?" I suggested. We both loved it. The middle name had always been a given—Edward, after Bill's beloved father and my father, Eduardo. But at the last minute, we made Edward his first name and Duke his middle name, leaving it up to him to decide which one he preferred later in life based on whatever career path he went down. Duke would be our son's NFL name, and Edward could be his CEO name. Done and done. Our happiness felt solid and true, something that could hold us up without shattering and drifting away.

Cancer is an algorithm: plug in the data, calculate the risks, spit out the options. I had a cancerous tumor and was HER-2 positive. That was the not-so-good news. The better news was that the cancer was extremely small—not billions of cells but a number you could actually count. If cancer is an invading army, I had the advantage that this one didn't seem to have sent out draft notices yet.

I'll admit it: Vanity was a factor in my first gut reaction to chemo. Avoid chemo. Chemo is ugly. No way was I going to lose my hair. My long blond cascade of waves had always been a signature part of my look. If I had to have cancer, I wasn't going to have Ugly Cancer. (Nor, for that matter, was I going to have

Playmate of the Year Cancer—when I had elected to have breast reconstruction at the same time as my mastectomy to avoid another surgery down the road, Bill was way more amused than he'll ever admit by the prospect of shopping for implants. It got a couple of cups less exciting when he realized it was my choice, not his!) I knew that if my hair fell out, it would grow back, and I knew Bill genuinely meant it when he said what I looked like didn't matter to him. He would love me bald as much as he loved me with hair. Hollywood is full of wigs and extensions; it's not like all of those full, glorious manes you see on the screen or in the pages of your favorite magazine actually belong to the stars whose heads they grace. I supplemented with my fair share of extensions, too. Fakery can be fabulous, I knew that. But losing my hair, becoming one of those courageous do-rag women, made my cancer too real, as if the disease had slipped its internal borders and stormed my "real" world on the outside. I thought I had outsmarted it by undergoing the mastectomy; one of the big "pros" on that legal pad had been that I wouldn't have to keep looking over my shoulder with mammograms every six months, or undergo round after round of chemo and radiation. I had wanted it to be over and done with.

But it wasn't, and now I had a new decision to make.

Early on in my diagnosis, Bill had tried to ban me from the Internet because I was obsessively reading every forum, website, blog, and article I could find about breast cancer, without rationally trying to separate fact from fiction, or educated experts from batshit nut jobs. I hadn't stopped, of course, but I had gotten a lot more discerning, and I was no longer just blindly searching for answers; I was learning how to ask questions, too. Remembering how close I came to an unnecessary blood transfusion the time my ovaries had overstimulated, we began making the rounds of cancer experts for a second, then a third opinion.

When my brother-in-law used his connections to get me in to see one of the country's top cancer doctors, I was deflated when he told me he would recommend chemo, too.

"Why?" I pressed.

He surprised me with his frank answer: Chemo was a crapshoot, and there was no way of knowing whether you would be one of the lucky ones. It wasn't a matter of me *needing* chemo, the way you might need an antibiotic, or need iron. Because HER-2 was so aggressive, chemo was *always* prescribed, regardless of the size of the cancer or any other factors in that algorithm. In my particular battle, it was starting to sound more like an offensive measure more than a defensive tactic.

"I want a number," I insisted. What were the odds of chemo changing my prognosis?

"I can't give you a number," the oncologist said.

"I want to know what the percentage is of it helping me," I tried again. I kept asking and asking, reframing the question any way I could. I was in journalist mode. Finally, the doctor saw I wasn't going to stop. He looked across at me and answered.

"Two percent."

I performed my own quick algorithm: Given the mastectomy, the small number of cancer cells found, and the early stage of the cancer, I had already been told that my survival rate was 94 percent. Going through chemo would bump that to 96 percent. What nobody could tell me, and no algorithm could predict, was what that extra 2 percent advantage would cost my body in the long run. Pumping toxins into your body affects the healthy parts of you as well as the diseased parts being targeted. Things like nerve damage, heart disease, and forgetfulness—known as "chemo brain"—are all common side effects. I was going to be a mother now. The unknown, for me, was far more terrifying than sacrificing that 2 percent margin. But why, if the pros were so tiny here, were the doctors pushing chemo so hard?

At the National Institutes of Health, I finally got that answer.

"No one is going to tell you not to do it," an expert we saw there confided. "Every doctor will tell you to do chemo because they don't want to be the one not to, and be wrong. Yes, this is HER-2, but it's so early and there are so few cells, and given your age, I can't imagine it ever coming back, but most every doctor will still prescribe you chemo and now it's up to you to decide what you want to do."

"I guess we'll call the doctor when we get back to L.A. and get you started," Bill said as we completed our educational tour of cancer experts. "I'm so sorry, honey."

"Or not," I said.

"What do you mean?" Bill asked. I took a deep breath.

"You heard the doctor," I went on. "I do chemo, or . . . I do nothing."

I just had a gut feeling. I had to ask and ask, and dig and dig, to get my odds. But now I had them, and going from 94 to 96 percent was not enough reason for me. When I put it like that, Bill tended to agree and, shifting into executive mode, assembled a personal "board of directors," as we called them, to guide us further. Our "board" consisted of the doctor who had given me the 2 percent figure as well as Dr. Devchand Paul, a top oncologist with the Rocky Mountain Cancer Centers; Dr. Richard Childs, a cancer researcher from the National Institutes of Health who at one time had treated Bill's father; and my surgeon, Dr. Armando Giuliano. Bill arranged for all four experts and the two of us to jump on a call together. Not an easy feat, but Bill is nothing if not persistent.

I took the call in my dressing room at E!, quietly listening to the experts discuss whether or not I should do chemo, and what my treatment should be now that we had all the pathology results in front of us. By the end of the hour-long conversation, a decision had been made: I would opt out of chemo and go on a five-year regimen of the oral cancer drug tamoxifen. The decision had been a unanimous one.

Shortly after, I embarked on night one of my 1,825 nights of tamoxifen. It took me twenty minutes of staring at that little white pill to finally muster up the courage to swallow it. I'm that girl who never has a headache and never takes medicine unless she absolutely has to, so to take that first pill, knowing there would be 1,824 pills to follow, was daunting, to say the least. I took it, and continued to reluctantly take it night after night, dreading the reported side effects it could carry: hot flashes, blood clots, and a decreased interest in sex, among others. Then a few months in, I was reaching for my pillbox and had a moment of enlightenment: *Don't think of this little white pill anymore as a cancer drug,* I coached myself. *Think of it as a vitamin that is nourishing your body and making you stronger and more vibrant.* And that was it: after that moment and still today, I actually look forward to taking my little white vitamin—a life lesson in the power of perception and how your attitude toward something can make all the difference in the world.

But the biggest difference of all in my world arrived six months later.

We flew to Colorado the last week of August as Delphine's due date approached. Bill and I tried to work off our nervous energy by hiking in the mountains until it was time to go to the hospital. As Delphine labored in the delivery room, Bill and I went stir-crazy in an exam room down the hall, giddy and goofy, blowing up gloves like balloons and generally acting like hyperactive idiots until a nurse knocked on the door and told us it was time. Our son was about to be born. We quietly slipped into the delivery room and stood at Delphine's head, crying and offering her encouragement while her husband and a nurse hovered at her feet and coached her. Everything happened so quickly. I heard the baby screaming and started crying hysterically. Bill cut the cord, and the next thing I knew, I was holding my newborn son against my chest, skin to skin, our hearts beating together at last. It was August 29, 2012, and Edward Duke Rancic had entered the world.

As I held our baby in that Denver delivery room, it was truly remarkable to think that in the course of eleven swift months, I had experienced the darkest day of my life and now, the brightest, most beautiful day of my life. I finally had what I wanted most, and every minute felt too precious to waste.

I sat down one night soon after to write my next chapter. I had been thinking about it off and on since I got married, but now it had taken on a new urgency. It was addressed to the top brass at E!

"This is the hardest letter I have ever written," I began, "but it's also the most meaningful. For the past 11 years, E! has been my home and there is no place I would have rather been. With that said, this letter is not one I would have ever imagined I would write. Not in my wildest dreams."

I went on to recount the feeling that the world had instantly crashed down around me when those four words—*you have breast cancer*—forced me to face my own mortality at thirty-six years young.

"I instantaneously began sobbing and couldn't stop sobbing while the doctor said words like mastectomy, radiation and chemotherapy," I wrote. "I could only think about dying. I was truly distraught. Once I picked myself up, what did I do? I got in my car and I drove to work . . . I went to the place I had gone every morning for the past 10 years. My home . . . E! I wiped my tears and walked through the newsroom at *E! News* like I did every day. I went to my office and instead of closing the door, I left it open and put a big smile on my face as if it was just another Tuesday. I walked onto the set of *E! News* with Ryan that day and made a promise to myself beforehand that I would be overly enthusiastic and peppy to overcompensate for the incomprehensible pain I was feeling inside. Not a single soul on that set or watching the monitors in the building had any hunch at all that I had just received the worst news of my life."

But I had gone back months later to watch the tape of that episode, and what I saw broke my heart.

"I had expected to see some sign of duress, a sign of a woman trying to hide a painful secret," I wrote my bosses. "Instead, I witnessed the complete opposite. And it made me realize I have always put my job first. Even in the most strained moment of my life.

"After 11 years at *E! News*, I have decided to resign as lead anchor. This has been a difficult decision for me to make but one that will allow me to spend more time with my growing family and to devote more time to my charitable efforts, particularly those that focus on women battling breast cancer."

I slipped it into my handbag to drop on the desk of the E! president the next morning.

It was time to leave on top and find my purpose in life.

chapter eleven

I couldn't believe I was quitting my job. My dream job, no less. It felt strange to think of myself not being at E!, no longer part of the daily adrenaline rush of a newsroom covering the ever-shifting landscape of pop culture. What would my life feel like without all these amazing people who filled my working hours? Was I really cut out to be the suburban stay-at-home wife and mother I liked to imagine myself becoming, or would that fantasy get snuffed out with my first snowbound week of a Midwestern winter? Who was going to gossip with me in the real world about Kim Kardashian's latest selfie with the kind of insider knowledge Ryan Seacrest provided? Or offer up the kind of hilarious wisdom that only Joan Rivers could? If I retreated from the public eye, would I lose that treasured connection with fans whose prayers had carried me through more dark tunnels than they could possibly know?

On the other hand, I felt excited and relieved that I was taking this drastic step.

My crazy career simply never allowed me to pour 100 percent of myself into taking care of my family or myself. Whatever I'm doing, I want to be all in, fully present. The last few years had been so busy, juggling four shows as well as my endorsements and business ventures. Whenever I left the office and walked through my front door at home, my heart would be singing, "I'm all yours now!" to my family, but in truth, there wasn't nearly as much of me left to give my son and my husband as I wanted, or as they needed. And I needed more of them, too, to nurture myself. Walking away from Hollywood was a choice I was ready to make. Pam read the draft of my resignation later and urged me not to deliver it. "Are you sure you want to do this?" she asked, as both my manager and friend of nearly twenty years. "Sleep on it." I did, then went back and told her my decision was still the same. "Okay," Pam said. "I'll set up a meeting." Pam, my agent, Nancy, and my lawyer would go with me to tell my bosses I would not be staying when my contract was up in a year and a half. I owed it to them to deliver the news in person. I didn't know how I was going to be able to hold it together. The little girl who had rehearsed every moment of her dream career back in her pink Laura Ashley bedroom had never thought to practice saying good-bye.

Ted Harbert had been promoted by our parent company to chairman of NBC, and Suzanne Kolb was E!'s president at the time. "What brings you all here?" she asked as our respective teams settled in. Tears were already stinging my eyes, and I momentarily regretted not just taking the chicken's way out and sending the resignation letter via e-mail. My agent took the lead, conveying my gratitude for the wonderful years I had spent at E! before telling Suzanne that I had decided it was time to leave. The new baby, my recovery from the mastectomy, and a commuter marriage were too much to juggle. I braced myself for the next part, where the E! brass would thank me, wish me luck, and tell me they'd make arrangements for me to clear out my dressing room and turn in my parking pass. Their response caught me by surprise.

Hold on, hold on, hold on! What can we do to make your life better? What would make it easier for you?

"Ummm, well . . . I haven't thought about that," I admitted. I had seen this as an all-or-nothing situation.

Suzanne and the other executives urged me to go figure out if there was a scenario that might entice me to stay. I left the office and called Bill.

"So that didn't go quite like I thought it was going to go," I said, filling him in on what had just happened. He was looking forward to both of us living full time in Chicago even more than I was, and had been waiting several years for me to deliver on my pre-engagement promise that we would spend no more than one year in L.A.

"Okay, that's interesting," he said neutrally. Hating L.A. was the third character on our reality show, and every time my contract had come up, we would discuss whether I should renew it. Our conclusion had always been "not yet." It is the kind of job people kill for in Hollywood. Besides, Bill had TV gigs in L.A., too, hosting the newsmagazine *America Now* opposite Leeza Gibbons, and going on to do a Food Network show. But with the baby and my health to consider, the decision to fold our tent and leave had seemed crystal clear this time.

Bill and I met with my managers the next day in our backyard to analyze this latest twist. I knew his philosophy as a businessman was that "everything has its price," but what was ours? I couldn't pay to get a clone of myself, so living in both L.A. and Chicago full time was an impossibility. What if I could spend more time in Chicago, though, short of moving there altogether? We sketched out a proposal that would allow me to occasionally shoot *E! News* from a studio in the Windy City. I would also be taking vacation and personal days—no more going for eight or ten years without asking for time off! There's a difference between dedication and blind devotion. Like most career women, I had fallen into the habit of overcompensating. We're always considered less reliable than men, because our lives seem so much messier—we're the ones who miss an important business meeting when the school nurse tells us to come pick up a feverish child, we're the ones who get pregnant and go on maternity leave, or take personal time when someone in our family needs us. We're insecure about our jobs because anyone could swoop in and snatch them away from our uncertain grasp.

Even as I was recovering from my double mastectomy, my responsibility to *E! News* had overshadowed my sense of responsibility to myself, and I went back on air just two weeks after surgery. It was a mistake. My body had suffered major trauma, and I did not really have the physical or emotional reserves to jump right back onto the treadmill, full speed ahead. I cried out in pain my first day back at work when my stylist lifted my arms over my head so I could slip into a dress. On day two I was relieved when she wheeled in a rack of new clothes—nothing but button-up shirts I could wear with pants or skirts. I worried whether I looked different. I needed more time than I allowed myself to heal. But so many fans had reached out, always telling me I was so brave. I couldn't let them down. I felt like I needed to show myself as soon as possible. *See? I'm fine, I'm okay, nothing to worry about!* It was what Brave Giuliana would do, and as much as I longed to, I couldn't banish her yet. Maybe I needed the illusion as much as my audience did.

E! generously agreed to let me spend ten weeks a year away from set, either on vacation or shooting from Chicago—enough to make Bill and me feel we could manage the back-and-forth a while longer. But it wasn't just how much time I would spend working that needed some adjustment.

Battling cancer and becoming a mother at the same time changed not only how I looked at the world, but how I moved through it. There wasn't room in my life anymore for cynicism or selfishness. Having purpose moved into the space that ambition had long inhabited, and now I consulted God more often than agents.

The time had also come to face the fact that anxiety had gained the upper hand in my lifelong battle against unseen disaster. Specifically, my phobia about flying. My life was revolving around it, and if anything, it was getting worse, not better.

Even my joy over Duke's birth had been overshadowed by my certainty that we would all die in the private plane Bill had chartered from a friend to take the three of us from Denver to Chicago, where we planned to introduce the baby to family and spend a few weeks relaxing and enjoying the beautiful summer on the shores of Lake Michigan.

We had reserved two private suites at the medical center where Duke was born—one on the maternity wing for Delphine, and another two rooms down the hall for us. We were able to bring Duke back with us to our suite right after he was cleaned up and pronounced healthy by the medical team. Bill and I gave him his first bath and celebrated parenthood over a steak and lobster dinner. We would spend one more day in Denver, then board the small plane for the two-hour flight to Illinois. The thought of taking my newborn on a plane increased my fear of flying a thousand fold. I frantically began researching how much it would cost to charter a tour bus, instead. One that no rock bands, sports teams, or bachelor parties had ever been inside. I would consider Michael Bublé's bus, if he had one. He seemed clean and trustworthy. Or Gwen Stefani. Yes! Gwen Stefani would be perfect: I had interviewed her before,

and she was lovely. Plus she was a mom, too! She would understand. If she had a bus, it probably already had a changing
table, bottle sterilizer, air purifiers, and blackout shades on the
windows, right? I scrolled through the contacts on my phone,
only to find that I had three different numbers for Paris Hilton
(definitely not her bus) but none for Gwen. Okay, so scrap that.
I would just have to be very specific with the charter company
about what kind of bus I wanted to rent: a virgin bus. One that
no one had ever smoked in. Or sneezed in. And what about
the drivers? Were they polygraphed and run through Interpol's
global databank of criminals, or at least Googled to make sure
they hadn't been the subject of a *48 Hours* mystery? Barring that,
did we still have that list of questions we'd asked Delphine before
choosing her? Maybe I could just use those to weed out sketchy
bus drivers, if I took out any uterus references. Bill thought the
whole bus idea was completely nutso, and we argued about it
nonstop. Finally, we agreed to let the baby's doctor settle the
transportation debate. "Sixteen hours on a bus versus two hours
on a plane?" he said. "Hands down, the plane. You want to get
there the quickest and safest way possible." I was so anxious the
day of our flight that I insisted we stop for a quick drink first,
even though it was only eleven a.m.

"That's nice, Mommy's already a drinker," Bill remarked sar-
castically to Duke.

"Bill, I am a bigger problem to you sober than drunk once we
get on that plane," I reminded him.

The flight was fine, and we were given a hero's welcome in
Chicago, where our friends and family had decorated the hangar
with balloons and signs welcoming Duke home. Having long
since sold the cavernous, painfully empty house in Hinsdale, we
had settled into a two-bedroom suite at a nice hotel for the next
few weeks, and they had set up a little nursery for us.

Overjoyed as I was to finally have the baby I had wanted for so long, I was confused when a dark cloud settled over me. It came as a shock when I found myself struggling with many of the classic symptoms of postpartum depression, even though I hadn't physically given birth. I spent my first week of mother-hood in a weird funk, not bothering to shower or change out of my white robe, and tugged down into a suffocating quicksand of sad emotions—regret, guilt, dread. Why did I bring some-one into this crazy world? What was I thinking? How selfish I had been! I kept looking at my tiny son and weeping over how helpless he was, how pure and innocent. There was so much he would have to learn, and so much evil out there he would have to avoid or outrun!

"Honey, it's okay, you're going to be stressed out. It's perfectly natural," Bill comforted me. He had seen his sisters go through this. "You're doing a great job."

The fear consuming me was very much like the paranoia I used to feel as a latchkey kid watching the evening news night after night back in Bethesda, except now I felt the panic not for myself, but for my child. I kept mentally hitting the fast-forward button, weeping over the everyday hurdles of an ordinary life: What if Duke got sick? What if bullies picked on him at the playground? What if he got drunk with his high school buddies and got behind the wheel of a car? What if his wife left him for his best friend? What if he got laid off and started drinking too much? What if he grew old and broke his hip? How could I ever protect him from a life's worth of pain? One day, the fear just overtook me, smashing me like blown glass into a million shards. I lay on the floor in my robe, sobbing my eyes out, feel-ing totally unworthy of this amazing gift God had entrusted me with. *I can't be a mom!*

My feelings of inadequacy weren't helped by the night nanny we had lined up to help take care of Duke. Cynthia was a Jamai-can nurse who had worked for my sister occasionally and came highly recommended. We flew her to Chicago, and the two of us immediately became locked in passive-aggressive warfare. I wasn't a natural at the mechanics of caring for a baby—I was the youngest in my family and had zero experience with infants—and Cynthia picked up on my uncertainty and started tsk-tsking and correcting everything I did. I appreciated the necessary tutorials, like how to properly swaddle the baby, but I felt my hackles rise over the constant minor adjustments. Really? Was every single bottle a little too warm or a little too cold, every single diaper I changed a little too snug or a little too loose?

The first night, as I put Duke to bed, Cynthia made the first of her many pronouncements: "Miss G, we are going to need to get a white noise machine, trust me."

"What is that?" I asked.

"Oh, it will make him sleep better," she promised. Insomnia didn't seem to be a problem for Duke, but I went along with the nanny's white noise plan.

It turned out to be a stupid machine going SSSSHH-HSHSHSHHSHSHSHSHS all night long. How are you supposed to have sweet little baby dreams with this annoying soundtrack playing all night? I would sneak in and turn it off. Cynthia would turn it back on. I decided it was going to cause brain damage, or make him grow up thinking extraterrestrials were trying to contact him. He would be the kid wearing a homemade foil receiver on his head to third grade. I went Googling in search of scientific proof of the white-noise menace to wave in Cynthia's face. There wasn't any. I knew why she wanted it—it was so she could make phone calls, take showers, and move around the room while on night duty without waking Duke up. But Duke himself didn't need it, and I resented her insisting he did. I thought about flinging the thing out the window and pretending it had fallen, but I was a little afraid of Cynthia and sure she would find out. I couldn't just throw it away because she probably had Dumpster informants. I asked our doctor if he would tell her it was bad for the baby.

"I can tell her that you feel it's bad for the baby and don't want her to use it," he offered.

"No, she can't know it's me!" I said. I had fallen into that mommy trap of denial, where the more you despise your nanny, the nicer you are to her. How do they do that? I finally gave up. Cynthia went on to a new job four months later, but the noise machine lasted longer. I still use it. I need to have a life when he's sleeping, and grab a shower or call my friends, but most important, we travel so much with Duke that the sound machine serves as a constant no matter where we go, which is comforting to the little guy. It doesn't seem to have affected Duke's brain. Mine, I'm not so sure about.

Comfort in numbers is what pulled me up off the floor from my particular strain of baby blues; I started feeling better when it registered that every other mom I spoke to had felt the exact same way, and every article and book I read by or about new mothers confirmed it. The despair lifted after a month or two, but the sheer terror of motherhood held fast. I had more than thirty years' experience being the world's biggest scaredy-cat, and now I was responsible for this vulnerable little person whose life was more precious to me than my own. The stress of being on live TV was a walk in the park next to the stress of being home alone all day with a baby.

Even as Duke grew into a healthy, resilient toddler, I remained on constant alert for all the potential dangers surrounding him. I'm no longer merely paranoid; I'm proactive. What scares me most about motherhood? Everything!!! There isn't a thing that doesn't scare the shit out of me or keep me up at night. Every day and every moment, I question if what I'm doing is right as far as raising Duke. Am I an unfit mother if I feed him pretzels instead of kale chips, or find myself cracking up instead of cracking down when he does something naughty? Will I be able to fake appropriate shock if a preschool teacher calls us in to complain that Duke is swearing in two languages? I look not twice or three times before crossing the street with Duke. Oh, no! I look four times, then I keep looking left and right and forward and behind me as I am walking across the street, my head and eyes in constant motion. If I'm not worrying that a car is going to hit his stroller in the street, then I'm imagining a bus jumping the curb and hitting him while we are walking peacefully down the sidewalk. Or a wild animal getting out of its cage the one day we are at the zoo. When we go to a trampoline park, I get nervous that he's going to snap his neck from an overly aggressive jump and end up paralyzed from the waist down for the rest of his life. Or that he's going to stick his hands in a fan at the car dealership service center and lose his fingers. I must muster up about twenty crazy and highly unlikely scenarios a day, and even though I know it's illogical and unhealthy and unproductive to think this way, I can't help it, and I'm accustomed to negotiating my life around my ever-present worries.

Now that I was a mother, I became more sensitive to the celebrities I interviewed, and their pain. There was no conscious decision to approach things differently. Being diagnosed with cancer and having the baby, experiencing those extremes of despair and triumph on top of each other, had shifted my priorities and buffed away some of the jagged edges. I found myself wanting to dive deeper in my interviews and connect with my subjects on a level that was raw and real. I was more attuned to people's vulnerability than I had let myself be before.

I was even second-guessing my weekly appearance on *Fash-*

ion Police with Joan. Was the show too mean? "The fashion is secondary," Joan would argue when doubters posed that question. "This is *comedy*." Still, I found randomly criticizing people too difficult—even the celebs I privately regarded with some disdain. Paris Hilton, for example. I considered anything Paris was wearing fair game for a well-deserved zinger or two, but I couldn't attack her personally, even though she had tried to have me fired once over a question she didn't comprehend when I interviewed her on the red carpet. (I officially apologize to the world for helping to launch the Paris Hilton celebrity juggernaut when I was made managing editor at *E! News.* Surely there was another way to boost ratings . . .) My conflicting feelings about *Fashion Police* reminded me how fickle perspective can be, and how it ultimately impacts every interview I do. How do you get someone who's used to performing in movies or onstage for a living to be authentic? I was eager to explore this deeper, and experiment with my platform. Demi Lovato provided the perfect opportunity.

About five weeks after my mastectomy, I sat down to interview Demi for a half-hour special. Lovato had experienced depression, an eating disorder, and self-harm before going into rehab after withdrawing from the Jonas Brothers tour. Word was, she had decided to enter treatment after punching a female backup dancer, which led to an intervention by her management and her family. She took "100 percent, full responsibility" for the incident. She was owning her mistakes and issues, and was hoping to serve as an inspiration to other young women. So I was surprised and irritated when the publicist who sat in on the session kept interrupting the interview and saying, "too personal." I had not been told anything was off-limits. I couldn't figure out why they were being so cagey, even with innocuous questions like how Demi and her old roommates she once lived with when she moved to L.A. divvied up the household bills, like groceries and electricity. "You're getting too personal!" the publicist snapped again. *I asked who paid the cable bill, not her account number, asshole,* I silently seethed.

I later learned that Demi was still struggling with her demons and had, in fact, moved herself into a sober living facility right before the interview. I get it that it's the publicist's job to be the bad guy so the star isn't put in an unflattering light by saying "no comment," but it was troubling to think that a young celebrity with an important story to share couldn't because handlers around her considered it too risky. I wasn't Geraldo Rivera attempting an ambush interview. I *know* how hard it is to let the world see you at your most desperate, how scary it is to share the intimate details of your life in case it can spare even one stranger out there the same anguish you've endured. And I know firsthand that making that connection isn't just altruistic—it's therapeutic, and even miraculous. If Bill and I had kept our struggles with infertility private, I never would have had people approach me and urge me to seek out Dr. Schoolcraft because he had helped them have babies.

As I was pondering all this, the idea for *Beyond Candid* suddenly popped into my head. I wanted a more intimate platform for in-depth celebrity interviews. I envisioned a setting that was safe and comfortable—their own homes, where we could kick our feet up and chat. There would be no publicists cutting in, and nothing would be off-limits. If someone didn't want to answer a question, fine, just tell me yourself. The network loved the idea, and I began lining up guests. When former Disney kid Amanda Bynes started to implode in very public fashion, I reached out to her people and began lobbying hard for her to tell her story on *Beyond Candid*. I promised empathy and a safe place. She was receptive, but before the final details could get worked out, she suffered another episode and ended up involuntarily committed to a psychiatric ward. All I could do then was keep praying for her.

When I went back to Demi Lovato to ask her to do *Beyond Candid*, she readily agreed, and I interviewed her this time in her own living room, where we sat under comfy throws in front of her fireplace. I told my team I wanted the room clear: only the camera people allowed, no distractions, and no one in our sight line. "If the tape runs out, don't stop the interview, just put in another tape and if we miss something, we miss something," I instructed. I turned to Demi. "Demi, if you don't want to answer something, just tell me. I'm cool with it. I'll move on." She shook her head.

"You know what? Ask me whatever you want. I think this is a really good platform to get an important message out to a lot of young women." The difference was like night and day. She opened up and talked all about cutting herself, bulimia, depression. The interview was amazing and got picked up all over the world.

Motherhood didn't just make me mush, though: it made me fiercer than I've ever been, too. When I got caught in the social media war between LeAnn Rimes and her new husband's ex, Brandi Glanville, shit got real.

It started back in the summer of 2011, when Bill and I were opening our first restaurant, RPM Italian, in Chicago. A reporter asked me which celebrity I would most love to feed at RPM, and I said LeAnn, because she looked a little thin, what with all the stress in her life. She and Eddie Cibrian had carried on a very public adulterous affair before divorcing their respective spouses and getting married a couple of months earlier. LeAnn fired back at me on Twitter, and Brandi chalked me up as being on Team Brandi. LeAnn's representative left a message one day with the singer's number, saying she'd like me to text or call her. I ended up texting her. "We should get together," she answered back. "This is so crazy!" We met for drinks and ended up talking about how people love to tear others apart over their weight. Too skinny or too fat—it doesn't matter which. Body size is a hot-button topic in our society, and people in the public eye, especially, are considered fair game to attack.

I ended up interviewing LeAnn for *Beyond Candid*. She broke down in tears when talking about her affair with Eddie and the firestorm of public criticism that followed, saying she had never known such pain, nor had she meant to cause any. I found myself not as quick to disapprove of her behavior as I had been. I mentioned this on an episode of *Fashion Police* when we were discussing LeAnn frolicking in a bikini on a beach with Eddie, and her home-wrecker reputation came up again.

"I used to totally poo-poo this relationship, then I watched his ex-wife on *The Real Housewives of Beverly Hills*. She is batshit *crazy!*"

Next thing I heard, Brandi was tweeting away about me. "Hopefully her man doesn't leave her and give her surrogate baby to a bonus wife," she wrote.

Surrogate baby? Not only was I personally offended, but I was offended on behalf of all the other women who had to rely on surrogacy to have a child and saw it as a gift, not something to be ashamed of or held up for public ridicule. I did exactly what I knew full well would make crazy Brandi even crazier: I didn't respond, even though she was trying and trying to get me to react. Respond to a D-lister, and you become a D-lister. Brandi's celebrity exists largely within her own twittersphere, and is based almost entirely on her feuds with LeAnn or fellow Housewives. I had no intention of entering her unhappy little world, but months later, I was on *Watch What Happens Live* with Andy

Cohen, and he read this tweet out of nowhere from a viewer wondering if I had cleared things up with Brandi.

"If she ever mentions my baby again, I'll cut her," I said without hesitation.

Having a child puts the future of our own reality show into question. Neither Bill nor I want to raise an attention-seeking brat, and Duke deserves his own life without the public scrutiny that Mommy and Daddy signed up for. Besides, we ask ourselves all the time, what more do we have that anyone would want to watch? We've already shared so much. And the one hard-and-fast rule we have about our reality show is that it remain real.

Authentic is one of those words people like to throw around a lot, but after you've spent a decade or two in Hollywood, you genuinely appreciate it on the rare occasion that you see it. After thousands of celebrity interviews, party chats, and red carpet drive-bys over the years, my admiration for the stars who are genuine grows deeper by the day, especially when I've had the opportunity to watch them evolve over the years. Some, like Dakota and Elle Fanning, I first met as child stars, and now they're beautiful young women every bit as sweet and unspoiled as they were back when a seven-year-old Dakota invited me to color with her. I wish I could bottle what they have and spritz it on some emerging young celebrities. Ariana Grande has made several headlines for her reported junior diva moves. I got my own dose of the twenty-one-year-old new-comer when I was on the red carpet for the Grammy Awards and was told by producers that Ariana was on her way to my position for an interview. I always stand on the same side at every red carpet event, and a big red X is placed on the spot next to me so the celebrity knows exactly where to stand. Suddenly, Ariana and her team came flying over to me, and the next thing I knew, she had jumped into my spot. When my floor director told the publicist to please have Ariana move over and stand on the X, the publicist angrily issued an ultimatum: Either she stands where she is, or she doesn't do the interview.

I was flabbergasted by the exchange, and shot Ariana a conspiratorial look as if to say "How crazy is this?" She feigned ignorance, looked at me with those Bambi eyes, smiled, and didn't budge. I was about to say, "Fine. Then we are pulling the interview, screw you!" but everything was happening so quickly, and the next thing I knew, the red light was on, we were live in more than one hundred countries, and Ariana had successfully planted herself with her preferred left side facing the camera. (Which, BTW, would be the side I fought for thirteen years to get. Earn your stripes, girl.) If Mariah Carey wants to shove me off the platform, I'll take the face-plant and gladly interview her from the floor.

Authentic doesn't mean perfect: Probably my worst interview ever was with the late Gary Coleman, the four-foot-eight actor best known for his childhood role as Arnold on the hit sitcom *Diff'rent Strokes*, which I had loved as a kid. In 2003, Coleman, then thirty-five, tossed his hat in the ring to run for governor of California in a recall election that Arnold Schwarzenegger ended up winning. But Gary, may he rest in peace, was kinda out of his fucking mind. He was seriously committed to winning, even though his candidacy had been sponsored as a satirical gesture by an alternative weekly newspaper in Oakland and his platform pretty much amounted to "why not me?" When we sat down for our one-on-one, I immediately asked if he really thought he could win:

"Yes, I do," he said.

Hate me if you must, but I couldn't resist, and responded with a not-bad imitation of his famous catchphrase from *Diff'rent Strokes*:

"What'chu talkin' 'bout, Gary?"

I thought he might roll his eyes, at the most. Obviously he'd heard the same cheesy joke fourteen jillion times over the years. But I guess mine was the tipping point.

"Oh, man! Really? That's it!" Gary ripped off his microphone and stormed off.

"I was kidding!" I called after him. "That was a joke! Sit down!"

"No!" Gary pouted.

"Are you serious right now?" I asked. This had to be a great act, joke on me. Gary was glowering.

"Do I look serious?" he said. End of interview.

His tantrum was egomaniacal, unprofessional, and 110 percent stupid, but I grudgingly had to give him some props. Gary's political ambitions may have been dubious, but he let his true self show that day, and in the end, I had to salute his crazy flag.

Angelina Jolie is one star whose authenticity I find inspirational. Keep in mind, she was my first major celeb interview from my short-lived starter job at LOAD, so I've watched her evolve from wild child to UN goodwill ambassador, mother, wife, and now director and producer. Interviewing her for the Christmas 2014 release of *Unbroken*, her second movie behind the camera as producer and director, I could see that Angelina had changed yet again. There was a difference in her eyes, a soulfulness I had never felt before from her. This woman who could have any—literally, *any*—movie role she wanted in the world, chose instead to follow her own heart instead of public and industry expectations, and stepped off the big screen.

Sitting across from her, no longer an ingénue but a woman just shy of forty, I had never seen Angelina look so beautiful.

She radiated a sense of joy and accomplishment that no makeup, lighting, or camera angle could ever create. I envied her courage to reach beyond people's expectations of her and take charge not of a single role, but of the whole epic story of one prisoner of war's incredible survival. When you've spent so much time in front of the camera, being taken seriously when you step behind it is a challenge, far more so for actresses than actors.

Whenever I hint at my own hopes of expanding my producer role, the three Fs—my friends, family, and fans—shoot the idea down. Why wouldn't I want to be on TV? Was I being forced off? Was I secretly being fired for someone younger? To which I have three responses:

1. Because I've done it so long, I know it so well, and I'm eager to apply all that experience to see some of my own ideas for shows through from inception to the TV screen.
2. No, I have more contract extensions than hair extensions.
3. Isn't there more to life than reporting the "breaking news" that Jennifer Lawrence is single again?

Which brings me to Joan.

Joan would fly in from New York every Wednesday afternoon, then go to Melissa's house to eat something, look at our binder full of pictures for that week's *Fashion Police* show, and start writing jokes until she went to bed. She'd be up again at 3:30 in the morning and at E! an hour later, then in hair and makeup by 5:30. I would come in and see her sitting on the set by herself with the teleprompter girl, going over every line, making the tiniest adjustments until every word was perfect. This was a seventy-eight-year-old woman staying on top of pop culture. She had to know who Kesha was and why Justin Bieber was in the gossip columns again. She was the only grandmother on earth who knew the difference between Demi Lovato and

Demi Moore. Joan always did her homework. We'd all go on set at 8:30 and roll the cameras at 9:00. We'd wrap at noon, and Joan would go straight to LAX for her flight back to New York. Sometimes she would land at JFK and get in a town car to drive to Philadelphia to do QVC, or jump on another plane to go on a book tour, or fly to London to do a stand-up show. Joan was on fire 24/7. She was unstoppable.

I never once saw Joan yawn or say she was tired.

About every fifth show, she'd have issues with her voice.

"Joan, you have to get some rest," I'd scold her.

"Stop, I'm good!" she'd rasp. She had her tea and her lozenges, and she would soldier on. I remember venting to her when my father, at seventy-five, signed a ten-year lease to open a new tailor shop. "It's ridiculous!" I complained.

"No, it's not," Joan replied. "If you love what you do, why would you stop? He enjoys it. Just support it."

She would walk onto set with a huge basket full of mini chocolate bars to give to our small studio audience and spend fifteen minutes treating them to a one-woman show, even though we had a warm-up guy. She'd answer any question a fan wanted to ask. She couldn't take a compliment. If I complimented her hair, she'd shrug it off and say it was extensions. Credit was always deflected to her glam squad or stylists for perfect makeup or a beautiful outfit. This went on for years. The very last time I saw her, just two days before she went in for routine throat surgery and never woke up, I remember Joan had her hair clipped back prettily on one side.

"Joan, you look beautiful today," George remarked. "Giuliana, doesn't Joan look beautiful?"

"Yeah, you really do. You look beautiful, Joan," I agreed. I waited a few seconds for her self-deprecating reply, thinking to myself, *here it comes*!

"Thank you," she said and gave me a big, beautiful smile.

That day, we were having this conversation on set about tragic deaths in Hollywood. We were talking about actor Paul Walker's car crash the previous winter, and how sad and shocking his sudden death had been. Everyone was still reeling from Robin Williams's suicide just the week before, followed the very next day by the death of screen legend Lauren Bacall.

"We're so lucky, knock wood," Joan said. "We're all so lucky. Never forget how lucky we are. We get to work with people we like. We genuinely love each other, not that fake Hollywood shit." We agreed with her. We always did. It wasn't ass-kissing. She was just right, and whenever we all had this sense of a shared vibe or feeling, Joan had this way of speaking up and giving voice to it. That sort of sixth sense is what made her such an amazing comedienne. She could, and would, say what everyone else was thinking.

She finished her work in L.A, then went to New York as usual. That night, she did a book-signing event with a Q and A. The following night, it was an hour-long stand-up show. The next morning, she went in for her throat procedure. I was selling my clothing line live on HSN in Tampa. Lisa, our *Fashion Police* executive producer, kept calling and calling, but I didn't have my phone on the air with me. As I was walking off the HSN set, one of the show handlers approached me.

"Um, a couple of developments," she stammered. "Joan Rivers is in a coma."

"What?" My knees gave out and I hit the floor. I saw all the missed calls on my phone, and knew it had to be true. I got through to Lisa but was too hysterical to talk.

"Calm down! Giuliana, you need to calm down!" Lisa told me in her tough New York accent. "She's in the hospital. Melissa is flying to New York with her son right now."

I dialed Melissa, frantic for news. She picked up and told me she was still en route.

"Melissa, she has to be okay," I cried.

"We don't know. We just don't know," she answered. She sounded stoic but stunned. I knew she was holding it together for her son. Melissa and Cooper were Joan's life; the three of them were a tight little family. Joan would know they were there no matter how deep the coma, and she would fight like hell to stay with them, I told myself.

I was a mess. I called George, and he was crying, too. Thus began what-the-fuck-is-going-on week. If that sounds irreverent, I promise you Joan would have approved.

Suzanne had been E! president for two years, and her impending exit was widely rumored as the parent company underwent a management overhaul. As the star of one of her biggest hits clung to life, she was determined to own the story, and I ended up being treated like a "get" instead of an anchor, a coworker, and, most important, a friend of thirteen years to the woman our mutual boss was now badgering me to cover. I was surprised and hurt by how shockingly insensitive my bosses were being. I kept thinking I could reason with them. No, I wouldn't do a special, or be interviewed for one. Joan was going to make it. I wanted to get to New York and be there for her. Melissa and I had been texting back and forth when Melissa had any updates, and she was determined to remain positive. "Praying," I texted her, "love you."

"Keep praying," she wrote back.

Duke's second birthday was August 29, the day after Joan went into cardiac arrest while undergoing the endoscopy at her doctor's office. I had made plans with E! long before to shoot the news from Chicago so I could spend the special day with family. Bill and the baby were already there, and I needed to be with them now more than ever. The network wanted me back on our set in L.A. immediately, but I stood firm, and they finally relented.

Then we got a glimmer of hopeful news: On Sunday, the doctors would know a lot more about Joan's prognosis. They were going to start bringing her out of the medically induced coma to see if there was brain damage. Kelly, George, and I were still talking and crying together every day, and I was upset when they didn't latch on to this new development with the same optimism I did. "Guys, keep praying. Keep visualizing her waking up," I urged. I was on my knees praying for Joan every night before bed, and I convinced myself that Sunday was going to bring us the miracle we all wanted so badly.

On Sunday, E! called and told me I had to be on set in L.A. the next day.

"That doesn't make sense!" I protested. "I'm an hour from New York, where Joan is. I should report from there."

"No," I was told. "There may not be a good outcome and if she gets worse, we want our main anchor in L.A. fronting the story. We want you on set in L.A." They wanted the gravitas our big, glossy set would convey.

I dug in my heels again. "I have to go see Joan and Melissa," I insisted.

"This is how it's going to work—" one of the executives started to argue.

"No! *This* is how it's going to work," I yelled back. "I am going to New York. I'm not coming back to L.A. You can deal with your damn L.A. set and I will report from New York, where I am headed to see my friends Joan and Melissa!" Click.

E! then appealed to my agent and manager to secretly have Bill convince me to go to L.A. Pam didn't even bother—she knew Bill would never do that—and just told them he'd said no. The E! executives were getting nastier, she added.

"Tell them they can fire me," I said.

"You know, they really can fire you," Pam reminded me. "Technically you're not performing your duties."

E! had another idea. It was Fashion Week in New York, and I had already been scheduled to go for months. I assumed they were pulling all coverage out of Fashion Week, but I was wrong. The network said they were still moving forward with shooting the two *Fashion Police* specials, obviously without Joan. My fingers couldn't dial Kelly and George quickly enough. Thankfully, the three of us banded together. We weren't doing *Fashion Police* without its star. The network ended up changing the name of the broadcast from *Fashion Police* to *E! from Fashion Week* and recasting it with the always camera-ready Kimora Simmons.

After refusing to go to L.A., I went to New York to see Melissa and report for E! There were reports that Joan had been moved out of the ICU and was in stable condition.

"Happy to hear things are looking up, even though there's a long recovery," I texted Melissa on my way. "Praying every day."

"Keep praying," she texted back. "Please come by the hospital and say hi. I need it." Her assistant later reached out and said Melissa wanted me to come by the hospital at nine that night. George was in town, so I called him. "They're making me go to the *Fashion Police* Fashion Week party," he told me miserably. I had refused to go and kept telling the producers how disrespectful it was not to cancel the party immediately. The network felt it was too late to call it off and maintained there was still hope Joan was going to come out of this.

"Just go for five minutes and come back out," I advised George. "Don't take pictures or smile for them." He slipped away from the event and came to fetch me at my hotel to go see Joan. When I got into the car, I didn't expect to see him crying hysterically.

"What's going on?" I asked.

"I don't think it's good, G," he said.

When we got there, Melissa walked out of her mother's room

and hugged us. I felt embarrassed that she was the one comforting us, but she was her mother's daughter through and through, and Joan never liked unhappy people: it was her job, and her joy, to make them feel good.

"In the morning we're taking her off the ventilator," Melissa said bravely.

What? Wow, this is it, I thought, *I'm here to say good-bye.*

George went in first. I followed Melissa into another room to sit. They'd been there for a week, but Melissa was still so strong. Everything that came out of her mouth was kind, and honest, and sure. She was so calm under unbearable pressure. Then it was my turn to go see Joan.

"Are you coming with me?" I asked Melissa.

"No," she said gently. "You go."

"I'll be really quick and respectful of your time," I promised as she left me at the door.

Melissa turned around.

"No, you take as long as you want in there," she urged me. "Talk to her, hold her hand. My mom would love it."

Melissa had taken exquisite care to make sure her mother was comfortable. The room was filled with beautiful flowers and thoughtful decorative details by Preston Bailey, the celebrity event planner who had designed Melissa's wedding and had become a close family friend. Joan lay beneath her favorite faux-mink blanket. I sat in a chair next to her and reached under the covers to pull out her hand and hold it in mine.

Joan always had the most gorgeous hands. Even at eighty-one, they were supple and baby smooth. I would often reach out for one of Joan's hands during commercial breaks so I could admire them. "My mom gave me these hands," she used to say to me, deflecting compliments as usual. She loved to wear trendy nail polish and big, shiny rings. On her deathbed, her nails were perfectly manicured and painted a deep vampy purple. Her hair and makeup were done, as well. Joan was just Joan, sleeping. Her favorite show tunes played in the background. I came in the middle of *A Chorus Line*. I spent the first few minutes with my eyes tightly closed, envisioning her suddenly waking up and asking why the hell she was in a hospital room with people crying all around her. When I sadly realized that wasn't going to happen, I spent the next fifteen minutes talking to her and thanking her for taking a chance on me, for all the invaluable advice, and for making me feel loved each week. Finally, I said one last good-bye through my tears, then walked out and hugged Melissa tightly.

"Thank you for this gift," I told her. "I'll never forget your generosity tonight."

The drive back to the hotel was a blur, and as Bill opened the door to let me in, I fell crying into his arms.

"Bill, Joan's dying tomorrow." I wept myself to sleep. I spent the entire next day in bed, buried beneath the covers, crying until there were no tears left. E! kept calling and leaving messages for me to prepare to go on air later that night.

I never picked up the phone.

When is enough, enough?

Bill and I used to ponder this even before we were married, when we would lie in each other's arms and plan the future we imagined together. We debated the meaning of life, and how we would know whether we were getting it right. Was true success a matter of looking back and saying you had accomplished everything you set out to do? Even then, I wasn't so sure. "It's not that complex," I told Bill. "You know how you know you've lived life to the fullest, and you've won? If you can say, I woke up happy most days, and I went to bed happy most nights."

We're settling into a new house again. We move, Bill and I, from one house to the next. Nine times in as many years, between Chicago and Los Angeles, trying to find the right place, the right time, to put our roots down. We design, shop, decorate, move in, and then out again, restless and unsettled. This house was too big, that street was too busy, this place grew too small, that one too sad. There are boxes marked "miscellaneous" that seem to exist just to shift with us from place to place without ever getting opened. We both want to leave L.A. but can't seem to pull anchor. "I don't want you to resent me later," Bill says when I swear that Chicago will be a permanent move this time: I want to stop working so much. The plan for now is for me to retire from the shows I work on that require me to be in Los Angeles every day. It's easier to leave than I imagined, maybe because I have been doing it for almost 15 years and have outgrown the content I am reporting on. Simply put, I've evolved. Until my contract is up, I will commute to L.A. and New York occasionally for shows that are less demanding of my time but still exciting to be part of. After that, who knows? Chill on a beach or do a daytime show with my husband out of Chicago. Both sound good. The sky's the limit. We keep our place in L.A. but bring all our good stuff to Chicago, including Duke's crib and most of his toys. We hope he'll have a sibling soon.

Three perfect embryos remained frozen after we had him. Three more chances.

In the meantime, we redouble our efforts to build our other businesses, determined to secure a post-Hollywood future for our family. Bill takes the driver's seat for the both of us on opening RPM's sister restaurants in Washington, D.C., and Las Vegas. I decide to import Italian and French wines in unique single-serve glasses that snap together to form a bottle, and am thrilled when my XO, G wine lands a deal with the biggest retailer in the world, Walmart. Whatever city I happen to be in, I search out the nearest Walmart to check the display. *It's come to this*, I think, *now you're stalking yourself.* I take quick trips every six weeks to Tampa to sell my G by Giuliana clothing line at HSN, and thank Duke for all the practice he's given me at being alert between two and four in the morning, one of their prime times for sales. If I leave television, there's always a chance these other ventures will dry up and blow away. And there it is again, that word. Chance.

There are weeks when I'm on ten different airplanes. No exaggeration. I spend hours before each flight obsessively checking the weather reports. "Bill, it's saying the winds are 19 mph, is that bad?" I text my husband from the airport before yet another flight from L.A. to Chicago, where he waits with the rest of the family for me to join them for the holidays. "The planes are built to withstand that," he assures me, but it doesn't calm my nerves, ever.

"How's your flight, Boo?" he messages me another time, knowing the panic doesn't subside once I'm airborne. "This anxiety is too much," I respond. "Clenching the seat belt for three hours. Praying so hard. There are storms left and right, I'm so scared. There's lightning out the window." Only three things make flying tolerable for me once we are on the runway and about to take off. Three things that keep me from pushing the attendant button and making up some bullshit about needing to get off because I suddenly have Ebola or the measles and don't want to be a threat to the other passengers. Those three things are half a Xanax, red wine, and iPhone videos of my son. I have about 320 videos of him that I watch to calm my nerves once we are in the sky. I never get tired of them, and fall deeper in love every time I hear his giggle or see him playing or making a grand mess out of lunch, or excitedly repeating his first word, "Bar? Bar?" to strangers on the street, who are aghast until I explain that he's looking for his favorite granola bar, not a pub. I fantasize again about life as a full-time mom, walking Duke to school every day with that little hand in mine, going to his soccer games, all three of us cuddling together on the couch under blankets while the wind blows outside and the sound of it brings me peace instead of panic.

We ask our surrogate, Delphine, if she would carry another

baby for us, and she happily agrees. We have two of our remaining three embryos implanted. The good news comes. We're pregnant! But like many times before, the joy is quickly turned into sadness when Dr. Schoolcraft calls to tell us the embryo detached from the uterine sac and after eight weeks of pregnancy, the baby is gone. I put him on speakerphone so Bill can hear, too. "It seems so illogical sometimes," the doctor says in his soft-spoken way. "There is a little bit of a random chance. Ultimately, it's up to the universe."

"So it didn't work?" I ask him.

"It's obviously such an emotional thing when it doesn't work," he replies. "It's statistically like flipping a coin. It doesn't mean the next time won't be a success."

I trusted more than ever in God's plan for us. I remember when I hit my lowest point after learning I had cancer, when doctors told me I would have to do chemotherapy even after my double mastectomy. I had already sacrificed both breasts to this disease—how could that not be enough? The levee burst, and all the fear, anger, and resentment I already had been struggling so hard to hold back suddenly swallowed me whole. I was in a place too deep, dark, and lonely for even Bill to reach me. Alone, I went to church and knelt down before the Virgin Mary to cry and pray. *Mary, please take care of me in this time of need. I am grateful to have you watching over me and never ask you to do anything but to look over my family and friends. Today I ask you to please grant me a miracle and let me receive some good news in this time of darkness.* The very next day is when we got news from the NIH that a pathologist had determined that the cancer had been caught so early, there were fewer cells than they thought—not billions—and the likelihood that a rogue cell had escaped into my bloodstream was virtually nil. That meant no chemo.

My hair has always been my vanity, always long and wavy, so long it would flow over my breasts like a mermaid's. I started using extensions at E! because if more is always better, then more and free must be best. About two years after my surgery, I feel stronger, braver, bolder than I ever have. It's true what they say about time being the best healer; I feel less sad with every passing day. "I need to cut my hair," I tell my stylist one day. "I want to cut it off." I don't want to think about it, discuss it, or second-guess it. I am excited. *Are you sure?* everyone keeps asking me as I sit in the chair.

"Yes," I insist. I need a break. I just want to be me for a minute.

Piles of hair fall to the floor, until a sleek, angular bob grazes my jawline. Bill has no clue what I'm doing. I just walk through the door—surprise, what do you think? He and I both love it, and I take it a step further, impulsively dying it bright blond one night after work. It takes my colorist four hours to get it so light. I love it, but E! hates it. The president of E! calls my manager and orders it dyed back—I suppose the network has "reasonable consultation" regarding my hair, but the demands seem any-thing but reasonable. "We want her brunette by the Emmys," Suzanne warns Pam.

I don't go darker. I go even lighter. I'm talking so platinum it was as if I had bleached my scalp to ensure I would have no roots and be as shockingly blond as possible.

Before I hit the red carpet, Suzanne asks the producers on Emmy day whether I'm brunette, and they're too scared to say, so she comes looking for me as I prepare for the big show. She says nothing about my hair, but I can see her seething as she asks how I'm feeling and if I'm ready for the show today. I'm just as angry as she is. How dare she mess with me on Game Day? Both of us are smiling and cordial. Suzanne calls Pam right afterward: *She showed up blonder! You have to reel her in and get her to change it back immediately.* Maybe she had a point, but I've never been someone who likes to be told what to do . . . especially when it comes to something as personal as the color of my hair.

I turn forty in triumph. I feel more beautiful than I ever have, gloriously alive in this body that's been crooked, infertile, cancerous.

I realize that something inside me has been shifting, that what I'm seeking now is affirmation, not approval, a gift I can only give myself. I remember the time I was on the red carpet covering the Emmys when I felt someone reach up and tap me from behind. I looked down from my platform at Jerry O'Connell, who was lingering while his wife Rebecca was doing an interview. "You look beautiful, homegirl," he said. "You really do." I said thank you without really meaning it, and turned my back on him.

A Hollywood life is filled with loyal fans and rabid haters. I've learned to say what I want to say, do what I want to do, and let the chips fall where they may. When I post a cute picture of Duke in his car seat with chocolate all over his face, the comments instantly fly: *The straps aren't tight enough, you have him facing the wrong way.* The pic ignites a feud, and people fight all day long on my Instagram page about the different state laws regarding car seats, and what the correct age is to face forward instead of backward. I post a picture of Duke on Santa's lap like any proud mama who wants to show off how precious her two-year-old is in his little white sweater, and suddenly, the haters pounce on Santa Claus. *Is that Santa's hat on the chair instead of his head? That's the worst-ever Santa! What mall is that, someone should complain!*

Even when the reality cameras aren't following us for the four months it takes to film a season of *Giuliana and Bill*, my everyday life sometimes feels like a documentary in progress that anyone can just step in to start filming.

I'm in the public restroom changing my baby and realize a woman behind me is surreptitiously taking photographs. I turn around and she slips out the door. It happens in the waiting room at the doctor's office. I see a flash go off at the airport when I'm chasing Duke around trying to get him to eat oatmeal from McDonald's and look up to see a sheepish couple who say "sorry," and I smile with gritted teeth and say, "No, it's fine. Just trying to be a mom, here. Just trying to be a mom."

We're at the airport again when I notice the woman sitting across from us in the lounge pretending to text while I hear the familiar click of a camera. She calls her daughter over to show her, and they grab a few more shots. My blood begins to boil. Here's the thing, taking pictures isn't the issue, it's the covert way in which some people take them that makes it feel like an invasion of privacy sometimes. When people come up and say hi and ask for a picture, I always oblige. I remember when I was seven or so, and my soccer team was called the A-Team. Our coach heard Mr. T was filming in D.C. and piled us into a big van to go see him. It was raining, but we waited hours for Mr. T to surface. Finally he came out of his trailer, and we all rushed up to the fence with our little noses pressed through the chain link, shouting, "Mr. T! Mr. T! We're the A-Team!" and he walked right past us without even waving. "Mr. T! Mr. T! You suck!" we started shouting. "All right, stop yelling shit at Mr. T," our coach said, as he herded us, betrayed and humiliated, back into the van.

I confront the sneaky woman in the airport lounge.

"Are you taking pictures of me?" I demand.

"I don't know what you're talking about," she blusters.

"I saw the flash," I say. I feel invaded, and I'm not going to let go. I pick up my phone and begin furiously taking pictures of her. "So I'll have pictures of you to show all my friends," I say. Bill gets up and walks away. He comes back. I know I've embarrassed him. He keeps his voice low and even, not wanting to create more of a scene.

"Why are you being such a brat?" he wants to know. "You

know what? You signed up for this. Welcome to Hollywood, honey!"

I'm surprised and a little angry that he isn't on my side this time.

I've never met him, but I still half hope, sometimes, that Mr. T has a brief comeback and merits coverage by E! I promise my long-lost A-Team that I will punch him in the nose.

Our new place in Chicago is a townhouse on the Gold Coast. We can walk to shops and restaurants and run into old elementary school friends of Bill who beckon us into a wine bar to relax. We spend raucous evenings playing Cards Against Humanity in the basement rec room of friends who have nothing to do with "the industry." Duke runs wild with the other kids, and I hear him laughing as he dives into the cushions of an old sofa with them. *He needs this*, I think.

At two, Duke is growing by leaps and bounds. One morning, I'm on a business call when he asks for his blanket. "Do you want the monkey blankie or the cow blankie?" I ask, searching the chaos of our still-unpacked kitchen while trying to finish up on the phone. Without missing a beat, he answers me like a kid three years older. "Mommy, what happened to my monkey blankie?" I apologize to Duke. I'm so amazed, I forget my caller and excitedly yell to Bill in the next room: "Did you hear that, Bill? He wants to know what happened to his monkey blankie!" Bill doesn't get it at first, and says he doesn't know where it is. "No!" I say. "He said it perfectly, not me! Duke, say it again!"

Duke repeats it. I'm amazed all over again. Not just a full sentence, but a complicated thought, this little two-year-old mind suddenly able to put together pieces and not just want something, but wonder about it. We've been so consumed with asking God for the big miracles these past few years, I forgot what we really are, what I see now in my child, this constant gathering of small miracles.

The boxes marked "miscellaneous" are still waiting to be un-packed when we make another decision. Dr. Schoolcraft trans-fers our last embryo into Delphine. Maybe life is about just this, a series of chances, of boxes unopened, of terrifying journeys you can't be sure of surviving. So we do what we've learned to after too many tears and so many blessings. We wait, and we pray. The stress of the move, of too many plane trips, of all the uncertainty I feel about my career, all takes a toll on my body. The few pounds I lose send me into a panic: What if the can-cer is back? Was I wrong to opt out of chemo? Is it too late to do it now? When my angular shoulder blades are revealed by a strapless gown I wear to the Golden Globes and then again by a black jumpsuit I wear at the Grammys, I'm body-shamed in the media, falsely accused of being anorexic when really I'm under immense stress and my cancer medication has caused me to lose weight. It's been hard to see myself lose the fit and toned body I had before treatment yet all people on Twitter can say is "eat a burger."

When my father gets ready to open his new store—that ten-year lease that amounts to his declaration to continue working until he's nearly ninety—I promise to come for the gala grand-opening party. Bill and I are in New York, where Bill is running the New York City marathon, his third marathon. This time, he is doing it to raise money for my charity, Fab-U-Wish, which offers women who are going through breast cancer treatment a wish, like a makeover or shopping spree, or a dream trip to Hollywood for a day of pampering with me. It is a tough day for the marathon, with bitter cold winds. Bill is exhausted by the time he gets to the finish line, frozen to the bone. We have a friend's plane waiting to get us to D.C. in time for my dad's big event. "You should stay here and rest," I urge Bill. "Babbo will understand. I'll go."

"No, no, I want to support your dad," Bill insists. He takes a two-second shower and we fly to Washington.

When we rush in, the store is already packed. All of my father's customers are there, along with the family doctor, the dentist, and the usual cast of Italian relatives. Babbo even has a red carpet out front, and beams with joy when I walk down it.

"Honey, we have a surprise for you," Bill says excitedly.

"For me?" I am confused. Is there a cake or something?

"It's someone from your childhood," says my sister-in-law, Nikki, who has orchestrated it all. I have a flash of fear: my parents have remained friends with Richard D. and his family.

"Wait, who, an ex?" I urgently ask.

"No, are you kidding?" Bill says. "Turn around."

And there she is in person. Barbara Harrison. She is exactly how I remember her, not a second older. The same blue eyes that gazed at me from my television set for so many years look at me in person now. I literally gasp, and she smiles. I start crying. I don't know what to say.

"Hi, Giuliana, I'm Barbara," she says.

"Oh my God, Barbara, you don't understand," I say, finally finding my voice. "I've worshipped you since I was a little girl. You taught me English! Once when I was at the mall, I was on the third level and someone said you were downstairs, and I tried chasing you but I couldn't catch up!" I am babbling like an idiot, but can't stop. It is such an emotional moment for me, bigger than interviewing an A-lister, bigger than meeting Madonna or even Clooney.

"I don't want to sound weird and stalkerish, but I literally talk about you all the time," I go on. "You're such a big part of my story."

Barbara Harrison is taken aback. She looks like she is fighting tears now as she thanks me for the compliments and tells me how incredible she thinks my journey is. She tells me to look at what I have done and all that I have achieved. Not only am I seen by viewers in Washington, D.C., like I dreamed of as a little girl, but, Barbara reminds me, I am seen all over the world.

"I'm so proud of you," she says.

I look around the room and take in the moment. Some people say you have to change to make it big, that success always comes with a price. That you have to leave your old life behind in order to get the shiny new one you've always dreamed of. But as I look around the room at my lifelong friends, my incredible family, and my soul mate who has given me the greatest gift of all, my son Duke, I realize Barbara is right.

I did it.

It's New Year's Eve again, three years to the hour since Bill and I clung to each other anxiously in Times Square and got the joyful news that we were going to have a baby. This time, half a world away in Dubai, we are again waiting for Dr. School-craft to call us with the news we so desperately want to hear. It's a perfect night in the Middle East—seventy-five degrees with no desert winds, just the electrifying energy of ten thousand people waiting in the arena for me and Bill to host their version of the Times Square ball drop. I'm wearing a beautiful red couture gown. I feel grateful for the past year full of laughs and love and good health, certain that even more awaits us in the new year. It's a cool coincidence, Bill and I tell ourselves, that things are playing out the exact same way; that come August, we will once again welcome a baby into our lives and into our home. We secretly decorated the guest room next to Duke's room in pink florals, knowing it would be a nursery for the daughter we would one day have. It's the promise that our last embryo, which we recently discovered is a little girl, will come to life and complete our family.

The phone rings. It's Dr. Schoolcraft.

"Hi Giuliana and Bill. First of all, Happy New Year," he says.

"Happy New Year to you, Doctor! We can't wait to hear the news." And then, a pause, followed by the two words we've heard too many times, yet still they stun me. *I'm sorry.*

"I'm sorry, but unfortunately six weeks into pregnancy, the embryo is not developing and therefore we have determined this is not a viable pregnancy. There is no baby."

Bill and I keep the conversation short. All I can say to the doctor as I fight back tears is, "You can't win them all." He agrees. We thank the doctor and look at each other. We are sad. Bill tells me that it's okay. That our family is already complete. He's right, but it doesn't make the pain that's quickly building inside of me go away.

Duke has stayed back in Chicago at Bill's sister's house, and at that moment, a text comes through to both of us from her. It's a video. She is driving Duke around the neighborhood to look at the Christmas lights that are still up. Duke is singing "Jingle Bells" happily in his car seat. He's holding his blankie and looking at the lights as he sings. He suddenly notices the camera and stops, almost as if he knows we are looking at him, and says, "Mama . . . Dada . . . Home." I smile through my tears; he's right, it's time to go home. Life is never the perfect fairy tale, and mine will no doubt have more ups and downs before it's over. But no matter what, I know I will live happily ever after.

ACKNOWLEDGMENTS

Thank you to the following people who, if they hadn't played a part in my life, this book would be a lot thinner.

My fabulous editor, Suzanne O'Neill, and the rest of the gang at Crown Archetype. Thank you for believing in this book even before I walked into our first meeting and for giving me the freedom to tell my story. And sorry for missing a couple of deadlines. This whole memoir-writing thing isn't easy!

Thank you to my literary manager, Richard Abate, for convincing me to write my story. Why are you always right?

To my longtime friend and manager Pam Kohl. I can't imagine not speaking to you 100 times a day. I love you Pam!

Ted Harbert for plucking me out of my cubicle and onto the anchor desk. More important, thank you for your friendship and all the laughs. I am forever grateful.

Niki Ugel for teaching me the importance of higher education and being the first to tell me that education is the one thing no one can take away from you. Thank you for your guidance when I needed it most.

Melissa Rivers for always believing in me and for being the superwoman you are. I am eternally grateful to you for your friendship and generosity.

Joan Rivers. Thank you for your candor and honesty and willingness to take a chance on a girl with a funny name. I will always remember your favorite story of the bumble bee. The bumble bee wasn't supposed to fly, but no one ever told the bumble bee that. And that's exactly what he did. Fly. I love you.

To the little sister I never had, Tara Bassi. At twenty-four, you were taken from us too soon because God needed you in Heaven. You will forever live on in my heart. Until we meet again.

Sarah Knight, Catalina Su, Brenda Kovar, Monica Rose, and Melissa Brown. Thank you for years of loyalty and friendship and for making me laugh so damn hard every day. I love you girls!

Colet Abedi, since the day we gave each other the stink eye at the fax machine you have been my most trusted and loyal friend. You are a beautiful soul and I am so lucky to have you in my life.

My parents, Eduardo and Anna. I can't imagine more perfect role models. Thank you for loving me, shaping me, and always rescuing me. My brother, Pasquale, for keeping me in line when we were kids, and Monica, you are more than just my big sister. You are my first mentor and idol. Thank you for teaching me the ropes. I love you.

Delphine for giving us the greatest gift, carrying our son, Duke. And Brett, Mason, and Ewan for supporting Delphine and us throughout the nine months. Friends forever!

My *E! News* family . . . the most talented bunch in the biz. Thank you for making me look good every day. And Lee Schneller for always having my back. Love you, Lee!

My *Live from the Red Carpet* and *Fashion Police* families. Thank you for being so damn talented. And Lisa Bacon for all the late-night texts and for always believing in me.

Bill's loving family, Gail, Karen, Katie, and Beth. Thank you for treating me like a member of the family from day one. I definitely hit the in-law lottery! And to the memory of Dr. Edward Rancic; I never had the privilege to meet you in person, but I feel your love every single day in your son Bill and your grandson, Edward Duke. One day we will meet.

My nieces and nephews, Eddie, Olivia, Alexa, Maxine, Jordana, Jasper, Zack, Luke, Noah, Jake, Ben, Sara, Rachael, and Liam. Life is waiting for you to make what you want of it. Carpe diem.

Dr. John Kostuik for making me straight, Dr. Armando Giuliano for making me healthy and Dr. Devchand Paul for keeping me healthy. Also, Dr. Richard Childs and Dr. Maria Merino for treating me like a person, not a patient. Thank you.

Donald Trump for choosing Bill to be your first apprentice. We wouldn't have met if you hadn't said "You're hired" to him.

To the memory of my grandparents, Antonio and Maria Santillo, Pasquale and Enrichetta DePandi, as well as my uncle Michele Santillo and my aunt Angela Santillo. Thank you for watching over me from Heaven.

My favorite beeeech, Tamara. What an incredible gift you have. Thank you for sharing it with me. I'm in awe of you.

Barbara Harrison, thank you for being the epitome of class and elegance and for inspiring my career path.

I thank God, my Father in Heaven, and Jesus Christ, my Lord and Savior, for holding my hand each day and blessing me with this beautiful life.

To my son, Duke. It took many years and many tears to get you here, but it was worth every moment. I can't wait to see the wonderful man you will become one day.

And finally, Bill. You are not only my husband, but you're also my best friend, confidante, and partner in crime. You're my dream come true and your love is intoxicating. I thank God every day for bringing us together. I love you until the end of time.